Bent Arms & Dodgy Wickets

England's Troubled Reign as Test Match Kings during the Fifties

By Tim Quelch

Pitch Publishing Ltd
A2 Yeoman Gate
Yeoman Way
Durrington
BN13 3QZ

Email: info@pitchpublishing.co.uk
Web: www.pitchpublishing.co.uk

First published in the UK by Pitch Publishing, 2012

Text © 2012 Tim Quelch

A CIP catalogue record for this book is available from the British Library.

13-digit ISBN: 978-1908051837

Cover design by Brilliant Orange Creative Services.

Typesetting by Liz Short.

Printed in Great Britain by TJ International.

CONTENTS

THANKS

I would like to thank all those who helped me so much in writing this book. I am very appreciative of the helpfulness of all the publishing companies who have given me permission to reproduce extracts from copyright work, namely: Andre Deutsch, Aurum Press, Constable & Robinson Ltd, Harper Collins, The History Press, Hodder & Stoughton Ltd, Ian Randle Publishers, Octopus Publishing, Pan Macmillan (London), Random House Group Ltd, Robert Hale Ltd and Souvenir Press. References to copyright sources are made in the text with a full account of each work given in the References section at the end of the book.

Please note that for all copyright material reproduced in this book, no part of these publications may be reproduced or transmitted in any form or by any means, electronic or mechanical, including photocopy, recording, or any information storage and retrieval system, without permission in writing from the publisher.

If I have inadvertently infringed copyright at any place in this book please accept my sincere apology. Some of the material used has lost its reference source, and/or the current rights ownership could not be identified. Nevertheless, I have endeavoured to seek permission before using any copyright material. I am writing this book to raise funds for the Parkinson's UK charity. All of my royalties will be donated to this source. I hope, therefore, that if I have inadvertently breached copyright this will be considered kindly by the rights owner. Should any owner identify their work they are asked to please contact: Pitch Publishing, A2 Yeoman Gate, Yeoman Way, Worthing, West Sussex, BN13 3QZ.

I am also greatly indebted to Huw Turbervill who granted me permission to use extracts from his book *The Toughest Tour: The Ashes away series since the war*. National radio, newspapers and cricket magazines have provided rich sources of material. Thanks go to BBC Radio, *Daily*

Express, Daily Mail, Daily Mirror, Daily Telegraph, Guardian, Independent, Mail on Sunday, Melbourne Herald, News of the World, Sunday Pictorial, Daily Sketch, The Age (Melbourne), *The Times, Observer* and *Observer Magazine, Sunday Express, The Sunday Times, The Cricketer* magazines and to *espn.cricinfo.com*, and also *Bodacious.com,* notably for Rob Steen's article on the D'Oliveira affair. All of the above sources have helped me to present, hopefully, a more rounded portrait, not only of the cricket, but also of life in Britain during the 1940s and 1950s.

I would like to express my gratitude to my wife, Liz, for her tireless attempts to identify all owners of copyright material, seeking their permission to use extracts from their work in this book. If some sources could not be traced it has not been through want of trying. I am also greatly indebted to my friends: Ray Pavey, for his prudent advice in writing the book, and to Rob Woodmore for the loan of very useful background material; and I am also most grateful to my publishers for their supportive and experienced guidance throughout the production of this book.

Tim Quelch, August 2012

'REELING IN THE YEARS':
AN INTRODUCTION

When Andrew Strauss's team seized the world Test match number one position in the summer of 2011 they finally recovered what had been lost at the Adelaide Oval in February 1959. England had previously been top of the world during the mid 1950s. In *Bent Arms and Dodgy Wickets* the story is told of English cricket's slow recovery from the dislocation of the Second World War, of its time of triumph after Queen Elizabeth II's Coronation in 1953, and of its undignified fall from grace five-and-a-half years later.

It is a tale of fluctuating fortunes recounted with reference to the memoirs of some of those who took part. For England, these include: Sir Len Hutton, Freddie Brown, Peter May, Colin Cowdrey, Trevor Bailey, Brian Statham, Bill Edrich, Denis Compton, Fred Trueman, Frank Tyson and Jim Laker. The Australian view is represented in the recollections of Ray Lindwall, Keith Miller, Ian Meckiff and Alan Davidson, while West Indian and South African perspectives are provided respectively by Sir Everton Weekes, and by Roy McLean and Jackie McGlew.

The book's title refers not only to sporting controversies of the time – notably suspect bowling actions and poor pitches – but also to the political sensitivities and class constraints impinging upon English Test cricketers' lives. Hampered by class snobbery, anachronistic fixations, and an uncompetitive domestic game, compounded, too, by unreliable playing surfaces, and limited coaching opportunities, England's post-war spell in the sun was destined to be short-lived.

This is a story of English cricket's rise and fall set against a backdrop of imperial decline; when Britain was about to lose an empire but had yet to find a role, to paraphrase the words of Dean Acheson, a former US Secretary of State. For cricket, like any other major sport, has always been more than a game. Celebrated cricket writer Sir Neville Cardus thought that "it somehow holds a mirror up to English society". However, cricket offers more than just a reflection of English society for it has also promoted social, religious and political change, albeit mainly abroad.

During the Victorian period, Australian national pride was stirred by its cricketing feats, as its leading players began to beat their English opponents regularly and decisively at their own game. Bradman's crushing batting successes during the 1930s and 1940s seemed to provide the perfect riposte to British cultural snobbishness. As Australian novelist Thomas Keneally observed: "No Australian had written *Paradise Lost*, but Bradman had made 100 before lunch at Lord's."

Cricket incentivised reform in pre-war India, too, enabling Palwankar Baloo, a shunned Dalit or 'untouchable', to rise from despised obscurity to become not only a hugely popular player, but in time a respected politician also, capable of challenging caste discrimination, alongside Gandhi, and supporting his campaign for Indian home rule. As with the Hindi film, cricket helped knit a newly-independent India, encouraging the emerging nation to rise above its class and religious divisions. Former broadcaster and journalist, John Arlott, concluded: "To say that cricket has nothing to do with politics and you say that cricket has nothing to do with life."

In the West Indies, cricket provided a means by which its black people could challenge white, colonial domination, complementing Caribbean campaigns for independence during the 1950s. Sir Frank Worrell not only became the first regular black captain of the West Indian side, he was also elected to the newly-independent Jamaican senate upon leaving the game in 1963. Here, he followed the example set by Lord Learie Constantine, whose popularity as a cricketer helped boost his political ambitions.

Lord Constantine served as Trinidad's High Commissioner to the United Kingdom during the 1960s, helping to combat racial discrimination and contributing to the passing of the first British Race Relations Act in 1965. West Indian CLR James wrote in his seminal work, *Beyond a Boundary*: "I haven't the slightest doubt that the clash of race, caste and class did not retard, but stimulated West Indian cricket. I am equally certain that in those years, social and political passions, denied normal outlets, expressed themselves so fiercely in cricket (and other games) precisely because they were games." When examining cricket, it is important to take a view 'beyond a boundary', as CLR James so aptly put it.

That said, the game of cricket has been commonly caricatured as a bastion of political and social conservatism. In Britain, during the two decades which followed the Second World War, this charge has considerable truth. For cricket's national and international ruling body, Marylebone Cricket Club, or MCC, continued to cling fervently to its Victorian and Edwardian principles. It seemed as if MCC's predilection for its illustrious past inhibited its ability to address its more challenging present. At home, these unanswered challenges included: fading public interest, suspect bowling, poor pitches and inadequate coaching.

MCC appeared to be in a state of denial about growing social mobility in Britain during the mid 1950s, and also about the inevitability of multiculturalism. Similarly, it sought to insulate itself from the implications of decolonisation. Most controversially of all, MCC attempted to turn a blind eye to South African apartheid until the D'Oliveira affair of 1968 forced upon it a cessation of sporting links. That said, even during the 1950s, MCC was not able to resist all forces for change.

Despite its obsessions with reviving the supposed 'golden age' of the heroically cavalier amateur, the Test team it selected found success with a contradictory, tough, combative, professional style of play that was practised as dutifully by its leading unpaid players as it was by its paid ones. It seemed as if this team's Test triumphs were achieved almost in spite of the actions of MCC's cricket administrators.

According to Karl Marx: "History repeats itself, first as tragedy, second as farce." Having spent over half a century recovering the long-lost world crown, England's Test cricket team relinquished it again 12 months later, to South Africa, in the saturated summer of 2012. England's celebration of restored glory was even shorter since Strauss's men had been thrashed by Pakistan in a three-match Test series played in Abu Dhabi and Dubai during January and February 2012. While England's sudden and unexpected demise against the itinerant Pakistanis had hardly seemed farcical, at least in the eyes of English supporters, there did seem to be a certain irony that Strauss's side should encounter, in microcosm, the fate which befell Peter May's side 53 years before.

For once again, English hubris was shattered on the back of complacency and, arguably, inadequate preparation. And once again the spectre of "chucking" was thrown into the mix as a possible explanation for failure, despite the obvious riposte of "sour grapes". Even in this vastly different 21st century world, in which Britain no longer had the world status it had in 1945, it is perhaps tempting to ask: "What's new, pussycat?"

'TOMORROW IS A LOVELY DAY': 1945-1951

"Come and feast your tear-dimmed eyes on tomorrow's clear blue skies..."
Tomorrow is a Lovely Day, written by Irving Berlin.

"The [Victory Tests] left me...with an unpleasant awareness of England's bowling weaknesses..."
Wally Hammond, 1945.

"Train? I just stubbed out my cigarette and ran..."
British Olympic athlete, 1948.

'WE'RE SO SHORT OF EVERYTHING'

'Let It Snow! Let It Snow! Let It Snow!'

Great Britain concluded its part in the Second World War battered, barren and bankrupt. After suffering six years of heartache and hardship, its working people were eager for something brighter and fairer, with greater protection against want and disease, better standards of living, and improved education. It was their deep-seated sense of entitlement, fed by 1930s impoverishment, which brought about the Labour landslide of 1945.

On the back of the excited VE Day celebrations, the British public flocked once again to our sad, neglected seaside resorts, and turned up in their thousands for the five vibrant Victory Tests of 1945, in which a creaking England side took on a scratch Australian Services XI. Wally Hammond recalled the occasion, in his 1958 book *Cricket My World*, with uncharacteristic euphoria: "There was a feeling of peace and happiness in the air that was very delightful to me. It seemed as though after years in the shadows, England was marching into the sunshine again."

Britain's cinemas, dance halls, race tracks, athletics stadia, boxing arenas and football grounds became packed, too, as the grim war years were cast aside with almost febrile glee. Writer and former diplomat Bruce Lockhart exclaimed in 1945: "Never have I seen a nation change so quickly from a war mentality to a peace mentality. The war [in the Far East] has disappeared from the news. Sport and the election now fill the front pages."

Nevertheless, the carefree mood did not last long. The country was £3bn in debt. Capital and overseas investments had taken huge hits. The nation's infrastructure was in tatters. Bombed-out housing had yet to be replaced. With servicemen about to return to their estranged families, and the first wave of 'baby boomers' already voicing their needs, there was an enormous and urgent housing shortage to address.

As an emergency response, 30,000 prefabricated dwellings were erected from kits financed by United States subsidies under the Lease-Lend programme. When that programme ceased in 1945, Britain had to cadge another £4bn loan in order to meet its "financial Dunkirk", as John Maynard Keynes so aptly put it. This wasn't charity. With the Cold War pressing ever closer, the Americans needed Britain to maintain its position as head of the Commonwealth in order to help stem the spread of international communism. In a statement resonant of Britain's position today, Labour minister Herbert Morrison declared: "We are in danger of paying more than we can afford for defences that are nevertheless inadequate, or even illusory."

Pumped up with wartime heroics, Britain professed to be still a world power. Its leading politicians continued to attend world summit conferences, and its servicemen undertook global policing duties in Malaya, the Mediterranean and the Middle East. These servicemen also helped defy the Berlin blockade and fought in Korea, too. Meanwhile, Britain was struggling to make and pay its way. Industrial production needed to be modernised, diversified and ramped up to deal with the vast balance of payments deficit.

The state of British agriculture was dismally primitive. Almost 80% of West Country farms lacked electrical power. Milking was done mostly by hand. The situation was scarcely better closer to London where only 50% of farms had electricity. With home-produced food needed also for export to help pay the huge national debt, a depressingly long list of rationed items was retained until the 1950s. The railway network was in a decrepit state. Because the railway companies found the remedial costs too high, the government stepped in. As radical as the welfare state reforms were, they had to be delivered on the cheap. The ascetic-looking Stafford Cripps seemed to epitomise the Labour government's grating self-denial.

David Lean's film *Brief Encounter* got the message; family duty came before passionate indulgence. Morale was worse than during the war years, not helped by the Arctic winter of 1947. Coal was short, so were other fuel supplies. Production halted, household pipes and geysers froze, and many shivering occupants took to their nightly beds in heavy woollens and balaclavas.

This was the scene as the country returned to its sporting life. If the

VE and VJ-celebrating crowds thought that military victory inferred prospective sporting triumphs, too, they were sorely mistaken. After all, the war had not been won by Britain's efforts alone. Without the colossal resources supplied by the USA, USSR and, indeed, the British Commonwealth, this nation's brave, lone stand in 1940 would not have resulted in victory.

Not that this inhibited the jaunty Pathe team, who flew the patriotic flag in Britain's smoky cinemas. Their message was that British was still best when it came to manufacturing, design, fashion and sport. At least the England football team was on message as it thrashed world champions Italy 4-0 in Turin in 1948. Nevertheless, a stern reality check came in the World Cup, two years later.

As for English cricket, at Lord's the Union Jack hung limply at half-mast. Both war and age had withered it. MCC's selectors were forced into picking "Dad's Army" to face a visiting All India team – the last of its kind – in the sopping summer of 1946. The average age of this England team was 34 years. Even its 'bright young things' – Alec Bedser, Godfrey Evans, Jack Ikin and Denis Compton – were nearer to their 30th birthdays than their 20th.

English county cricket ignored the wartime relaxation of class boundaries by preserving a hierarchical division between its amateur 'gentlemen' and its professional 'players', whereas the Indian visitors of 1946 managed to rise above the subcontinent's sectarian politics and religious and class divisions, selecting a unified team of Hindus, Muslims and Christians. Not that this achieved any political traction at home as India lurched towards partitioned independence.

The All India team included the imperious strokeplayer, Vijay Merchant, who scored a superb century in the drawn final Test at the Oval, and a gifted all-rounder, "Vinoo" Mankad, who scored a half-century at Lord's, and took seven wickets at Old Trafford with his probing left-arm spin. Their efforts were in vain, though, as the Indians were crushed in two of the three-day Test matches played in this series.

As emphatic as this victory was, MCC officials remained doubtful about sending what appeared to be an under-strength England side to Australia during the following winter. They knew how much had been lost to war. Fast bowler Ken Farnes had perished when his bomber crashed on take-off, and left-arm spinner Hedley Verity had been killed in action in Italy. Pace bowler Bill Bowes survived, but returned from three years as a POW in poor health. Fellow 'Bodyline' tourist Freddie Brown had also been detained at Hitler's displeasure.

The selectors were not spoilt for choice because younger, fitter talent was thin on the ground. Beating a novice Indian Test side at home was one thing, competing with a vibrant Australian team, including Bradman, was quite another. However, MCC eventually bowed to Australian political pressure, and reluctantly agreed to a hastily arranged tour.

England captain Wally Hammond, aged 43, wasn't even sure that he should be going. He had considered retiring after the Victory Tests, having realised how much the war years had diminished him. Nevertheless, having decided to commit himself to a further season, he enjoyed a magnificent summer in 1946, averaging 85 runs per innings.

Joe Hardstaff junior, another pre-war star, also gave him encouragement after hitting an immaculate double century against India. It was a glorious innings, full of wristy cuts and elegant drives. Len Hutton had apparently overcome his career-threatening injury, albeit with a shortened left arm which made batting uncomfortable.

Meanwhile, Compton and Washbrook had signalled their return to form by recording half-centuries against the Indians. The big, burly debutant Alec Bedser became the summer sensation, though, as he took 24 Indian wickets with his medium-fast bowling at a cost of only 12 runs each. It seemed as if a successor to Maurice Tate had been found.

Nevertheless, Hammond was doubtful about whether his bowlers carried enough punch to trouble Bradman et al. While the unstinting, stout-hearted Bedser bagged 16 wickets in the intense Australian heat, they proved costly at 54 runs each. This was a salutary experience for Bedser, but not one that daunted him as he learnt to deliver a lethal leg cutter on the parched Aussie pitches.

Brilliant stumper Godfrey Evans was in a good position to judge, recalling in a later BBC interview: "Alec rolled his fingers over the ball as he delivered it, and as it swung it pitched on the seam and became, as it were, a leg spinner."

Alec Bedser told Alan Hill, author of *The Bedsers: Twinning Triumphs*, that the sharp spin he imparted with his hefty fingers left a callous, a raw reminder of his long, sweated labours. He had some recompense, though, when he delivered the ball of the series at Adelaide, an in-dipper which jagged back to castle the great Don Bradman for a duck. Bradman reckoned it was the finest ball ever to take his wicket.

Doug Wright also performed well with his springy, quick leg breaks. Like Alec Bedser he bowled long, long spells in England's cause, deservedly taking 23 wickets, the best aggregate of any bowler in this series. Despite incurring a high average cost, as Wright's wickets came at 43 runs each, his command of vicious spin and bounce drew Bradman's respect. Had Wright been supported by more attacking fields and better catching, he might have exerted greater pressure. His highly impressive figures of seven wickets for 105, in the final Test, helped secure a narrow first innings lead. However, because Hutton was indisposed through illness, his splendid effort came to nothing.

As for Bill Edrich, Bedser's gutsy new-ball partner, his nine Aussie scalps were equally expensive. And, while medium-paced Norman Yardley managed ten at slightly improved cost, helping slow the run rate with his containing leg stump line of attack, this did not stop the Australians from stacking up formidable totals. Bradman averaged almost 100 runs per innings during the series, followed by openers Arthur Morris and Sidney Barnes, and all-rounder Keith Miller, each of whom recorded averages in excess of 70. Miller dominated with both bat and ball. His batting average of 77 was complemented with a 16-wicket haul at only 21 runs each.

Bill Voce, the 37-year-old 'Bodyline' veteran, made no impact at all, although Bradman controversially evaded his clutches at Brisbane when an apparently legitimate slip catch was turned down by umpire George Borwick. Bradman stood his ground, claiming that he had squeezed Voce's yorker into the turf before it ricocheted to Ikin at slip. An incensed Wally Hammond thought otherwise, hissing: "What a fine f***ing way to start a series!" At that point Bradman had only 28 runs to his name. He ended up with 187 as he and Lindsay Hassett (128) put together a 276-run stand. Australia racked up a devastating first innings total of 645.

Len Hutton recalled in his 1956 autobiography *Just My Story:* "Bradman could put the ball exactly where he wanted. His footwork was still so quick, his balance so perfect, his sighting so early, putting himself in the best position to make the shot he wanted. He aimed for the maximum result from each stroke, seeing no advantage in producing hard shots that might find a fielder. He could shut out everything except the task in hand."

According to David Hopps, author of *A Century of Cricket Quotes*, Harold Larwood added: "They said I was a killer with the ball without taking into account that Bradman with the bat was the greatest killer of all."

In terms of pace bowling, Bradman had much greater firepower at his disposal. He had the venomous speed and movement of Ray Lindwall, the steepling bounce and startling versatility of Keith Miller, plus the nagging accuracy of Ernie Toshack's swerve and spin. These three strike bowlers shared 51 England wickets during this unequal series, at a combined average of around 22 runs each.

Bradman deployed their greater potency ruthlessly. Norman Preston, then a journalist with Reuters, cabled home: "This was indeed bodyline. It showed that the Australian bowlers can exploit the short bumping ball to intimidate batsmen." It seemed a deliberate policy to curb Len Hutton who was considered vulnerable to short-pitched bowling.

Miller had noted this potential flaw during the Victory Tests. Lindwall sensed it also during MCC's match with New South Wales. Bradman did not think Hutton lacked the necessary technique. He considered it was Hutton's appetite that was in question. "The Don" thought that Hutton did not play the hook shot because he was discomforted by the quicker stuff. This was untrue. Hutton was reluctant to play the shot because it was harder to execute after his arm injury.

Having averaged only 20 runs after six Test innings, Hutton was told by his former team-mate, Bill Bowes: "Tha' knows what they're saying, Len? That tha's afeard on 'em." Hutton bridled at the very suggestion. In his next Test innings at Adelaide, Hutton immediately laid into the bumper barrage, scoring 94, as England posted 460 runs, their highest first innings total of the series.

When he followed this up with a second innings knock of 76, he had helped secure a worthy draw. Hutton carried the fight to the Australians in the final Test, too, scoring a brilliant 122 out of a first innings total of 280 runs before being struck down with tonsillitis. A temperature of 103 enforced his hospitalisation, and then an early return to England. However, it was not before he had confounded his doubters.

Denis Compton also made a spectacular return to form at the Adelaide Oval, scoring a brace of centuries in the hot, sticky conditions, but with the Aussie opener Arthur Morris following suit, England was unable to capitalise on a fine start. In fact, England's second innings collapse almost gifted Australia the game. Thanks to a plucky, unbroken 85-run partnership between Compton and Godfrey Evans the retreat was beaten. Renouncing his impish, breezy batting style, Evans dug in tenaciously, remaining scoreless for 95 minutes while Compton guided England to safety. This was 'Dunkirk' cricket, the calibre of resilience that England would need to produce, in tight spots, if the Ashes were to be recovered.

Australia was also better equipped in the spin department. Leg-break bowlers Colin McCool and Bruce Dooland, together with teasing off-spinner Ian Johnson, shared 36 wickets during the series. According to Gerry Cotter, author of *The Ashes Captains*, Denis Compton was critical of Hammond's instructions to play the Australian spinners from the crease. Compton thought this clamped-foot batting style played into

Australia's hands. It certainly hamstrung him. Not until the fourth Test, at Adelaide, did Compton throw off these shackles and show what damage he could inflict by playing his natural game.

It seemed odd that Hammond should have been so defensively minded. In the pre-war years he had been lauded for his daring, powerful stroke-play that had devastated the very best bowling attacks. On this tour, though, he seemed plagued with insecurity. His faltering batting ability troubled him greatly, as if his self-belief depended upon his supremacy at the crease. Besides, he deeply resented Bradman's greater success.

He distanced himself from his players, choosing to travel by car while his team took the train. He disliked his players fraternising with the Australians, instructing them not to share a drink with them. Like Bradman, he was experiencing regular pain on account of fibrositis. Then, there was the unwelcome publicity about his impending divorce. With the responsibility of captaincy weighing heavily on his sagging shoulders, he became increasingly introspective. Joe Hardstaff junior observed: "There was a worried look on his face when he failed. I thought it was a big mistake to make him captain: it was more than he could take."

This tour of Australia and New Zealand marked the end of Hammond's illustrious Test match career. Although he top-scored with 79 runs in his final Test innings in Christchurch, his finest display on this tour was given in the first Test match on a spiteful surface at Brisbane, where an apocalyptic tropical storm had made batting almost impossible.

In his 1954 autobiography *Flying Stumps*, Ray Lindwall expressed his admiration for Hammond's innings of 32 runs, remarking upon how the England captain used his longer reach to pick up the ball on the half-volley and lift it to the boundary. Lindwall considered this to be vintage batting that few Australians could match in such adverse conditions. Despite fading into melancholy retirement, Hammond later wrote in *Cricket My World*: "I revelled in the sight of Australia's dauntless, picturesque and happy youth, giving to the game we love something we older players could no longer offer it."

While Bradman did not pursue a deliberate 'Bodyline' policy to inflict humiliating defeat upon his old rivals, he made no attempt to restrain his head-hunters. Australian journalist Jack Fingleton reckoned that Lindwall and Miller bowled as many bouncers in 1946/47 as Larwood and Voce had done during the 'Bodyline' series of 1932/33. As a veteran of this infamous series, he was well-placed to judge. An unrepentant Ray Lindwall remarked: "There's no sitting duck like a scared duck."

Keith Miller testified to Bradman's unyielding pursuit of victory.

He told Mihir Bose, author of *Keith Miller: A Cricketing Biography*: "At Brisbane, where one ball would hit the batsman's ankle and the next endanger his head...I thought I was going to kill someone and eased off."

Even with Lindwall indisposed with chicken pox, Miller and Toshack managed to decimate the English batting by bowling medium-paced spinners on this hideous, spitting surface, but Bradman was not satisfied. "'Nugget', bowl fast," he told the reluctant Miller. "It makes it harder." Miller did as he was told, but later confessed to Bose: "If this is Test cricket, I don't like it. But I did bowl faster and Bill Edrich just stood there and took it. He scored 16 runs and it was one of the greatest innings I ever saw. It was worth 200 on any other wicket."

Although a fierce competitor, Miller did not subscribe to the 'cricket is war' mantra. After all, he'd experienced war at first hand having piloted a Mosquito on bombing raids at the end of the Second World War. He reckoned: "Pressure is a Messerschmitt up your arse. Playing cricket is not." Actually, Miller was never attacked by a Luftwaffe fighter, although he'd had several 'hairy' moments, including an enforced pancake landing which left him with a troublesome back.

Miller regarded Bill Edrich DFC as a kindred spirit. Both men had been RAF bomber pilots. And both men counted their blessings. They had survived, whereas many of their former RAF pals had not. Both men loved to party. They were determined to live life to the full. Perhaps Bradman did not understand this mentality, having been medically discharged from the RAF, allegedly on account of poor eyesight! Rumours circulated that he had been a war dodger. Whether this was true or not, Bradman often irked Miller. It was not just Bradman's pitiless attitude to winning. Bradman was, on occasions, officious, petty even, in enforcing his authority. While Bradman was hugely admired, he was not loved to the same degree, even within his own country.

According to Alan Hill, author of *Bill Edrich: A Biography*, in keeping with his wartime instincts, Edrich chose to go out for several drinks on the eve of the second Test match at Sydney. He caught up with an old RAF pal and together they sank a fair amount of alcohol. Bill did not return to his hotel until the morning of the match. His room-mate, Denis Compton, had to cover for him.

When an early wicket fell, a still groggy Edrich pulled himself together and marched out to face the rampant foe. True to form, he rose to the occasion splendidly. It didn't take him too long to find his feet or his pull. Edrich batted defiantly for over three hours. However, when he was in sight of a well-deserved century, McCool trapped him lbw. Wicketkeeper

Evans chirped: "Magnificent innings, Bill. But what did you get out for, you were playing so well." Wry as ever, Edrich quipped: "Godders, I think I'd sobered up by then."

Despite Miller's sobering view of what real pressure was, this did not lessen the intensity with which the games were played. Gone was what writer CLR James described as the "golden age of cricket". James was referring to the late Victorian and Edwardian periods when the game was supposedly played with an adventurous flourish, without the cramping fear of failure, when batsmen thrust or skipped forward to drive with confidence. The First World War, and its impoverished aftermath, destroyed that optimism and gallant sporting spirit, pressing not only the cricketers onto their back foot. As the dole queues multiplied, and wrecked nations sought restorative pride and economic salvation through hideous totalitarianism, cricket began to reflect the harshness of those times.

Arguably, the 'Bodyline' crisis was its ugliest manifestation. However, the legacy of 'Bodyline' was to confirm rather than decry the hard-nosed pursuit of success, despite MCC's hypocritical condemnation of Larwood's feats. The grinding accrual of gigantic scores, during the late 1930s, said as much.

During the hungry, vindictive 1930s, the primary objective of Ashes cricket seemed to be the demoralisation of the opposition, not just the seizure of victory. Journalist Jim Kilburn believed this was not just a reflection of the troubled times, it was a legacy of the Bradman phenomenon. Kilburn wrote: "Some challenged like Trumper, some charmed, like Ranjitsinhji; Bradman devastated – deliberately, coldly, ruthlessly."

At the Oval in 1938, Hammond was given a rare opportunity to place his boot on the Australian's windpipe. As Hutton's gigantic innings unfolded, Hammond looked on with growing, malicious satisfaction. Hammond had no intention of easing up, even with the depleted Aussies wilting in the Vauxhall heat, angrily reproaching Compton for "throwing away" his wicket with 550 runs already on the board. Not until the England total had exceeded 900 did Hammond call off the dogs. His side eventually won by a record margin of an innings and 579 runs.

The Second World War did nothing to erode that savage spirit despite the breezy manner in which the Victory Tests were played. After all, this was merely a cavalier, 'de-mob' carnival, a joyful parenthesis. What the England team found in Australia, a year later, was a resumption of pre-war hostilities. Don Bradman may have toyed with the idea of retirement, but once he'd decided to continue he went about his preparations as fastidiously as ever. His focus was undimmed, his appetite for runs as voracious as before, as was his relentless pursuit of victory. Despite his 38 years, he prowled the covers with predatory alertness and anticipation.

During the 1946/47 Ashes series, the Australians batted better and longer, bowled with greater penetration and fielded with superior athleticism and reliability. Crucially, their players were, on average, five years younger than the MCC tourists. They were also more accustomed to the suffocating heat. Alec Bedser, who sent down 246 eight-ball overs in the unforgiving conditions, lost six pounds during one scorching, humid day at Adelaide, not helped by the heavy woollen flannels he and his team-mates had to wear. It was no wonder that Bedser succumbed to heat exhaustion. England was well beaten in this rubber, losing 3-0, with Australia having the better of both drawn matches. Bill Edrich, who fought so bravely throughout this series, averaging 46 runs with the bat, concluded: "The Australian second and third XIs could give the England first XI very hard games."

That said, Hammond was true to his word when he promised his team "the happiest six months of their lives". Despite spending most of the winter chasing lashed leather on the sun-bleached outfields of Australia, the MCC tourists had been spared one of the coldest winters on record in drab, desolate, deprived Britain. And how they made the most of their reprieve!

There was fun aplenty to be had on the outward sea voyage, a trip which they shared with many wartime brides and fiancées of Australian servicemen. Party leader Bill Edrich was one to take advantage of the many opportunities for dancing and drinking. Denis Compton told Norman Giller, author of *Denis Compton: The Untold Stories of the Greatest Sporting Hero of the Century*, that on one evening Edrich had overindulged at the bar leaving Compton to haul him back to his cabin. Compton had his work cut out. Pausing for breath en route, Compton propped Edrich up against a cabin door, pressing himself against Edrich to prevent him from collapsing. A passing elderly woman must have misinterpreted what was going on, as she muttered disgustedly: "Quite disgraceful. Surely they could wait until they got into their cabin!"

When the team reached Australia they were astonished by the vast array of 'goodies' to be had. Australian broadcaster Cliff Cary wrote: "In between meals they were forever eating fruit, cakes and chocolates." Pace bowlers Bill Voce and Dick Pollard put on two stones in weight, while another player admitted eating more in one day than he had done in a week in his heavily-rationed homeland. As they marched, or perhaps waddled, on their full stomachs, any lingering thoughts of spam, snoek (the vilified canned South African fish) and powdered egg were torn from their collective memories. Abject defeat had never tasted so sweet.

'NEW LOOK'

'Summertime'

One thing that Britain wasn't short of, in 1947, was jobs. National Service was still in full swing and, with demand so strong at home and abroad for British food and manufactured goods, employment remained high. Between 1945 and 1947, the average wage increased by £8 per week, a rise of just over 12%. The bad news for English cricket was that talented youngsters were not attracted to the county game in sufficient numbers because of richer pickings to be had elsewhere. This left the first-class game largely populated by older stagers. So, when it came to choosing the national side, MCC's selectors were hardly spoilt for choice. And now they had to replace the departing skipper, Wally Hammond.

Ideally, his replacement needed to be as tough and shrewd as Don Bradman, even if the Australian's incredible talent was matchless. Arguably, Len Hutton should have been the favoured candidate. Technically and productively, he was England's best batsman. He was tactically astute and commanded huge international respect. He had no prior experience of captaincy, though. His county side, Yorkshire, was skippered by an amateur, as was every county side, bar one. Besides, it was an MCC tradition that the England side should always be captained by an amateur.

It mattered not that a professional, like Hutton, might have better credentials or potential to do the job. Hammond had only been appointed as England captain after he had renounced his professional status. By 1947, such exclusivity was anachronistic. MCC's eligibility criteria for the England captaincy did not even stipulate that the candidate should compel selection on playing ability.

MCC's adherence to amateur leaders had its roots in the Victorian period when professionalism in sport was a spurned working-class phenomenon. In 19th century Britain, senior positions within politics, the legal profession, the clergy, the armed forces and the civil service were the prerogative of the aristocracy or the upper middle classes. Typically, those selected had a public school education.

Many went to Oxbridge also. Their exclusive education was a reflection of their families' considerable wealth and influence. A talented cricketer from a privileged background was better equipped, financially, to play the first-class game as an amateur. Unlike the working-class professional, they were not reliant upon a wage to play. The cricket authorities required no demonstration of the higher intelligence or scholastic sophistication of an amateur to select one as captain. It was presumed that the higher born should lead. This elitist principle was reflected in the practice of purchasing British Army officer commissions, a custom that was not scrapped until 1871. The choice of British colonial administrators followed similar elitist principles.

Although the English game of cricket has been played and watched by all classes since its inception, the upper and upper middle classes have largely run the game, setting and maintaining its rules. Irrespective of the substantial changes taking place in post-war Britain, democracy infiltrated Lord's at glacial speed.

Lord Hawke, a powerful MCC administrator between 1914 and the late 1930s, denied that the game had an elitist class bias. In 1924, he stated: "High and low, rich and poor, greet one another practically on an equality, and sad will be the day for England if Socialism ever succeeds in putting class vs class and thus ending sports which have made England." The historian GM Trevelyan seemed to agree, concluding: "If the French noblesse had been capable of playing cricket with their peasants, their chateaux would never have been burnt."

The aristocratic Hawke revealed his true colours, though, when he remarked, condescendingly, in 1925: "I love professionals, every one of them, but we have always had an amateur skipper. If the time comes when we are to have no more amateurs captaining England, well I don't say England will become exactly like League football, but it will be a thousand pities and it will not be for the good of the game."

In 1947, only one county side was captained by a professional – Les Berry at Leicestershire – although he was soon replaced by an amateur who had not played first-class cricket previously. In the immediate post war years many, though not all, county cricket teams still had separate dressing rooms for their amateur and professional players. While the relatively few amateurs generally enjoyed spacious changing facilities their professional team mates were often squeezed into cramped accommodation. In Victorian times, and in some instances beyond, there were separate pavilion entrances for players and amateurs. On tour, amateurs or 'gentlemen', as they were then known, roomed separately from the 'professionals' or 'players'.

Up until 1962, a team of 'gentlemen', largely comprising ex-public school and Oxbridge amateurs, played an annual fixture at Lord's against the professional 'players'. By then, the distinction was not only socially outmoded, it was also economically inaccurate, since most 'amateurs' earned a living from the game, albeit through tax-deductible expense payments or via club-related employment. 'Shamateurism' was not new, though. It preceded the Second World War. England's captain, Wally Hammond, might have renounced his professional status, but his cricketing career was bankrolled by a commercial firm.

There was also the issue of correct etiquette. The professional was expected to address his amateur captain as "Mr" or as "skipper", and not by his forename, while the amateur had no such constraint. The amateur Gloucestershire captain, Basil Allen, felt it was necessary to apologise to Cambridge University batsman David Sheppard after Tom Graveney had the 'impertinence' to say to Sheppard: "Well played, David." Allen assured Sheppard: "I think you'll find it won't happen again." In 1959, with the more egalitarian 1960s just around the corner, MCC tour manager Freddie Brown insisted that his players abide by this convention.

According to these fusty rules of etiquette, an amateur's initials preceded his surname, whereas for a professional, it was the other way round. On one occasion at Lord's, in 1950, the public address announcer felt compelled to correct a scorecard error: "This should read Titmus FJ not FJ Titmus."

It was hard to believe that Britain had just been through a war in which people of different classes had been thrown together in chaotic and intimate proximity. Despite Lord Hawke's assertions of cricket's 'one nation' characteristics, the amateurs' customary politeness towards their professional colleagues was often underpinned by condescension or contempt, whereas the professionals' deference towards their so-called 'betters' relapsed frequently into suspicion or mockery, at least when out of earshot.

Although Lord Hawke died just before the Second World War, his soul went marching on. In the *1949 Playfair Cricket Annual*, the *Daily Telegraph* cricket correspondent EW (Jim) Swanton wrote: "From the amateur strain is to be expected, in general, the enterprise, the ready acceptance of risks which cannot reasonably be looked for, in the same degree, from one whose livelihood bears relation to his batting average: also, normally, and in the natural course, one looks to the amateur for the sense of leadership which makes captains, and later, perhaps, legislators and administrators."

The famous former professional Sir Jack Hobbs seemed to agree, stating: "[The amateur players] were a great asset to the game, much appreciated by all of us because they were able to come in and play freely, whereas many professionals did not feel they could take chances."

Lest it be thought that the amateur player was either a carefree maverick or a glimmerous fop, it is worth remembering that the fiercely competitive Douglas Jardine was one. So was Bill Edrich, although he, like Hammond, was the 'elective' kind, with ambitions of the England captaincy.

In 1947, the England selectors were not minded to abandon Lord Hawke's principle, so they appointed Yorkshire's personable amateur, Norman Yardley, to lead the national side against the visiting South Africans in that sumptuous summer. Christian Dior had defied the age of austerity, in creating his Parisian 'New Look' fashion, but at Lord's, it was strictly 'Old Look' once more.

Yardley was cast in a traditional mould, in that he had enjoyed a public school and Oxbridge education. His privileged upbringing had not spared him the horror of war, though, having fought in Italy alongside Hedley Verity. Unlike the famous Yorkshire left-arm spinner, Yardley survived his war wounds. He was a useful batsman and a noted partnership-breaker with his gentle medium-paced bowling. He had performed satisfactorily in Australia without achieving startling success.

Despite having limited experience of captaincy at a first-class level – Yardley captained the Cambridge University team in his fourth year – he was chosen to deputise for Hammond in the final Test in Australia. Nevertheless, Yardley was well-liked by his players. He was more approachable and responsive to their needs than the distant Hammond. Len Hutton said of him: "A kinder or more considerate captain never walked on to a cricket field."

Having assumed the Yorkshire captaincy in 1948, he gained a reputation quickly for tactical shrewdness. He became adept at denying batsmen runs in their preferred areas. He prepared well, scrutinising his opponents for potential weaknesses. With England facing defeat at Nottingham, Yardley ordered an hour of net practice prior to play starting on the final day. This was not customary in these more 'amateurish' times. Practice made perfect as his batsmen saved the match. And Yardley led from the front, complementing Denis Compton's match-saving innings of 163, with 99 runs of his own.

Apart from his vital innings at Nottingham, Yardley batted satisfactorily throughout the series averaging 39 runs per innings, at number five or six in the order. He fielded consistently well, too, in contrast to many of his colleagues who performed fitfully in the field; on too many occasions brilliant catches were interspersed with spilt sitters. Yardley deployed his bowling attack intelligently, making frequent changes in order to unsettle the South Africans.

However, he was said to struggle when dealing with the stronger personalities in his Yorkshire side. In his autobiography *As It Was*, Freddie Trueman explained that Johnny Wardle and Bob Appleyard were too often laws unto themselves, frequently defying Yardley when he had decided upon a change in the bowling. Trueman thought that because Yardley was unable to stamp his authority upon these dissident elements, the resultant disharmony sapped Yorkshire's competitiveness.

The summer of 1947 was a glorious distraction from infernal rationing and months of Arctic cold. Neville Cardus wrote in the *Manchester Guardian*: "[Compton's] cricket, in 1947 gave a nationwide pleasure which was somehow symbolical. In a world tired, disillusioned and threadbare, heavy with age and deprivation, this happy cricketer spread his favours everywhere, and thousands of us, young and old, ran his runs with him. Here at any rate was something un-rationed.

"There were no coupons in an innings by Denis Compton. He was contagious; he liberated impulses checked for so long amongst all sorts and conditions of English folk – women as well as men and girls as well as boys. He embraced a new public in search of entertainment and release, a public which knows nothing of the old divisions that restricted sport to 'men's games.' Denis hath his fans not less dewy eyed than those of Hollywood."

In 1947, Compton and Edrich provided the perfect antidote to glum privations, scoring 3,816 and 3,519 runs respectively. John Arlott said it was a "legendary time of gallant cricket, played in the glory of sunlight".

That said, the third Test, in early July, was played in bitterly cold weather as Old Trafford, once again, lived down to its reputation. The fourth Test at a dank Leeds was not much better. However, the two London Test matches, played in scorching heat, remained long in the light-sensitive memories of the British public.

Compton scored four Test centuries during the South African series, including a double ton at Lord's, while his Middlesex team-mate Edrich scored two, also chipping in with 16 Test wickets at 23 runs each – a just reward for Edrich bowled very quickly and accurately on some flat tracks. Wright delivered some fizzing leg breaks, too, capturing 19 Test wickets at 25 runs each, but the persevering Bedser lost his place after suffering wretched luck at Lord's. Frustratingly, England's catching proved as fallible as it had been in Australia.

England took the series 3-0, a surprisingly decisive victory given that they were second best for much of the first Test at Nottingham. Three South Africans excelled with the bat: Alan Melville, Bruce Mitchell and Dudley Nourse. Each scored a brace of centuries, but their bowlers let them down, particularly in the bowler-friendly conditions at Leeds. Here, Hutton (100) and Washbrook (75) batted sublimely on a kicking surface to help set up a ten-wicket English victory, and seal a series win.

Compton and Edrich were at their peak during that summer. They worked so well together. Despite Compton's suspect judgement of a safe run, they took short singles wherever possible, stretching the field and making it difficult for the tourists to bowl at them. When one scoring avenue was blocked another would be found.

Bill Edrich was the more powerful hitter, pummelling the leg-side with his brutal pulls, hooks and on-drives. Although competent against spin, he preferred to face the faster bowlers. He certainly wasn't frightened by the short-pitched stuff, as he demonstrated so bravely in Brisbane in 1946. He gave the bowlers more of a chance because he was prepared to hit over the top, whereas more of Compton's shots streaked across the bleached turf.

Compton was so quick on his feet. He seemed to get into position quicker than most. He would disturb the bowlers' rhythm and concentration by his speed of movement – first shifting forward, then back, and skipping into a drive if he had the chance. He refused to be contained. They called him "twinkle toes" for good reason. The bowlers weren't quite sure what he'd do next, or where they should aim.

He was so unorthodox, with his sweeps and late cuts, that he effectively re-wrote the coaching manual. The South African slow bowlers tried to outfox him by looping high balls over his head when he danced down the pitch, but he would just swat these away as if they were annoying flies.

As quoted in Norman Giller's book, *Denis Compton: the Untold Stories of the Greatest Sporting Hero of the Century*, Compton recalled: "The summer got off to a cold and miserable start, and so did I... If anybody had told me that by the end of the season I would have nearly 4,000 runs to my name, they would have been dismissed as quite dotty. Then the sun came out...From then on I could not stop scoring...Bill Edrich and I used to challenge each other saying, 'first one out buys the first round'. We got very thirsty that summer with all the running we did."

Bill Edrich added: "Both Denis and I got annoyed when [it was said later]...that the bowling we faced was of a poor standard. Tell that to the likes of Alec Bedser, Doug Wright, Trevor Bailey, Roy Tattersall, Cliff Gladwin, Tom Goddard and Jim Laker."

'AT LAST THE 1948 SHOW'

'My Happiness'

In his book *Beyond a Boundary*, author CLR James explained that "coloured" Caribbean people claimed superiority over the "ordinary blacks" since the days of slavery, while sharing the blacks' resentment of the "white assumption of superiority". After slavery was ended in 1834, a black and coloured middle class emerged. West Indian cricketers Sir Clyde Walcott and Sir Frank Worrell were brought up in this social grouping, whereas Sir Everton Weekes was a child of a working-class family.

James believed that "between the brown-skinned middle class and the black there is continual rivalry, distrust and ill-feeling, which, skilfully played upon by European peoples, poisons the life of the community". The "nearly-whites" were seen, by James, to cling desperately to the coat-tails of white society, often expressing greater hatred of the blacks than more liberally-minded whites. According to him, the rules of Caribbean social stratification were rigidly drawn, and those who broke these rules were ostracised for their supposed sins – such as those entering inter-racial or inter-class marriages, partnerships or friendships.

That said, cricket assisted the growth of West Indian democracy, helping instil and spread a desire for greater equality and freedom of opportunity. Their great batsman, Sir Everton Weekes, recalled in his autobiography, *Mastering the Craft*: "The society of the 1930s and 1940s was not designed to give working-class people like myself much support in pursuit of careers that conferred honour and status...You were not expected to acquire skills that took you too far from the needs of the

33

sugar fields and factories because it would be said that you had broken free.

"The Barbados Cricket League teams were built by cane cutters who were fit young men who loved the game. They respected cricket because it was built on the principle of equality and justice for all, and offered respect to achievers. This meant a great deal to young men who were daily degraded by the drudgery of the cane fields."

Lord Learie Constantine, from Trinidad, and "Mas" George Headley, the "Black Bradman", from Jamaica, were the heroes of young black West Indian cricketers such as the youthful Everton Weekes. They raised the profile of West Indian cricket, and the status of black Caribbean people, by their achievements and popularity.

Jamaicans referred to George Headley as "Atlas" because, during the late 1920s, 1930s and 1940s, he carried West Indian cricket upon his shoulders, challenging, with the colossal weight of his run-making, prevalent racial prejudices about the place of black people and what they could achieve – discrimination that, as CLR James described, was exercised as strongly within West Indian society as outside.

The English side chosen to tour the West Indies in 1947/48 was perhaps the strangest, weakest selection in post-war times. Seven players made their England debuts during the series, including spinners Jim Laker and Johnny Wardle. Hutton, Edrich, Washbrook, Yardley, Bedser, Wright, Pollard and Hollies remained at home though, as did Compton who was due to undergo an operation on his increasingly troublesome right knee. This was a legacy of a pre-war football injury. However, Compton still played 14 times for Arsenal during the winter of 1947/48.

An MCC squad of 14 was captained and managed by 46-year-old "Gubby" Allen, a 'conscientious objector' under Jardine in 1932/33. Allen and his under-strength party set out for the Caribbean in a poorly-ballasted banana boat in late 1947. With the ship pitching and rolling violently in the Atlantic storms, it was a ghastly voyage. To make matters worse, Allen pulled a muscle en route which incapacitated him for much of the series.

The party seemed cursed with injury and sickness. Dennis Brookes damaged his finger while fielding in the first Test match at Bridgetown. He contributed little, to what seemed a losing cause, until a tropical downpour saved England's bacon. Joe Hardstaff junior did better, top-scoring at Bridgetown with a first innings knock of 98 runs, but he then injured a hamstring which ruled him out of the second Test match in Trinidad.

The 34-year-old Nottinghamshire fast bowler, Harold Butler, made just one Test appearance. He went down with malaria after the second Test at Port-of-Spain. Described in the *Complete Who's Who of Test Cricketers* as "carrying considerable weight with a sag-kneed, uninspiring run-up", Butler struggled to make an impression on the true Trinidad surface. He and new-ball partner Allen took a fearful pummelling as Carew (107), one-cap wonder Ganteaume (112), Worrell (97) and Gomez (62) created carnage.

Allen's side was indebted to Jack Robertson's second innings century (133), which held up the West Indians sufficiently for England to escape with another draw. Given the multitude of injuries, Godfrey Evans' deputy, 33-year-old Billy Griffiths, had to be pressed into service as a makeshift opener. Griffiths did his team proud, though, scoring a superb maiden first-class century on his Test match debut.

Another of England's new caps, Gerald Smithson, was unfit to play after the Trinidad Test. He injured his arm so badly that he did not play at all during the following season. There were so many injuries that Hutton had to be summoned from England to play in the final two Tests. It was to no avail, though. The West Indies won both games easily by seven and ten wickets respectively. The West Indians were vastly superior in all respects.

Everton Weekes and Frank Worrell made spectacular Test debuts, notching their first Test match tons during the series. Meanwhile, the third W, wicketkeeper Clyde Walcott, was responsible for 16 smart dismissals as the West Indies rammed home their superiority. Although Jim Laker, the Surrey off-spinner, took 18 wickets, and Dick Howorth, the Worcestershire slow left-arm bowler, claimed 13, they had very little support from their colleagues.

In a later BBC interview, Walcott seemed affronted by the weakness of the English side. And yet he understood that Karl Nunes, then the president of the West Indian Board, had hoodwinked MCC's Sir Pelham Warner into selecting an under-strength side by pointing out that the West Indians were not yet strong enough to do battle with England's best XI. It seemed as if Warner had been duped on account of his enduring Caribbean loyalties – he had been born in Trinidad and was part-educated in Barbados.

Walcott was, perhaps, quick to seize offence because of his enduring resentment at the superior, imperialist attitude he perceived among the English ruling classes. Barbadians, like himself, were not conceded the vote until 1948, while the island remained under British colonial control until 1966. He was equally critical of MCC's autocratic administration of the rules of cricket, which he attributed to their haughty patenting of the game. Walcott might have been affronted more, though, had he known about the reception that the West Indian immigrants, aboard the *Empire Windrush*, experienced upon their arrival in Britain in 1948.

Britain was experiencing an acute labour shortage, notably in the textile trade, mining and construction work, but the Ministry of Labour was dubious whether Caribbean migrant labourers were "constitutionally suitable" for "cold, outdoor work" or the heat of the coalfaces. The Ministry of Labour thought that black Caribbean men tended to be "lazy" and "unreliable", and "susceptible to colds and serious chest infections".

So, while the *Windrush* passenger Aldwyn Roberts (aka "Lord Kitchener") performed his chirpy calypso, 'London is the Place for Me', to accompany the immigrants' arrival, certain Labour backbenchers looked on in dismay. Those representing constituencies such as Stepney and Camden Town, less blessed with jobs, were worried about the strains an immigrant influx might impose. Prime Minister Clement Attlee had to move quickly to allay their anxieties.

The chastened MCC squad returned from the blazing tropics to a cool, largely overcast English spring. Fortunately, the British press was preoccupied with the birth of Israel, after British troops had found their Palestinian Mandate too hot to handle. Emotions were running high, too, over the Soviets' attempted blockade of Berlin until a massive airlift thwarted the crisis. The creation of a National Health Service was a cause for celebration, though, as was the opening of London's "austerity Olympics", the first Olympic event to be held since the "Nazi Games" of 1936.

The opening day of the Olympics began dank and drab, but by the time the torch-bearer was ready to light the flame at Wembley, the packed stadium was bathed in unaccustomed sunlight. Behind the squinting torch-bearer, the Olympic banner read: "The important thing in the Olympic Games is not the winning but taking part. The essential thing in life is not conquering but fighting well."

It was a modest expectation, but one that was beyond the capabilities of England's abject cricketers. For meanwhile, at the Oval, England had just been dismissed on a placid, sodden wicket for only 52 runs. Ray Lindwall's 'slinging' speed, bewildering changes of pace, and devastating movement had hit them for six – six for 20, to be precise.

This was England's second lowest total in Test cricket. Bradman's "Invincibles" were on course for a 4-0 series win and an undefeated tour. Only the peerless Len Hutton, with 30 runs, had managed to achieve double figures. The public execution had been dragged out over 42 excruciating overs during two-and-a-half hours of play. The Pathe newsreel commentator described the dismal procession in hushed, funereal tones: "Dewes, one, Edrich, three, Compton, four, Crapp, nought, Yardley, seven, Watkins, nought, Evans, one, Bedser, nought and Young, nought."

The sky remained solemnly overcast throughout their grim parade. Large patches of sawdust were scattered around the burial site. "Ashes to ashes, dust to dust, if Lindwall does not get you, then Miller (or Johnston) must." Amazingly, MCC officials had agreed that, for this series alone, a new ball could be claimed after only 55 overs. The mighty Australian pace attack hardly needed a helping hand.

The series started badly. Yardley's decision to bat first at Nottingham backfired spectacularly, as the Australian quick bowlers exploited the damp, overcast conditions and the slightly green pitch to hustle England out for 165. It might have been worse. Helped by a lunchtime downpour, the ball skidded through alarmingly, leaving shell-shocked England in disarray at 74-8 by tea.

Only an 89-run stand between Laker (63) and Bedser (22), made in just 73 minutes, restored a smidgen of pride to a hapless performance. As well as Johnston bowled – taking five wickets for 36 runs in 25 overs of sustained accuracy and troubling swing – England contributed to their downfall by poor shot selection. Australia then nonchalantly rubbed in their advantage, in more benign batting conditions, accumulating 509 runs with Bradman (138) and Hassett (137) scoring patient centuries.

Despite having such a small total to defend, Yardley mistakenly replaced Laker after the off-spinner had reduced Australia to 121-3. With the new ball available, Yardley decided to revert to his plan A, based on Bedser producing late in-swingers from an off stump line of attack. Yardley explained in his book *Cricket Campaigns*: "Don's weakness was to make an opening single by tickling the ball behind to leg. We employed three short legs to wait for the catch. The great man's apprehensive feeling until he was fairly well off the mark was about the single weak joint in his shining armour."

At Nottingham, Bradman was caught twice by Hutton at backward short leg, off Bedser's late in-dippers. In an unattributed press interview "The Don" retorted: "I refused to be chained down into inactivity by an obvious plan, and paid the penalty with my eyes open, to the delight of some partisan spectators who thought they saw in this old-fashioned device some new theory which would save England." Being 'bored out' was as much as he would concede.

Ray Lindwall added, in his 1954 autobiography *Flying Stumps*: "After

Australia had taken the lead, Norman Yardley switched to a defensive policy. Alec Bedser bowled to Bradman and Hassett with most fieldsmen on the boundary. Charlie Barnett, Norman Yardley and Jack Young pitched eight to ten inches outside the leg stump to a packed leg-side field. The Australian batsmen replied to these tactics by not attempting to play a stroke, and at one period Jack Young bowled 11 successive maiden overs, mostly to Lindsay Hassett. This was my first sight of bowlers concentrating on wearing down the batsman's patience by preventing him from scoring without trying to take his wicket...such methods...just aren't cricket."

There wasn't much for the 35,000 England fans to celebrate at Trent Bridge, but Compton's stupendous second innings of 184 runs was a startling exception. Arriving at the wicket with England's second innings score at 39-2, he and Hutton set about the Australian attack, scoring 82 runs in the last 70 minutes of play on the third day. As well as Compton batted against Australia's depleted attack – Lindwall was incapacitated with a groin strain – Australia cantered to an eight-wicket victory.

At Lord's, England's performance was even worse, despite the Australian bowling attack being deprived of the injured Keith Miller. "Nugget", so called because of his 'golden boy', debonair image, was suffering back pain, a legacy of his war-time crash landing. His marathon spell at Nottingham hadn't helped, although he was fit enough to smite 74 glorious runs in the Australian second innings. Morris and Barnes scored centuries as Australia aggregated 810 runs.

With Lindwall bowling at fearsome speed, and Johnston and Toshack applying a stranglehold, England was blown away for a brace of low scores, losing by 409 runs. Hutton probably played his worst Test innings here. Lindwall and Johnston psyched him out with a succession of short deliveries, which he slashed wildly at before losing his wicket. After his second failure, Hutton returned to the pavilion in accusatory silence. He paid with his place at Old Trafford.

The selectors argued that Hutton's anxieties had undermined the confidence of his team-mates. Hutton was blamed not only for his own failure but for those of others, too. Hutton kept his own counsel over the affair, refusing to be drawn into an argument that he knew he could not win. His admirable discretion was justly rewarded four years later, when he was given the England captaincy. To his credit, Norman Yardley admitted, in later years, that dropping Hutton was a mistake.

Despite the absence of Hutton, England produced a much better performance in the third Test at Old Trafford. Denis Compton completed a century which bristled with bravery and brilliance. Having hooked a short no-ball from Lindwall into his face, Compton had to retire hurt, but with England in deep trouble, he was stitched up and returned to the fray, though not before undergoing a precautionary net session. After a few minutes of Dick Pollard's pace and Jack Young's spin, Compton insisted: "I can see them all right and now for Lindwall."

Compton resumed his innings to ecstatic applause, with England tottering at 119-5. Lindwall gave him no quarter, neither did Johnston, but Compton was unruffled, playing both with assurance. With a mixture of sound and perky support from the lower order, Compton biffed and blunted for over five hours. He remained unbeaten on 148, as England recovered well to reach a total of 363 runs.

Pollard and Bedser then cut a swathe through the mighty Australian batting line-up to help England seize an unexpected 142-run first innings lead. However, with the fourth day rained off, there was insufficient time for Yardley to press home their advantage on an unresponsive pudding of a pitch. Although the draw confirmed that the Ashes would remain with Australia, some honour had been restored.

Pelham Warner was unhappy about the Australian short-pitched bowling, though. As MCC's manager on the infamous 'Bodyline' tour, he had to stomach the angry denunciations of Woodfull and the cold contempt of Jardine. Prickling at the hypocrisy of Bradman's tactics he announced: "To condemn uncompromisingly a form of bowling and later to give any suspicion that it is being used again, if only occasionally, is, to put it mildly, not only illogical to a degree but greatly weakens the arguments in favour of the original protest."

He received unexpected support from Australian Test legend and journalist Bill O'Reilly, who observed: "There were several occasions when the only difference I could see between our bowling and that of Jardine's team was the disposition of the field." The British public were no less intolerant, having booed the Australians' bumper barrage at Trent Bridge, forcing the public address announcer to demand that the crowd cease their abuse.

Hutton returned to the side at Leeds, immediately confirming the imprudence of dropping him. At Manchester he had been replaced by Gloucestershire's George Emmett, a novice at Test level. Emmett scored 10 and 0 in his only Test appearance. Having sussed out his vulnerability in a preceding county fixture, Lindwall cannily holstered his guns until the big day. Emmett's lack of technique against the short, rising ball was exposed cruelly in a more testing contest.

While Emmett had a decent county batting average of 39 runs per innings, Hutton's record was almost twice as good. Only Cyril Washbrook, who averaged 70 runs, had done better that year. Driving home the point, the English openers, Hutton and Washbrook, put together a pair of century opening partnerships at Leeds.

After ditching his troublesome hook shot, Washbrook achieved his best Test returns of the summer, making scores of 143 and 65 at Leeds. Hutton reached 81 and 57 in his two innings. With Bill Edrich chipping in with a first innings ton (111), and a half-century, England produced their best batting form of the series.

Despite making a rocky start to their first innings, Australia recovered strongly with young Neil Harvey (112) and Sam Loxton (98) setting about the England attack with malicious glee. Loxton lashed five sixes in an incandescent showpiece. However, a powerful riposte from the English batsmen set up an outstanding opportunity of victory, on a wicket beginning to produce alarming bounce and spin.

Yardley's decision to omit spinner Jack Young was regrettable. Punishing England for a succession of missed chances, Australia romped home on the final day, scoring a record 404 for the loss of just three wickets. Morris scored 182, while Bradman was 173 not out at the finishing line.

Yardley's shortage of spin prompted him to use Hutton's raw leg breaks. It was a catastrophic decision. Morris and Bradman plundered 64 runs in 30 minutes. Lindwall remarked with withering contempt: "The Australians required no ground-bait to try to win."

At Leeds, Bradman scored his 9,666th and final run in Test cricket. For at the Oval he failed to spot Eric Hollies' googly and was bowled, second ball, for a duck. Had he scored just four runs, he would have averaged 100 in his Test career. He professed to be unaware of this, as he strode to the wicket in the beaming evening sunlight, to the acclaim of the crowd and the respectful English fielders. "It's not easy to bat with tears in your eyes," he explained. Wicketkeeper Godfrey Evans scoffed at the suggestion: "I didn't see any tears, and I was standing behind the stumps, right up close." Bradman was such a hard-nosed competitor that no opponent believed he had a heart.

Bill Edrich observed: "All England feels that now, at last, we may be able to fight for the Ashes on more equal terms again." They wouldn't without matching Bradman's dedicated professionalism, though. Despite claiming that he was never coached, Bradman prepared assiduously, forensically examining others' weaknesses. For him, as for Sir Alf Ramsey: "Winning wasn't everything, it was the only thing."

In a newspaper article, entitled "Preserving the Amateur", Jim

Swanton chivalrously credited the Australian side with honorary 'amateur spirit'. He wrote: "The Australians, strictly, are not amateurs: the tour to England, for them is a very profitable enterprise. But if their ways are not exactly our ways, the approach to the game of most of them has a zest and freshness which is something apart from that of those for whom cricket is their bread-and-butter."

Nostalgic for a supposedly more colourful, artistic age, unencumbered by an "excessive emphasis on figures", Swanton seemed to miss the point. The Australians weren't successful because they were better at playing the 'amateur' way. Leaving aside a crucial imbalance in skill, it was actually the other way about. England failed to match the Australians' greater professionalism.

Keith Miller suggested as much, albeit in a passing swipe at Bradman's unrelenting competitiveness. In Mihir Bose's biography of Miller, he recounted a conversation the Aussie all-rounder held with Jim Laker at a festival game at the end of the tour. "Don't think we're all as prim as this little man, Jim," said Miller. "This is no way to play festival cricket and I'm f***ed if I'm going to support this 'head down' idea. I don't care if I don't score a run." True to his word, Miller promptly surrendered his wicket.

England's weaknesses during the late 1940s were not just due to the ravages of war, although parallels could be drawn with what had happened after the Great War. Nor were these deficits due to an absence of "amateur gaiety, spontaneity and spirit of adventure", as Swanton seemed to believe.

Anthony Sampson seemed to get the picture. In his seminal work *Anatomy of Britain,* published in 1962, he examined the archaic, privileged, political and social networks that continued to dominate British life after the Second World War. He concluded that although Britain remained as a highly civilised, compassionate and pleasant country to live in, it was lagging behind the leading world nations in terms of commercial drive, efficiency and innovation, seemingly beset by complacency, snobbery and a predilection for outmoded practices.

He criticised Britain's "club amateur outlook" which appeared to treasure the nation's past at the expense of planning its future. Sampson exhorted British politicians and captains of industry to invest in a new breed of meritocratic experts, scientists, managers and technicians to carry the country into the 1960s. While Sampson's analysis focused on the political and commercial aspects of the British way of life, it also had resonance for the way English cricket was organised and played in the immediate post-war period.

Even the avowedly conservative MCC realised that some remedial action was called for after England had been thrashed by the Australians. In time-honoured fashion, they set up a committee to enquire how the nation's young cricketing talent could be nurtured into becoming world-beaters.

Cricket writer RC Robertson-Glasgow commented in the *1949 Playfair Cricket Annual*: "Cricket needs help...Anyone since the Education Act, can sign an order. It takes a man to see it's carried out. So it is with cricket. The Australians, with the kindest intentions, suggested last summer that concrete cricket pitches in parks would help our young players. Maybe they would...But to put a concrete pitch in a park and expect it to produce cricketers is like putting a piano in a school and expecting boys to practise on it...Happily, attention is being directed towards raising the standard of cricket in those many schools where skilled coaching is impossible and space to play unobtainable...It is here that we lag far behind Australia."

Not that there was any shortage of good facilities and coaching at Britain's top-notch public schools. Some of England's leading batsmen of the 1950s and 1960s – Peter May, Colin Cowdrey, Ted Dexter and David Sheppard – had the best environments in which to maximise their talents. So it seemed that Swanton's impassioned plea for more amateur players of Test stature amounted to a cry for Britain's public schools to produce a larger yield. This overlooked what MCC's "Gubby" Allen creditably recognised as the untapped talent existing within the state schools. Allen chided the MCC general committee with his question: "What has MCC ever done to help the boys of this country as a whole over their cricket?"

However, it was Harry Altham, a former public school housemaster and a renowned cricket historian, who was appointed to chair the committee of enquiry. Moreover, starved of resources in this time of rationing, the recommended group coaching schemes achieved little, with pupils given few opportunities to practise what was taught. The *London Evening News* also arranged trials for hundreds of young cricketers, sifting out the best for the county sides to consider, but there was little chance that these limited initiatives would help restore the strength of English cricket.

'YOU'VE GOT TO BE CAREFULLY TAUGHT'

'That Lucky Old Sun'

During the winter of 1948/49, MCC were due to tour South Africa. Once again, Norman Yardley declared his unavailability, so George Mann, the Middlesex captain, was chosen in his place, making him the fourth England skipper in two years. If it was a peculiarly English amateur phenomenon to chop and change the helmsman, it hardly served the national interest. Certainly, it was not the Australian way.

And yet George Mann's MCC party managed to redeem lost pride, defeating the South Africans by two Tests to none, albeit with a pair of narrow victories, and remaining unbeaten in all first-class games. Led by their trio of prolific run-makers, Hutton, Washbrook and "Brylcreem boy" Denis Compton, England batted with consistent brilliance. Admittedly, the Union's plumb wickets granted little movement to either the spinners or the seamers. Importantly, Mann managed to help eradicate the fielding errors which had let the Aussies off the hook at crucial moments. In fact, his team fielded so well that the South African press acclaimed them as the best seen in the Union.

The bowling proved steady and persevering, too, with the medium-fast pairing of Bedser and Cliff Gladwin sharing 27 wickets, and leg-spinner Roley Jenkins heading the Test averages with 16 wickets at 30 runs each. Jenkins' success was attributable to Mann's canny captaincy, for Mann encouraged the debutant Worcestershire leg-spinner to give the ball flight despite the South Africans' determination to get after him. Mann's concealment of Jenkins in the provincial games also helped the bowler to spin his web of deceit. Mann was highly regarded by his players. He was a firm, but sympathetic, leader of men. He might have been an amateur, but he captained England with superb 'professionalism'.

As doggedly as "Tufty" Mann and Athol Rowan, the two South African spinners, performed in sharing 41 Test wickets during the series, they often struggled to restrain the run-hungry English batsmen. Cricket journalist and broadcaster John Arlott, quipped after England skipper, George Mann, had slammed a six off his namesake: "[It is] Mann's inhumanity to Mann."

The only other South African bowler to make any impact was Cuan McCarthy, a tall, young fast bowler. McCarthy had impressed on his Test debut, in Durban, taking 6-40 and almost denying England their two-wicket victory. In an article published by the *1949 Playfair Cricket Annual*, Arlott reported: "McCarthy, with a slingy action was faster than any member of MCC team and when the wicket gave him any assistance, he could be extremely hostile." The legality of this 'slingy' action would arouse suspicion when he toured England two years later.

However, Mann's team confronted a much bigger controversy upon arrival in the Union. Apartheid had been declared to be a South African government policy. This followed the National Party's victory at the polls in May 1948. Its leader was Daniel Malan, a Protestant cleric. As with other extremist ideologies, it was one founded in fear. It was perpetrated principally by Afrikaners, whose roots lay within Boer farmer traditions. Unlike the English-speaking South Africans, who tended to be more liberal-minded about racial integration, the Afrikaners saw co-existence with black and other non-white ethnic groups as threatening their way of life.

The reasons for the Afrikaners' fears lay both in their past and their 1948 present. The Boers believed that their South African lands had been a gift from God, and yet, for much of the 19th century, they had to fight for a place of their own, not only with native tribes, but with British colonialists also. The British had seized control of Cape colony from the Dutch during the Napoleonic Wars, prompting a Boer evacuation. Then, Britain annexed Natal in 1843, after many Boers had set up home there.

Feeling compelled to move on, yet again, the Boers established independent republics in the Transvaal and Orange Free State. But here they were drawn into further conflict with Britain. In 1871, diamonds were discovered in the disputed territory of Griqualand West, and in 1886, gold was found in the Boer republic of the Transvaal. This prompted a rush of mainly British prospectors, who arrived in such large numbers as to threaten Boer political control. The Transvaal Boers responded by refusing the *Uitlanders* (foreigners) the vote. Britain objected. An ultimatum was issued, and in 1899 the Boers reacted by declaring war.

Although the Boers' makeshift army proved surprisingly resilient, Lord Kitchener's extreme brutality ultimately brought them to their knees. While his scorched earth policy starved the Boer soldiers into submission, tens of thousands of Boer women and children died of disease or malnutrition in the appalling concentration camps. After surrendering in May 1902, the two Boer republics were absorbed into the British Empire, although limited self-government was restored in 1910.

The residual mistrust or hatred of Britain felt by many Boers was manifest in the National Party's opposition to South African involvement in the Second World War, and in its desire to break away from the Commonwealth and establish a South African Republic. Further immigration of Britons was resisted, too. Unlike the English-speaking, more liberal white South Africans, few Afrikaners played first-class cricket, until the likes of Hansie Cronje and Allan "White Lightning" Donald emerged around 40 years later. Cricket, for many Afrikaners, was a vestige of loathed British imperialism.

However, the roots of apartheid were not solely located in the Afrikaners' past struggles. Religiously-minded Afrikaners insisted that they had God on their side as they strove to carve out a 'promised land' for themselves. However, white South Africans represented a minority within these appropriated territories. They comprised a mere 20% of the population whereas blacks constituted 70%, with Asians and other "coloured" people making up the remaining 10%.

The political and economic difficulties associated with this ethnic imbalance caught Jim Laker's attention, during an MCC tour made eight years later. In his 1960 book *Over To Me*, he wrote, rather equivocally: "It's easy to sit back in England and condemn apartheid. In South Africa coloured people outnumber the whites many times over. The white people have got themselves into a position of the utmost difficulty; it's easy to blame them, but less easy to suggest what they ought reasonably to do. Whatever views you hold on the subject and mine are probably the same as those of most Englishmen, you find you have to readjust your thinking once you get to South Africa."

As much as white South Africans wanted a secure, prosperous homeland of their own, they recognised they were reliant upon black labour in order to thrive. The Afrikaners, in particular, were fearful that this reliance would enable the indigenous people to enhance their economic, and, thereby, their political power, threatening white interests. As repugnant as it was, the fearful white factions, many of whom then supported the National Party, sought to deprive the black people of voting rights in order to avert a potential loss of white power. This seemed analogous, politically, if not racially, to the *Uitlander* threat which precipitated the Boer War. Driven by ruthless self-interest, apartheid was promulgated to maintain white supremacy.

With mechanised production growing principally within the towns and cities, large numbers of black labourers migrated from the rural areas. Soon, indigenous people comprised 50% or more of the urban populations, developing manufacturing skills, and replacing white master-craftsmen of previous generations. Once South Africa gained independence from Britain in 1910, racial discrimination intensified leaving black labourers consigned to living in shanty towns. While a Civilized Labour Policy protected the wage levels of white workers, employers were free to hire black people at wages as low as possible. This was a slave economy.

Given its ethnic and tribal mix, South Africa was a highly divided society well before the ruinous impact of apartheid. England all-rounder Trevor Bailey observed, in his 1986 autobiography *Wickets, Catches and the Odd Run*: "There are many black tribes and the differences, apart from language, are considerable. The Indians do not meld easily with native Africans, nor do Hindu with Muslim. The Cape Coloureds are understandably suspicious of everybody. The English-speaking South Africans tend to dislike the Afrikaners, many of whom were still thinking in terms of the Boer War when I was there [in 1956/57]...It wasn't the clear-cut, black-versus-white situation so misunderstood by those who have never been to South Africa."

Jan Smuts, and his United Party, were defeated in the 1948 election because they failed to convince white farmers, manufacturers and working people that his party was addressing the consequences of increased black power, and a perceived threat of communism. Smuts' United Party was criticised for being 'soft' on racial integration. It was true that the United Party had relaxed enforcement of existing segregationist laws, causing consternation among urban working-class whites who feared for their job prospects. White farmers also wanted stricter segregation retained in order to help keep black wages low, thereby improving their profits.

The National Party exploited these anxieties, slyly linking the supposed "Black" and "Red" perils. They flooded their campaign with emotive slogans which included "the Kaffir in his place" and "the coolies out of the country", ratcheting up racist and xenophobic sentiments. Capitalising upon the febrile mood, the Nationalists claimed that Smuts' appreciation of Stalin's war effort was proof of his communist sympathies. The irony was that Jan Christian Smuts was a Boer farmer's son. As a guerilla leader, he had fought the "Soldiers of the Queen". Although he later became a staunch friend of Britain, he was also a South African hero. Electoral campaigns don't come much grubbier than this.

Malan's apartheid policy was predicated upon disenfranchisement of non-white voters. It formalised racial classification, and introduced an identity card for all persons over the age of 18, specifying their racial group. Each race was allotted its own area. Compliance was rigidly enforced. Mixed marriages were forbidden as were interracial sexual relations. Municipal amenities were reserved for particular races, creating, among other things, separate beaches, buses, hospitals, schools and universities. Signboards such as "whites only" applied to public areas, even park benches. All opposition to government policy was deemed illegal. It was hard to imagine Rodgers' and Hammerstein's 1949 musical, *South Pacific,* being well-received by Malan's government given its liberal treatment of interracial marriage, as illustrated by its anti-racist song, 'You've Got To Be Carefully Taught'.

Although interracial sport was not criminalised it was certainly frowned upon. Basil D'Oliveira was then a highly talented 17-year-old all-rounder, playing in a team of non-white cricketers. He watched the top white cricketers at Newlands but knew he could never represent his country at either cricket or football, another sport at which he shined. However, D'Oliveira would be permitted to represent his disenfranchised "caste" – the South African "coloureds" or non-Europeans – in international competition. Twenty years later, his dignified stand in an undignified affair helped bring about the end of apartheid – first in sport and then more widely. Meanwhile, the South African Cricket Board insisted haughtily: "There can be no normal sport in an abnormal society."

Apart from deputy wicketkeeper Billy Griffith, it is unknown whether any other MCC tourist in George Mann's party was exposed to the spectre of apartheid. Its evil certainly left a horrific impression upon Griffith, as it did for broadcaster and journalist John Arlott, who had been invited to cover the 1948/49 Test series for South African radio.

Arlott's experience was recalled in his 1990 biography *Basingstoke Boy.* "[On his first day in Johannesburg] he saw a black man walking towards him in an ordinary fashion on the outside of the pavement. Suddenly, a white man walking in the opposite direction swung his leg and kicked the coloured man into the gutter. The victim got up and, apparently apologetically, walked away. JA's stomach turned over."

47

The country that had treated him so well appeared in a very different light. Later, Arlott encountered a coloured taxi driver – an unusual occurrence. He asked the driver to take him to one of the coloured towns. The driver needed considerable persuasion. Arlott recounted: "It was an amazing sight: the poverty, the filth. The houses were built of tar barrels hammered flat; single room hovels for whole families. A narrow stream ran down through the settlement. The inhabitants used its head waters for drinking and washing water, its end as a sewer."

Arlott might have missed Denis Compton's incandescent triple hundred at Benoni, but he discovered a lifetime cause. When asked his race by a South African customs officer, Arlott replied "human". It was due to Arlott's relentless efforts that Basil D'Oliveira was given an opportunity to shine at the highest level in first-class cricket.

Arlott was so distressed at what he saw in that squalid shanty town that he invited Billy Griffith to accompany him on a repeat visit "to ensure I had not been mistaken in the appalling degradation". Griffith suffered it and even long afterwards as secretary of MCC said, unasked: "I shall never forget what we saw in that compound in South Africa." Griffith had been decorated for his bravery in wartime. He was no stranger to abhorrent sights. Unlike Arlott, he made no public pronouncement about what he saw in South Africa. Perhaps he felt more constrained to toe a reticent MCC line.

Arlott had no intention of remaining silent, though, even in the heart of the British establishment. Upon his return from the tour in March 1950, he remarked on the BBC Radio programme, *Any Questions,* that the pro-apartheid South African government "was predominantly a Nazi one". Predictably, his comment caused a diplomatic row. South Africa was then still a Commonwealth member, and the BBC was, of course, a government-sponsored broadcasting service.

To his enormous credit, Sir William Haley, the director-general of the BBC, refused to suspend Arlott. Recognising that Arlott was better placed to "express editorial opinion" as a freelance operator, rather than as a member of his staff, Haley released Arlott from his contract, but ensured he was paid as well in his liberated role. Gratifyingly, Haley did not consider deference to be the better part of valour. Twenty years later, Arlott concluded: "Few of those within the world of first-class cricket are political animals. That, however, is no excuse for being politically unconscious."

Following the returning MCC party was a ship transporting a young Rhodesian writer. She had with her the manuscript of her first novel,

The Grass is Singing. Known to have communist sympathies, England was meant to represent a safe haven from the strife of South African life. However, first appearances were not prepossessing ones for Doris Lessing. The world-renowned novelist remarked in an interview with the BBC's Sue McGregor in 2002: "[London was] dull and grey...clothes were still 'austerity'...dismal and ugly [although clothes rationing ended in March 1949]. Everyone was indoors by ten, and the streets were empty. The dining rooms...served good meat, terrible vegetables and nursery puddings. The war still lingered, not only in the bombed places, but in people's minds and behaviour. Any conversation tended to drift towards the war, like an animal licking a sore place."

And if life was not gloomy enough, during the winter of 1948/49 the nation's big cities became engulfed by filthy, sulphurous smog. In London, it lasted for six consecutive days. Its citizens shuffled through the filthy shroud with scarves wrapped around their downcast faces, trying to filter out the noxious fumes. These indeed were the dark ages. Railway signalmen were depicted peering hopelessly into the impenetrable gloom. Trains collided, so did cars, buses and lorries as street flares failed to disperse the murk. Worse was to follow. The pound was devalued by 30 per cent in September.

With the 'mother country' ailing so badly, the Australian government donated £8m towards its future well-being, which amounts to £400m in today's currency. It was probably just enough for a large English council to pay for its new social welfare services for a year, but a welcome gift, nevertheless. How different was this from the days of 'Bodyline' when an indignant British government threatened to recall its loans if Australia persisted with their acrimonious protests.

The Aussies were then so strapped for cash that on their next Ashes tour, captain Bill Woodfull was pressed into making a plea for English shoppers to buy more Australian produce – butter, tinned peaches and the like. The patently ill-at-ease Woodfull seemed to have an unseen hand up his back as he stiffly delivered his script to a Pathe cameraman. Now the tables were turned.

At the least the summer of 1949 restored a ray of light to the insufferably dismal British way of life. Dry, summer warmth lasted well into September, and Len Hutton, our finest wet wicket batsman, duly made hay, scoring an incredible 3,429 runs, only bettered by Compton and Edrich in the equally glorious summer of 1947, and by Tom Hayward in his Edwardian heyday of 1906. Two of Hutton's dozen centuries came in the four-match Test series with New Zealand. Because MCC condescendingly granted the visiting New Zealanders only three-day contests, neither of Hutton's Test tons were in a winning cause. In fact, all four Tests were drawn. The New Zealand side had a selection of batting stars, too, including Bert Sutcliffe, Martin Donnelly and John Reid. They all enjoyed productive summers.

George Mann began the series as England's skipper, but after the first two Tests were drawn, he was replaced by Northamptonshire captain and all-rounder Freddie Brown, who had not played Test match cricket for 12 years. It seemed an odd decision given Mann's success in South Africa. Test debutant Trevor Bailey regarded Mann very highly indeed, but Brown less so.

Brown recalled in his autobiography *Cricket Musketeer* that he had been selected in place of Mann to see if he could achieve a definite result. The selectors made five changes. Washbrook replaced Robertson, Simpson came in for Watkins, and Les Jackson took over from Gladwin, while 18-year-old Brian Close – the youngest player ever to win an English cap – replaced Jack Young of Middlesex.

Brown won the toss, and noticing a slight greenness in the Old Trafford wicket, put the New Zealanders in to bat, which was a more unorthodox decision in those days. He was justly rewarded, too, as New Zealand struggled to 82-4 at lunch with Bailey, in his debut series, clean-bowling Sutcliffe, Scott and Kiwi skipper Wally Hadlee. In improving batting conditions, though, Donnelly and Reid shared a 116-run stand for the fifth wicket, allowing New Zealand to achieve respectability at 293 all out. Bailey was the pick of the English bowlers with a fine analysis of 6-84 from 30.2 overs. He had already grabbed 6-118 on his debut at Leeds.

Bailey commented in a later BBC radio interview: "What I liked about being an all-rounder was that I was always in the game. It was less demanding because I always had the chance to redress, with the ball, what I failed to do with the bat or vice versa. Len Hutton lamented that the press always expected too much of him. Anything less than a hundred in a county game was considered a failure. I could be quite content with scoring a fifty or by taking three wickets, say."

Bailey 'arrived' in 1949. It was his first full season for Essex. Having taken 63 wickets for them at 31 runs each in 1948, he more than doubled that haul in the 1949 season, taking 130 at an average of just over 24. During that summer of rich pickings, he once took all ten wickets in an innings, and completed the season by performing the 'double', scoring over 1,000 runs to go with his hundred-plus victims.

He narrowly missed out on a debut Test century at Lord's, too, where he accompanied Denis Compton (116) in a 189-run partnership, which averted a disastrous start to the English innings. Uncharacteristically, Bailey smote ten fours, mostly from sweeps to the square-leg boundary, in his first 50, made in just over an hour. He had yet to grasp his dour destiny. Unfortunately, a freakish dismissal ended his innings seven short of his ton. A firm cut from Rabone's medium-paced offbreak hit the boot of Kiwi stumper Mooney, and rebounded to Bert Sutcliffe at second slip.

Freddie Brown could do no better than George Mann in his two games in charge. He attributed this, in part, to the defensive bowling employed by the tourists. At Manchester he recalled: "When Hutton and Washbrook began the English innings, Cowie dispensed with an attacking field after a few overs and proceeded to bowl just short of a length on the offstump with one of his slips withdrawn to extra cover, his forward short leg dropped back to mid-on and another of his close leg side fielders retired to midwicket. Hutton and Washbrook did their utmost to penetrate the run-saving field, but they could not push ahead very quickly."

Even with Bedser, Wright, Hollies and Laker returning, England could not force victory on the perfect Oval pitch. Hutton scored a sublime double century, supported by exactly 100 runs from Bill Edrich, but even a 137-run first innings lead could not be converted into a decisive result as Reid and Wallace mounted a superb rearguard action on the final afternoon. While England's batting had performed well during the two previous series, this was against bowling considerably inferior to that of the Australians. Bailey's introduction had helped improve its durability while reinforcing an attack that still relied too heavily upon Bedser. England's next visitors would prove to be a much harder proposition.

Hutton, Compton and Bedser apart, the state of English cricket during the 1940s seemed to reflect the nation's wan, woebegone and wanting disposition. English county cricket was inordinately low in quality during this period. As proof of that, Bradman's "Invincibles" inflicted innings defeats upon 13 out of the 17 county sides. The West Indian tourists of 1950 managed eight, too.

That said, Britain could still impress in other respects. Despite its meagre medal tally, Britain laid on an inexpensive, unpretentious, but undeniably successful Olympic Games. Claims made about the superiority of British technology in Pathe newsreels were somewhat overblown, but the launch of Britain's first jet airliner, the de Havilland Comet, in 1949 was a genuine cause for celebration, notwithstanding its later catastrophes. And, although British troops were unable to contain the violence in Palestine, they had more success in combating communist insurgents in Malaya. Devaluation proved not to be an unmitigated disaster, either.

Helped by the lower cost of its exports, Britain still controlled 25% of the world market. In the eyes of its leading politicians and military chiefs, Britain remained a world power. And, despite the independence granted to India and Pakistan in 1947, the Empire seemed largely intact, if not loved as much, at least by ordinary working folk. On top of this, the Clement Attlee administration had instigated one of the most radical reform programmes ever undertaken by a British government. Although created on a shoestring, there was no denying the welfare state's value to the nation's well-being.

The resumption of global hostilities in Korea during 1950 was a dismal prospect so soon after 72 million had perished in the 1939–45 conflict. The 1951 Festival of Britain, though, would mark an unexpected watershed between the hungry 1940s and better times ahead. Confounding the doom-mongers, the Festival was a massive success as a fun event and as a celebration of civic pride. The balm of spring had arrived. Sponsored by American Marshall Aid, and assisted by modernisation of the UK's major industries, the economy began to deliver more disposable income.

In 1947, one long-suffering Brit was heard to say: "Whatever picture is on, whatever drivel it is, the queues are there. Dogs, pictures, tobacco, drink, football pools, crooners – what an indifferent lot of pastimes there are for our people. To do a monotonous repetition job you loathe, and to use these anodynes to help you forget tomorrow's work!"

However, with more cash becoming available to spend on leisure items, options widened, and habits began to change. TV ownership shot up after the successful coverage of the 1953 coronation of Queen Elizabeth II. The downside, of course, was a decline in cinema admissions. With British professional football also losing popularity, English county cricket was soon exposed to the cold blast of competition.

'ARE YOU SITTING COMFORTABLY?'

'Cricket Lovely Cricket'

In her interview with the BBC's Sue McGregor in 2002, Doris Lessing recalled a troubling incident she witnessed in 1949: "In Oxford Street underground, I watched a little bully of an official hectoring and insulting a recently arrived West Indian who could not get the hang of the ticket mechanism. He was exactly like the whites I had watched all my life in Southern Rhodesia shouting at blacks. He was compensating for his own feelings of inferiority."

Outside many English boarding houses and apartments to let, were signs stating: "No coloureds." Because of such restrictions, 'ghettos' began to emerge, as in Brixton and in Cardiff's Bute Town, with black immigrants congregating for security and mutual support. There were occasional racial disturbances, as in Liverpool in 1948, but fortunately these were rare. Nevertheless, there was little to suggest that racial integration was operating smoothly.

Fear and ignorance lay at the heart of the matter. While in Nottingham, on the 1950 tour, the West Indian wicketkeeper/batsman Sir Clyde Walcott was approached by "a little old lady". She asked to touch his skin, having never met a black person before. Walcott recalled that she rubbed her fingers on his hand to see whether the blackness would come off.

As chronicled in David Kynaston's social history *Austerity Britain 1945-51*, attitudinal surveys conducted with British people during the late 1940s and early 1950s revealed that a third of the population expressed an antipathy to "coloured" people (as they were then known). The most strongly discriminative of the three groups comprised largely older people, and those of limited means or in low-status occupations. While the second group was not overtly hostile, many of them held "uncertain" or "unfavourable" views about "coloured" people.

Even the least antipathetic group, ostensibly the most liberally-minded respondents, demonstrated a disinclination to meet a coloured person socially or let a room to one. With public servants commonly stereotyping black Caribbean people as "lazy" and "unreliable", with "lower living standards", there was little effort made by British authorities to combat this racism. Even 30 years later, most British football managers held such prejudices despite three black players playing superbly for one top flight team.

When the West Indian Test party arrived in England in May 1950, they had two stern challenges: firstly, to beat England in their own back yard for the first time and, secondly, to convince the British people that black Caribbean people had greater worth than was commonly perceived. They achieved the first objective brilliantly, thrashing England in the full view of the British media. And, by virtue of their pyrotechnic power with the bat and their mesmerising guile with the ball, they shattered the presumption of white supremacy in a prestigious test of sporting skill. Sir Everton Weekes excitedly called it "the end of empire".

Although George Headley had captained the 1947/48 West Indian side, albeit for one Test only, it had become established practice that their team should be led by a white man, directly reflecting the Caribbean social hierarchy. In 1950, John Goddard was appointed as team captain.

Weekes commented in *Mastering the Craft*: "John Goddard was a rugged, business-like sort of person. He played the game hard, and he was respected as a good player...He could have made the Barbados team as a bowler or batsman, and he was one the finest fielders in the country... Goddard was respected but he was not the type of person who would sit down with players over a beer and go through an innings after a day's play. He would come into the dressing room, say what he had to say, and off he went. [Tom Pierce, another white Barbadian captain was quite different, though. Both he and Goddard had an enormous influence over the future course of Barbadian cricket, unifying the separate factions and shaping the careers of its cricketers.]

"Goddard was part of the Barbados merchant class...We had nothing in common in terms of social understanding...He was part of the Barbados elite system that had conspired to keep people like me in the margins. I did not hold these things against anyone personally. It was a system from the past that we inherited...Those of us who suffered from it wanted it changed. In such a circumstance relations would have been a little tense...There was no doubt that they did a magnificent job setting up West Indian cricket...But they built it for themselves...we ended up with cricket being a place where a race and class war was being waged."

When Weekes was first selected to play for the West Indies, he was ineligible to vote on account of his limited financial means. Not until 1950 did he gain that right – five years after winning his first Test cap. He said pithily: "So I was representing my country but my country was not representing me."

Clyde Walcott recalled that the succession of official functions on the 1950 tour was excessive. He also thought it insulting when one speaker thought that the series provided an opportunity for MCC to try out some young English players in preparation for the forthcoming Ashes tour. Walcott found this attitude patronising, but felt that it helped harden his team's resolve to beat England.

Walcott remembered with distaste the "awful food" they were served, an unchanging menu of "roast beef, boiled potatoes and soggy cabbage". His request for savoury rice was met with a sweet rice pudding. Bowing to resultant pressure, the West Indian team manager eventually permitted his side to eat at Chinese restaurants.

The West Indians were angry at the standard of pitch prepared for the first Test at Old Trafford. Although a belated decision was made to use another strip, this was scarcely better – dry, dusty and badly cracked. After England batted first, scoring 302, with Evans recording his debut first-class century, the pitch turned into a dust bowl. English spinners Bob Berry and Roley Jenkins took 17 wickets between them as the West Indians were crushed in a 202-run defeat. That was as good as it got for the injury-ravaged home side.

Weekes, Worrell and Walcott then blasted the England bowling into infinity, running up huge scores, and leaving the 'novice' spin twins, Ramadhin and Valentine, to sweep away the bemused English batting. The West Indies won by 326 runs at Lord's, by ten wickets at Nottingham, and by an innings and 56 runs at the Oval, where only a masterly innings of 202 not out by Len Hutton salvaged some English pride.

Frank Worrell scored 539 runs in the four-match series at an average of almost 90 per innings, with a highest score of 261 made at Trent Bridge. While the dependable openers, Allan Rae and the elegant Jeff Stollmeyer, averaged 63 and 51 runs respectively, Everton Weekes managed an average score of 53, and Walcott, 45.

Worrell (261) and Weekes (129) put on 231 runs together at

Nottingham, in just three hours, helping the West Indies to post a match-winning total of 558 runs. In so doing, they underlined the value of their Lancashire League apprenticeships; Worrell played at Radcliffe and Weekes at Bacup. Not to be outdone, Walcott clubbed a furious unbeaten 168 at Lord's, helping set England another impossible victory target.

Opener Jeff Stollmeyer commented in his book, *Everything Under the Sun*: "I considered Worrell the sounder in defence, Weekes the greater attacking force; Worrell the more graceful, Weekes the more devastating; Worrell the more effective on soft wickets, Weekes the more so on hard wickets. Worrell gives the bowler less to work on. Weekes has a wider range of strokes. Both are good starters, but Weekes is the more business-like; Worrell appeared to be enjoying an afternoon's sport; whereas Weekes was on the job six hours a day.

"When Worrell went out to bat he was usually in a relaxed frame of mind, often as not having been asleep in the dressing room. He would wash his eyes out, wander to the crease, greet the wicketkeeper and then enjoy himself...Due possibly to his wider stroke range, Weekes took more chances than Worrell did...Worrell bowled left-handed either at a pace well above medium or slow-length stuff. He was quite equal to the task of opening our Test attack in 1950, and whenever he bowled his slows he kept the runs down." Both Weekes and Worrell were also brilliant close catchers.

Freddie Brown replaced Norman Yardley as England captain for the final Test, after Yardley had announced his unavailability to lead a MCC party Down Under during the following winter. Brown was not a conventional "amateur" in that he was employed by a Northampton firm, but he had the necessary credentials as a "gentleman" – a public school and Cambridge education and a British Army 'commission'; in short, he matched MCC's profile for an England captain.

Besides, a change of leader seemed warranted. Yardley had hardly distinguished himself against the West Indians, having averaged 18 runs in his six innings, and having taken only one wicket for 94 runs. As in 1948, he made the crucial error of batting first on a green and lively pitch at Nottingham. As a result of good bowling and undistinguished batting, England was reduced quickly to 25-4. The *1951 Playfair Cricket Annual* report suggested, kindly, that: "Yardley wished, no doubt, that Goddard had won the toss."

In choosing to bat first, though, he denied Bedser and Shackleton the opportunity to exploit the helpful conditions before the pitch flattened out. Instead, they had to endure Worrell and Weekes clattering their bowling to all points of the compass, as the savage pair racked up a mammoth score.

In his autobiography *Cricket Musketeer*, Freddie Brown commented: "Ramadhin and Valentine returned to their homeland as all-conquering heroes...It seems a strange thing that while Australia and India have been able to take their measure, our players have never been able to do so...Not even Len was able to go down the wicket to Ramadhin and hit him back over his head although I understand Miller and Harvey did. Valentine has a better temperament when things are not going quite his way.

"He spins the ball tremendously...He bowled at the off stump rather than the leg in the tradition of the great slow left-handers. He was quicker than most of his type, and one of his most dangerous deliveries – without any apparent change of grip or action – was the one that pitched on or just outside the off stump and came in with his arm. It was certainly not easy to get down the wicket to him...But it was Ramadhin who worried our batsmen more. His break from off or leg was extremely difficult to pick. He had no googly; there was no tell-tale drop of the wrist. It was all done with a finger-flick, with a predominantly leg-break bias and a very low trajectory. It was remarkable how he would come on to bowl with that funny shuffling run and quick action, and almost invariably at once drop on a good length."

Had Denis Compton been in his vintage form of 1947 or 1948, he might have exercised greater authority over the two West Indian spinners. Alas, his troublesome right knee was restricting his movement, and his appearances. He managed to appear in less than half of Middlesex's fixtures during this season.

Sir Everton Weekes added in his book *Mastering the Craft*: "Only two English batsmen were able to read Ram. Those two, funnily enough were Hutton, the opener, and Evans the keeper." Incredibly, Evans scored a maiden first-class century against Ramadhin and Valentine on the Old Trafford 'dirt track' where they were turning the ball square off middle stump. Evans decided to get after them using his shovel shot to mid-wicket with such great effect that he raced to his ton in two hours and 20 minutes.

As for Hutton, it was his patient, adroit technique which impressed stumper Clyde Walcott, who complimented the master batsman's relaxed grip on the handle, making sure there was no chance of a catch offered to a close fielder. Walcott seemed to be describing what are known today as 'soft hands'. In reporting on the series in the *1951 Playfair Cricket Annual*, John Arlott concluded: "Ramadhin's finger spin perplexed almost every batsman who opposed him. Only the best of technicians, prepared to use quick footwork, achieved anything like a solution."

This West Indian Test victory has gone down in West Indian folklore, immortalised by Egbert Moore's (aka "Lord Beginner") rendition of 'Victory Calypso', a jaunty reggae number, penned by Aldwyn Roberts. It celebrated the West Indian triumph, their Test first victory on English soil, at the citadel of English cricket, to boot.

> "*Cricket lovely Cricket,*
> *At Lord's where I saw it;*
> *Cricket lovely Cricket,*
> *At Lord's where I saw it;*
> *Yardley tried his best*
> *But Goddard won the Test.*
> *They gave the crowd plenty fun;*
> *Second Test and West Indies won.*
> *Chorus: With those two little pals of mine,*
> *Ramadhin and Valentine.*"

John Arlott was the BBC radio commentator on that final day, Thursday 29th June 1950. After watching England's meek capitulation before lunch, he told his listeners: "A crowd of West Indians rushed onto the field in a final skirmish of the delight which they had called out, from the balcony at the Nursery End, since the beginning of the game. Their happiness was such that no one in the ground could fail to notice them: it was of such quality that every spectator on the ground must have felt himself their friend.

"Their 'in, out, in, out', their calypsos, their delight in every turn of the game, their applause for players on both sides, were a higher brand of spirits than Lord's has known in modern times. It is one of the credit marks for MCC that, faced with all the possible forms which a celebration of victory might take, their only step was to ensure no portions of the wicket were seized as trophies. Otherwise, these vocal and instrumental supporters were allowed their dance and gallop of triumph."

The West Indian celebrants were not the mighty throngs of later years, as in the heydays of Sobers, Lloyd, Richards, Holding, Marshall or Ambrose. It was estimated that only some 30 West Indians took part in this 'ode to joy', all soberly dressed, perhaps understandably so, for the cost of admission was beyond the means of the many Caribbean immigrants, forced to eke out meagre livings on shrivelled wages.

Many years later, Aldwyn Roberts, the self-appointed 'Lord Kitchener', recalled in a BBC interview: "After we won the match, I took my guitar and I call a few West Indians, and I went round the cricket field, singing. And I had an answering chorus behind me, and we went around the field singing and dancing. That was the song that I made up. So, while we're a dancing, up come a policeman, and arrested me. And while he was taking me out of the field, the English people boo him, they said, 'leave him alone! Let him enjoy himself! They won the match, let him enjoy himself'. And he had to let me loose, because he was so embarrassed. So I took the crowd with me, singing and dancing from Lord's, into Piccadilly in the heart of London."

This was a day in which English sporting pride had taken a fearful battering. The news had just come through of England's humiliating football World Cup defeat by the USA part-timers. How gratifying it was, then, that the English spectators, together with MCC, the acme of British conservatism, should rise to the occasion so magnificently, and applaud both the West Indian triumph and their supporters' infectious joy. How different this was from the gratuitous racism sullying so many encounters between white British people and non-white folk.

Elsewhere, prospective landlords were turning away black people seeking homes, disingenuously laying the blame on "neighbours' disapproval". Prospective employers were turning away black people seeking work, fearing unrest among their employees. British sport might not have been up to much in June 1950, but British 'sportsmanship' had done rather better. In an uncharacteristically raucous corner of St John's Wood, there had been an extraordinary interlude of gleeful revolution.

"Those little pals of mine, Ramadhin and Valentine" took almost three-quarters of the English wickets to fall in this series (59 wickets) for little over 20 runs each. There was a bitter aftertaste, though. Doubts were raised as to whether Ramadhin had obtained his spoils legitimately. Len Hutton, for one, had his doubts, as he had about the apparently 'jerky' action of the Australian off-spinner, Ian Johnson. However, Hutton did not pursue his suspicions about either bowler, explaining in a later BBC radio interview that if he was an umpire, he would be very careful about taking action unless he was entirely convinced of the illegality of the action. He pointed out that what may look like a throw from one position can appear to be a perfectly legitimate delivery from another.

It was left to Ramadhin to come clean almost 50 years after the event. His confession came about when Muttiah Muralitharan's strange action was put under the spotlight. "It's about time I got it off my conscience," Ramadhin told a *Daily Mail* reporter in 1999. He then openly admitted that he threw his faster ball. "There was no way somebody of my build (5ft 4in) could have produced my faster ball without throwing it," he explained.

Ramadhin then revealed that he had attempted to conceal his suspect action by always keeping his shirt sleeve buttoned at the wrist. He thought that, had he played during the 1990s, the television cameras would have exposed his offence. Actually, a still photograph taken in 1957 should have given the game away. It seems churlish now, so long after the event, to re-write a legendary feat as grubby history. As the newspaper editor quipped, in John Ford's western, *The Man Who Shot Liberty Valance*: "When the legend becomes fact, print the legend."

As indicated by John Arlott's coverage of the West Indian triumph at Lord's, by 1950 cricket had pervaded the airwaves. *Test Match Special* had begun two years earlier, although the familiar ball-by-ball format was not adopted until 1957 when *TMS* was allocated the Third Programme's vacant daytime slot.

Although Arlott's BBC radio broadcast helped disseminate the news of the West Indians' unexpected success, because this was a midweek event, most of his listeners would have been women, few of whom then had much interest in cricket. Not that this had deterred fellow BBC cricket commentator Rex Alston. Two years before, he had made a jocular, if ham-fisted attempt to win over female listeners to the game when he had appeared on *Woman's Hour*.

The poor man seemed so sceptical of his persuasive powers that he began by admitting: "Yes, I'm one of the awful men you keep switching off" before urging his listeners to give him their attention for a few minutes, and not to "dash off into the kitchen to see if your cakes are burning". Digging a progressively deeper hole for himself, he promised, patronisingly, not to talk about "silly mid-on and gully and maiden overs and all other jargon that must perplex you", while confessing that he could not guarantee that "you won't be bowled over, completely stumped, or even badly caught out!"

With Alston's maladroit evangelism lost on most of his female listeners, Lord's remained a male-only domain until 1998, when Tony Blair and his Minister of Sport, Tony Banks, urged MCC to desist. In fairness, MCC had granted the Queen a special dispensation to enter the Lord's pavilion, their holy of holies, during the preceding years. Of course, few 1950s housewives would have had the time to indulge such fripperies as a regular day out at Lord's.

According to research of the period, housewives spent, on average, 15 hours a day, seven days per week immersed in a vast array of domestic duties, with few, if any, labour-saving devices. BBC radio commonly supplied their opiates with programmes such as *Housewives' Choice, Music While You Work* or *Listen with Mother*. As much as enlightened radio shows such as *Woman's Hour* offered a 'sisterhood of the airwaves', a lifeline to housebound women irrespective of class and race, 1950s BBC radio, notably the Home Service and the Third Programme, was aimed principally at a white, middle class, conservative, Home Counties audience.

Possibly, no programme epitomised this profile better than the long-running 'plummy' saga, *Mrs Dale's Diary*. Despite featuring the odd anarchic moment, as supplied by the splendidly outspoken John Arlott or the surrealistic *Goon Show*, this was essentially bland, predictable 'Establishment' radio that sought to present Britain in comforting, familiar and anodyne terms, as reflected by the rose-tinted programme, *Down Your Way*.

'BOMB CULTURE'

'Mockin' Bird Hill'

As the Cold War intensified during the late 1940s, so did the race for nuclear armaments. While an MCC party was embarking upon its Australian tour, the Americans were developing the hydrogen bomb, to be tested in the South Pacific in May 1951. The H-bomb, which taps the same source of energy as the sun, was a thousand times more powerful than the atomic bombs which destroyed Hiroshima and Nagasaki.

With the prospects of mutually assured destruction magnifying, the glacially grave consequences of the Korean conflict impressed themselves upon the world leaders, not helped by Douglas MacArthur's demand to attack the "privileged sanctuary" of Manchuria. Anxious to forestall a third world war, US President Harry Truman sacked his head of United Nations forces. Truman explained: "I fired him because he wouldn't respect the authority of the President. I didn't fire him because he was a dumb son-of-a-bitch, although he was, but that's not against the law for generals [although it might have been for MCC captains]."

Thousands of miles away from the Korean conflict, MCC selectors Sir Pelham Warner, TN Pearce, RS Wyatt and Norman Yardley sat in quiet, leafy seclusion ruminating over their choice of captain for the winter tour of Australia and New Zealand. They were hardly spoilt for choice. Yardley had declared his unavailability for "business reasons" and George Mann followed suit. Before 39-year-old Freddie Brown was invited to lead the England team, at the Oval, there had been another candidate – Tom Dollery, the 'professional' captain of Warwickshire.

At least that was the opinion of the *Daily Telegraph* cricket correspondent, Swanton. If there was any truth in Swanton's assertion, the annual Gentlemen versus Players fixture in late July settled the issue. Dollery struck a thoroughly competent century, but Brown blasted his way to three figures in just over an hour-and-a-half against the might of England's Test attack, comprising Bedser, Shackleton, Tattersall, Hollies and Wright. To cap it all, he reached his ton with a massive six.

Suitably inspired, Brown then dismissed Gimblett, Parkhouse and Kenyon at the top of the Players' order for just 11 runs. MCC members purred. Swanton wrote in the *Daily Telegraph*: "The more elderly were reminded of how cricket used to be played and especially how the ball used to be driven before the game's descent, as many would lament, to an age of over-sophistication and a dreary philosophy of safety first."

Brown's combustible hitting had once again stirred MCC's passion for the 'golden age' of the amateur. It seemed to matter not that most of the counties were then captained by amateurs or 'shamateurs' hardly worth their places, if playing ability was the primary consideration. As an employee of the considerately-minded Northampton firm British Timken Ltd, the able all-rounder Brown was probably more of a 'shamateur'. Being demonstrably the 'right type', in terms of breeding, education and spirit, the misty-eyed MCC selectors entrusted Brown to fly their flag on the parched plains of Australia.

The chairman of MCC selectors was 77-year-old Sir Pelham Warner, a suave, articulate, personable grandee, who had captained England during the Edwardian period. He prided himself on his ability to pick a young cricketer of great promise. Crucially, he was accustomed to getting his own way, albeit by always exercising due courtesy.

He was assisted by Bob Wyatt, who preceded Warner as chairman of the selectors. Wyatt had also captained England, but in the harsher climate of the 1930s. His background was not as privileged as Warner's, although he had family connections with the prosperous Woodrow Wyatt construction business. Wyatt was an Oxford graduate, and formerly played for Worcestershire as an amateur. Len Hutton thought well of him, stating that there was no cricketer he had known who had a greater love of cricket, or was more knowledgeable about the game.

The other named members of the selection committee were Tom Pearce, a recently retired Essex county captain, and the new skipper Freddie Brown. According to Brown the selection committee comprised seven other MCC members whose identities were not disclosed. The unwieldy size of the gathering led to tortuous decision-making.

MCC was rightly concerned about reducing the average age of the England side which was then over 30 years. New, young talent had to be found sooner rather than later. This hardly seemed the right time to experiment, though. Presumably, at Warner's behest, the selectors seized upon the notion that English pride could best be restored with an infusion of youthful sprightliness and cavalier amateur spirit. Consequently, three inexperienced Cambridge amateurs were chosen to combat Australia's might.

John Dewes and David Sheppard were Cambridge batsmen of huge promise. Dewes had scored 183 and Sheppard hit 227 as their university side racked up 504 runs on day one of their fixture against the West Indians. Admittedly, the tourists then replied with 730-3. The Fenner's wicket was a duvet, helping Dewes and Sheppard to become renowned 'flat track bullies'. When batting on more competitive surfaces, they still had much to learn.

Dewes had already been capped, but Test cricket had proved to be a grim experience. He had been blown away by Miller and Lindwall in 1948, and nonplussed by Valentine in 1950. His one Test innings of note (67) had been achieved on a Trent Bridge wicket which had flattened out in his side's second innings. Worrell had dismissed him for a duck in the first, when the wicket was still green. Sheppard's Test debut, at the Oval in 1950, had not been a conspicuous success either. He struggled badly against Ramadhin and Valentine, although he proved more dogged in defence than his Varsity colleague.

Dewes and Sheppard had occupied lofty positions in the 1950 batting averages. Only Weekes, Worrell, Willie Watson and Reg Simpson were better placed than Dewes, who even pipped Len Hutton for fifth spot. However, while Hutton ended a very testing Ashes series with a batting average of almost 89 runs, Dewes averaged less than six from his four Test innings. Sheppard did little better, averaging 17 runs in his three innings, although he resisted well at Adelaide. Here, he made 41 runs in his second innings, defying Lindwall, Miller, Johnston and Johnson for three-and-a-quarter hours, although, according to Freddie Brown, he had never looked comfortable.

Nevertheless, Sheppard's stoical rearguard action might have saved the game had it not been for his colleagues' injudicious shot selections, causing the last five wickets to tumble for just five runs. Both Dewes and Sheppard were fallible to extremes of pace. While Sheppard did enough to suggest that he might make the grade at Test level, Dewes seemed not to have the strokes to succeed against top bowling.

In a post-tour assessment, Brown expressed the belief that Sheppard, like Parkhouse, had a pronounced back lift which meant that both batsmen were fractionally late in dealing with extreme speed. Brown thought Dewes failed to get into line, playing too far away from his body. These technical limitations became apparent almost upon arrival in Australia. Brown thought that all three batsmen were troubled by the unfamiliar speed of the wickets, and consequently were late on the stroke. In order to sharpen their technique, while also protecting his quicker bowlers from overwork, Brown threw balls at all of his batsmen, bar Hutton, during the early net sessions.

Simpson seemed most at ease in these initial workouts although Hutton missed them on account of injury. Belatedly, Brown realised that several batsmen were not equipped to deal with the Australian quick bowlers. He must have regretted that Bill Edrich, a redoubtable player of high pace, had been left at home.

As for the selectors' other hunches, these proved equally imprudent. The 19-year-old Yorkshire all-rounder Brian Close was chosen because of his impressive county achievements in 1949. Because Close was completing his National Service, he had played little first-class cricket in 1950. Incapacitated by a thigh injury and a lack of match practice, his tour degenerated into a nightmare, despite scoring a classy hundred in the opening game at Perth.

Having been coerced by his captain into playing in the second Test at Melbourne with a torn ligament, Close contributed only nought and one to his country's cause. He completed an unhappy tour in the dog house after Freddie Brown discovered that he'd chosen the golf course in preference to cheering his team-mates on to victory at Melbourne. Brown was not amused.

As for Cambridge University's third man, John Warr, it was difficult to understand why he had been even shortlisted. According to the 1950 first-class averages, he had been the 55th best bowler in England, having taken 87 wickets with his lively fast-medium bowling at just under 25 runs each. There seemed to be better, albeit mostly older, candidates.

Cliff Gladwin had bowled his leg cutters and swingers with impressive steadiness on the dead South African wickets during the 1948/49 tour. His 1950 record of 94 wickets at just 17 each put him 37 places ahead of Warr, while his new-ball partner, Les Jackson, had taken 92 wickets at just under 21. Hampshire's Derek Shackleton, who, like Gladwin and Jackson, had already been capped by England, had taken 111 wickets at 22 runs each. Meanwhile, the whippy, undemonstrative, young Lancastrian,

Brian Statham, had done better than any of them, at least statistically. His 37 wickets had cost a mere 16.6 runs each.

Poor Warr was completely out of his depth in Australia. A 'yokker' yelled at him: "Warr, you have as much chance of taking a Test wicket on this tour as I have of pushing a pound of butter up a parrot's arse with a hot needle!" The harsh sledger was almost right. Warr played in two Tests, taking one wicket and conceding 281 runs. Warr never flagged, though, completing a mammoth spell at Sydney when England's attack had been reduced to three fit bowlers. Warr, like Dewes, did not recover from his drubbing in Australia. Neither player represented England again.

England was beaten 4-1 by Australia in the five-match series. Although the respective retirements of Bradman and Barnes meant that the gulf between the two sides was reducing, England was deservedly defeated. Captain Freddie Brown said as much, despite suffering catastrophic luck, not only with injuries and the toss, but in becoming caught on another 'sticky dog' at Brisbane. Here, England was undone once again by a cyclone – the meteorological kind. On their next tour MCC would take the precaution of bringing their own typhoon – the Tyson kind.

Brown certainly played his part, leading from the front with some wholehearted all-round performances. He averaged 26 runs with his big hitting, top-scoring at Sydney with an entertaining knock of 79; he also took 18 wickets with his medium-paced swing and leg-breaks, costing less than 22 runs each. Crucially, his five wickets in the Australian first innings in the final Test at Melbourne paved the way for England's first victory over Australia since 1938.

Apart from Brown, only the majestic Len Hutton, the indefatigable Bedser and the effervescent Evans performed consistently well, although Simpson played one stellar innings at Melbourne, a glorious, match-winning knock of 156 runs and, before succumbing to injury, Bailey bowled with great heart and penetration.

As for the others, it was a catalogue of lamentable failure. The young Glamorgan hopeful, Gilbert Parkhouse, averaged less than 20, scarcely better than Australian tail-enders Lindwall and Johnson. Even his poor return was good enough to secure him fourth place in the English Test batting averages. Below Parkhouse were Washbrook, with a very disappointing average of 17.30, Sheppard with 17, Bailey with only eight and, most distressing of all, Compton, with an embarrassing average of 7.57. The truth was that Compton was not fit – either in mind or body.

Compton ricked his troublesome knee the day before the team sailed to Australia. A specialist was summoned who strongly advised him not to tour. With the team relying so much upon him, both he and the MCC chairman of selectors pressed strongly for his inclusion. The specialist relented, but cautioned Compton that his knee could well break down altogether. Even the patently chancy selections of Michael Vaughan and Andrew Flintoff, in later years, could not compare with the risk taken here.

Predictably, Compton soon suffered further pain. He spent most of the voyage in considerable discomfort. Although there was a brief remission, upon arrival in Australia, it wasn't long before the partisan crowds were on his case, scoffing "peg-leg" as he struggled in the field and at the crease. Denied his habitual twinkling movement, Compton's assured, sunny countenance became clouded with self-doubt. He became heavily reliant upon painkillers. Because he was not confident that his knee would support him, he could not dance down the wicket as before. Lacking his customary movement, Compton was forced into playing a gawky, crease-bound game that was totally alien to him. The more he failed the less certain he became. Hobbling and short of runs, Denis Compton was a lame duck.

Ray Lindwall recalled in his biography, *Flying Stumps*, that he had never seen Compton in such an apprehensive mood. He thought that he lost his wicket on several occasions because he had to suppress his instinctive flair, and rely upon shots that were foreign to his style. Compton had another concern preying on this mind, too – his domestic troubles.

Once again, Lindwall castigated the English batsmen for their defensive outlook, a criticism which was endorsed by an exasperated Freddie Brown. Lindwall pointed out that England had a golden opportunity to win the second Test at Melbourne, after Brown, Bailey and Bedser had dismissed Australia for a paltry 181 in their second innings. Alas, England failed by 29 runs to reach their modest victory target of 179 having spent 64 overs on the back foot waiting for a bad ball to put away.

Lindwall wrote in *Flying Stumps*: "Seeing the batsmen were primarily concerned with defence, we were able to find and keep our lengths, to place an attacking field, and to experiment as we wished...The respect paid to Ian Johnson on this wicket must have made some Australian grade cricketers pinch themselves...Ian bowled 13 overs of his slow-flighted off breaks without a man behind him or a deep extra-cover and he gave away only 24 runs."

With the momentum firmly with Australia, and injuries disabling both Bailey (broken thumb) and Wright (groin injury), the home side overpowered the tourists' depleted bowling at Sydney, running up a first innings total of 426 to which Keith Miller contributed a circumspect 145 runs. England lost by an innings and 13 runs. Australia won by a mile at Adelaide, too, after 20-year-old Jimmy Burke had scored a patient, unbeaten century on his Test debut. Had England batted with more care, this game could and should have been saved. A whitewash beckoned.

At last the lion roared. Freddie Brown attributed victory to two turning points. Firstly, a last-wicket stand, between Simpson and the newly-recruited Tattersall, realised 74 runs, 64 of which were scored by Simpson with unaccustomed belligerence. Secondly, Wright produced a perfectly-pitched leg break to end Hassett's stubborn resistance with the Australians less than one hundred runs ahead in their second innings. Hutton's watchful 60 then helped England to a joyful eight-wicket victory. Although a corner had been turned, the series should have been much closer.

The reality was that Hutton carried the English batting, "Atlas"-like. His average of 88 remains one the highest achieved by an English batsman on an Australian tour. He often held the batting together almost single-handedly. He contributed 62 not out at Brisbane and 156 not out at Adelaide, both in losing causes, and 60 not out in the victorious run chase at Melbourne.

Meanwhile, Alec Bedser was by far the most penetrative of England's bowlers. His 30 wickets, at just over 16 runs each, was a remarkable performance, both in quelling runs and in taking wickets, although he enjoyed better support from his bowling colleagues, notably Brown and Bailey, than poor Hutton had from his fellow batsmen.

Freddie Brown commented: "To think [Bedser] has now taken 69 Australian wickets in two consecutive series! Superb stuff...No captain could ever have asked for a greater trier...Alec, if anything, is a better player in Australia because the wickets are quicker, and he feels looser in the dry sunshine."

Then, there was the world-class wicketkeeping of Godfrey Evans. He went through the entire series without dropping a catch, and, while he missed two wide leg-side stumpings, he pouched several chances that most competent 'keepers wouldn't have touched. Brown observed: "Godfrey Evans gave the finest exhibition of wicketkeeping I have ever seen...Even allowing for the great concentration which wicketkeeping entails, it is fair to say his batting was a disappointment, though."

Bedser was aggrieved at having to work so hard in a losing cause. For all his skill and stamina, he felt let down by the selections made by the men in St John's Wood. Even 60 years of reflection did nothing to dilute Alec Bedser's anger with them. In a scathing rebuke, made to Huw Turbervill, author of *The Toughest Tour: The Ashes Away Series Since The*

War, Bedser exclaimed: "We were a terrible side. We picked the worst squad that had ever been selected. The selectors thought the way to beat Australia at that time was to have young players: David Sheppard, Dewes, Gilbert Parkhouse and Brian Close, but that is no good if they can't play, is it? When you think of the men we left behind: Bill Edrich and Jack Robertson, my brother Eric, John Langridge and one or two Yorkshiremen – Willie Watson for certain." Watson was possibly omitted because he had spent a good chunk of the summer with England's hapless World Cup football squad in Brazil.

Equally inexplicable were the omissions of England's three best spinners in 1950: Roy Tattersall (although he was belatedly called upon as emergency cover for the ailing Wright), Jim Laker and Johnny Wardle. These three had taken 533 first-class wickets between them during the previous summer, and were placed in the top ten of the bowling averages which also included Ramadhin and Valentine.

Their exclusion made little sense. While Doug Wright produced a number of unplayable leg breaks, as he had on the previous Australian tour, he was also wildly erratic on occasions, as at Melbourne in the second Test when his eight overs were plundered for 63 runs. As for Hollies and Berry, they were not called upon at all for Test duties.

Bedser was not the only recriminatory voice; not by a long chalk. Former Aussie Test batsman Jack Fingleton wrote in *Brown and Company: The Tour in Australia (1950/51)*: "Those who missed their chances with bat and ball, and spilling innumerable catches in the field, were mostly youngsters upon whom England was relying for its cricket revival."

Too many of the beloved amateurs were too amateurish. The novelist and poet Rex Warner was moved to write, at the time, to an Australian friend: "Will one ever know what the selectors were thinking of? The abolition of the dictatorship of MCC is perhaps the only thing that might save English cricket."

England's heavy defeat was not just the product of a poorly-selected side, though. Australia managed to unearth a new match-winner in 35-year-old, 15 stone Jack Iverson, their "mystery bowler". Iverson devised a freakish method of using his thumb and middle finger like the trigger of a gun to propel his bewildering spinners – as if he was flicking away a used cigarette. Early on in the 1950/51 tour, Iverson, suddenly, turned a ball a good 12 inches on a typically hard Sydney pitch. It took England three Tests to fathom what he was doing. Ninety-five per cent of his deliveries were found to be googlies, but by then the series had been lost.

Iverson's strange grip was perfected, during the war, with the use of a table tennis ball. He introduced variations to produce the leg break, off break and top spinner without any apparent change in action. When not taking wickets – he took 21 in the series at only 15.23 each – he attacked the leg stump with five defenders on that side of the wicket.

Later, Len Hutton laughed at the irony, having suffered accusations of ultra-defensiveness when captaining England. After Iverson damaged his ankle badly, by inadvertently treading on a cricket ball, his career collapsed as quickly as it arose. Like Bob Massie, he became a one-series wonder.

As for Brown's captaincy, he was at his very best leading from the front, boldly defying the odds. Jack Fingleton remarked in *Brown and Company: The Tour in Australia (1950/51)*: "[At Melbourne, during the second Test] Australia were 151-7 and the man wreaking the havoc was FR Brown! One would not expect him to run through a first-class side of batsmen, yet here was his name on the board with three Test batsmen to his credit at a very small cost and at a very vital stage of the game. With his sun-hat on, a 'kerchief tied round his neck, and an ambling joviality, in the field, Freddie Brown lacked only a wisp of straw in his mouth to make him look like the original Farmer Brown."

An unnamed Australian journalist added: "Perhaps we are sticking our necks out by naming England's captain, Freddie Brown, our Cricketer of the Year? We don't think so. When he was first chosen to lead England all of Australia wondered why. Since then he has inspired his team by his own refusal ever to give up a losing fight. That, for our money, is what makes a real cricketer." Brown's 'up and at 'em' spirit certainly impressed a Sydney vegetable barrowman. "Fine lettuces," he yelled. "All for nine pence, with hearts as big as Freddie Brown's."

Not everyone was sold on Brown, though. Trevor Bailey dismissed Brown's leadership in a single word: "limited". Although Brown attempted to lift the standard of England's performance with a series of preparatory drills, these had a mixed effect. His "speed trials" in which he threw the ball at his batsmen did little to improve the quickness of their eye or feet. And while he paid a lot of attention to close-to-the-wicket fielding practice, he admitted that his team was not well-armed.

Nevertheless, Jim Swanton observed in the *Daily Telegraph*: "As to the fielding, although England could not match the exceptional speed and brilliance of Harvey, Archer and Miller on the off-side, their close catching was better than anyone could have hoped for."

So, Brown's efforts had not been in vain. However, Swanton chided Brown for his inattentiveness in the field. Swanton commented: "There was not sufficient appreciation of the importance of fielding specialists for key places in the field. Too often the field switches around so that the man occupies the nearest position."

As for the bowling, Brown spotted an immediate problem. He thought that he might have a difficulty in finding a bowler to keep one end tight. He had found that it was difficult to set a field for the leg spin of Hollies, and the orthodox slow left arm of Bob Berry because neither bowler seemed able to attack or to defend consistently. It was a case of *nil desperandum*, though, as Bedser and he stepped into that breach admirably, although their task became all the more demanding after Doug Wright succumbed to fibrositis and Bailey broke his thumb.

Brown was criticised for some of his tactical decisions, such as his allegedly premature declaration on Brisbane's 'sticky dog', and for dropping Hutton down the order in the second Test at Melbourne. Neither plan came off, but these were justifiable gambles. At Brisbane, he tried to mitigate his team's misfortunes by exposing the Australians to the troublesome pitch before it quietened. At Melbourne, he hoped that, by delaying Hutton's entrance, he might solidify his fragile middle order.

Fingleton was scornful at this decision, stating: "Hutton must never go in other than first because England cannot afford to lose a minute of him." Hutton was only too well aware of the weight of responsibility resting upon him and his opening partner Washbrook. He confessed: "When Cyril and me go out to bat, we are like a couple of window cleaners set to work on the top floor of a skyscraper. Only some silly so-and-so has whipped the ladder away."

Although inclined to be bombastic, Brown had sufficient sense and humility to make good use of Hutton's expertise. He recognised that Len Hutton was "the very greatest help to me throughout the tour, both on and off the field". Hutton's view of operations from first slip, where he held some grand catches, proved invaluable. Here he was able to observe a batsman's weaknesses. Brown greatly valued Hutton's tactical advice.

In an interview with the Bedsers' biographer, Alan Hill, John Dewes referred to the socially divisive aspect of Brown's captaincy, claiming that he distinguished the amateurs or "officer class" from the professionals or "men", as if he was conducting a military exercise. If that was so, Brown seemed unaware of the anachronism. Dewes added: "To those of us who were young and amateurs, he was friendly and fatherly. For others, I suspect, he adopted a different manner."

Harold Larwood was one to suffer from Brown's coldness. In 1950, Larwood was still a newcomer in Sydney, having recently emigrated from Britain. According to his biographer, Duncan Hamilton, Larwood expected to be cordially greeted when he visited Brown at the Sydney Cricket Ground. After all, they had been team-mates on the 'Bodyline' tour and Larwood remembered Brown as a big, beaming, affable chap. Brown gave the famous fast bowler a frosty reception, though, turning his back on him after a curt "hello", refusing to shake Larwood's hand and closing the dressing room door in his face. Hamilton interpreted Brown's behaviour as indicative of his distaste for the man who refused to apologise for his 'Bodyline' bowling.

It was true that Brown disapproved of the 'Bodyline' tactics. He said as much in his biography, but he also acknowledged that Larwood was a hired hand, responding dutifully to his skipper's bidding. So, that might not have been the reason for the perceived snub. It might have had more to do with unfortunate timing.

When Larwood called, Brown must have been preoccupied with the ghastly state of his team. Not only had he lost two of his leading bowlers to injury, his depleted side had just been thrashed, ensuring that the Ashes remained Down Under. Nevertheless, as Dewes intimated, Brown was prone to snobbery. His discourtesy might have been because he regarded the former miner to be 'beneath him', socially. Whatever the reason, it was evident that Larwood was regarded with greater respect by Australia's leading cricketers. Perhaps Jesus Christ was correct when he remarked: "A prophet is not without honour, but in his own country."

As for Brown's manner with the press, it ran the gamut of the brusque, the arrogant and the dismissive. Brown had arranged a conference with all the English and Australian reporters when he reached Perth, and suggested that each country should select one representative to whom he could give official statements, such as the selection of teams and reports on injured players. Brown reasoned that the two representatives could pass on his information to other members of the press. Given the highly competitive business of newspaper reporting, there was little prospect of this idea working, but Brown refused to consider any alternative.

Likewise, his suggestion to alternate his release of the Test team details, to suit both the morning and evening papers, was not received well, either. He dismissed the journalists' protests with an irritated comment: "Until they come to some understanding between themselves, they have no grounds for complaint against the touring team administration." Brown later became a journalist himself. It is not known how he reacted once the boot was on the other foot.

One of the least appealing aspects of this heavy defeat was the manner in which Sir Pelham Warner, as the chairman of the selectors, and Freddie Brown attempted to pass the buck for their poor squad selections. Brown confided to the deposed Bill Edrich that "had it been left to me, you would have been in this party", whereas, Warner insisted: "[Brown] made one very costly error in refusing to let the selectors give him Edrich, who would inevitably have made his mark, and would probably have tilted the series in England's favour. Brown should certainly have taken the risk." According to Alan Hill, Edrich's biographer, Warner had previously invited Edrich to withdraw his candidacy for the 1950/51 tour, as a disciplinary measure.

Hill recorded that Edrich had blotted his copybook in the previous summer by partying with typical boisterousness on the Saturday night of the Manchester Test. Sunday was then a rest day but Warner took a dim view. As Compton observed, Edrich was, perhaps, too accustomed to 'partying' his woes away, although Compton conceded that such habits were easily acquired after being confronted with the grotesque experiences of combat.

As an RAF pilot, Edrich had been decorated for his bravery, having led a low-level bombing raid in the face of intense enemy fire. He had proved equally redoubtable in standing up to the flak of Lindwall and Miller, although the twists and turns of Ramadhin and Valentine discomforted him.

Admittedly, Edrich could be tactless. However, as his county captain George Mann wisely said, in conversation with Alan Hill: "If a player is picked for England, it does not mean that he is naturally an easy, or even a nice person. What it does mean is that he is a bloody good cricketer. As a manager, or captain, you have to cope with misdemeanours and try to help players to avoid them." More's the pity that Mann hadn't called the shots in Australia, but Bill Edrich's time would come again.

In summing up the strength of Australian cricket, in 1951, *Daily Telegraph* correspondent Jim Swanton commented in the *1951 Playfair Cricket Annual*: "From the Australian viewpoint the season was slightly more auspicious for the immediate future in that Hole and Burke made a successful beginning in Test cricket as, up to a point, did Archer... Australian cricket has relapsed into an uncharacteristic defensive mould... [This] sprang from two roughly equal causes – the absence of Bradman, to give the lead, and dictate the tactics, and the skill with which Bedser, Brown and Bailey exploited the weaker points in the [Australian] armour.

"Even Miller was unable to counter concentrating of their attack on his leg stump...Apart from his double century at Adelaide, Morris was almost as out of touch as Compton. Harvey looked very much at sea when the ball was doing anything and the most consistent and tenacious performer was, therefore, Hassett...If Australia's bowling seemed to suffer slightly by comparison with 1948 the cause lay chiefly in the fast bowlers getting less lift than on the English wickets and also in their having to wait a more reasonable period before calling for the new ball."

The Australia team was definitely more fallible in 1951. It could no longer be taken for granted that they were still the best team in the world, particularly after the West Indies' triumphant tour of England. This Ashes series might well have ended 3-2 or even 2-2 rather than 4-1 had the English batsmen shown more pluck in the second Test and greater resilience in the fourth.

Changes needed to be made if England was to challenge Australian supremacy. The English middle order desperately needed a class performer, and the estimable Alec Bedser needed a new-ball partner who could share his heavy load – preferably one with high pace. After three emphatic Ashes defeats, it was clear that speed mattered. Much to their surprise and pleasure, England was about to find the men it needed.

After the fiasco at Sydney, MCC flew out two substitutes: off-spinner Roy Tattersall, who had topped the 1950 bowling averages with 193 scalps at a cost of only 13.59 runs each, and the promising pace bowler Brian Statham. Both played for Lancashire.

Statham recalled in his 1969 autobiography *A Spell at the Top*: "I did not believe it when asked can you and Roy fly out to Australia in four days' time. I could understand the request for Roy. He was unlucky to go out in the first place. But me! There were far more experienced seam bowlers around such as Derek Shackleton and Kent's Fred Ridgway who I thought should be given preference over me.

"The furthest I had been abroad was a trip to the Isle of Man! I had never flown before and when the plane was delayed at London Airport for two hours with an electrical fault, both Roy and myself felt distinctly queasy. Our nerves were not improved by an electrical storm as our plane approached Rome. Then there was more work on the electrical system.

"I had nothing in the way of exercise since the end of the English cricket season four months before. Because of the rain in Australia my work outs were limited, apart from one spell on the roof of the Sydney Cricket Club. Then I was launched into a two-day up-country game at Renmark on the River Murray. The temperature was 102. That was my first genuine bowl in Australia, and also the first time I had ever bowled an eight-ball over. After four overs I was whacked. I could not breathe. I knew how green and unfit I was for bowling in those conditions." MCC's contingency planning seemed to be in its infancy in 1950.

While Statham made little impact in Australia, he was given his debut in New Zealand, taking the first of his 252 Test wickets when he clean bowled centurion Bert Sutcliffe. On the lifeless Christchurch track, neither he nor his more experienced colleagues made much impact as New Zealand posted 417-8 declared. Once England replied with a total of 550, helped by Bailey's maiden Test century and Compton's return to form (79), the game fizzled out into stalemate.

Statham's fellow substitute Tattersall made a greater impact. After his heroic batting at Melbourne, Tattersall's impressive return of six wickets for 44 runs at Wellington enabled England to win the match by six wickets. Even an earthquake, on the final afternoon, could not halt England's victory march, whereupon their weary cricketers returned to Britain just in time for the opening of the prestigious Festival of Britain. Among the exhibits was the Skylon tower, a futuristic-looking, cigar-shaped steel structure with no obvious means of support. "Just like Britain," quipped one visitor.

The English summer of 1951 started coolly, and only became truly warm in late July, before relapsing into a chilly, wet August. Nonetheless, the heat was on in early June when two British diplomats, Guy Burgess and Donald MacLean, defected to the Soviet Union. This was espionage, but not as Ian Fleming knew it. In his view, Brits should always be on top. At least Randolph Turpin was on message as he beat his famous American opponent, Sugar Ray Robinson, to take the world middleweight crown. Not to be outdone, Peter May produced a wonderfully composed century on his Test debut, at Leeds, against the South Africans.

Despite losing consecutive home Test series to England (2-0) and Australia (4-0), South Africa began the 1951 rubber strongly. At Nottingham, Dudley Nourse scored a brilliant double hundred despite suffering with a broken thumb. His brave effort enabled the South Africans to reach a first innings total of 483 runs. Simpson (137) and Compton (112) then scored centuries as England replied with a total of 419-9 declared.

With the wearing wicket allowing increasing degrees of cut and turn, Bedser and Tattersall then dismissed South Africa for only 121 in their second innings. A winning target of 186 runs proved too high, though, on this tricky surface. Athol Rowan and "Tufty" Mann took nine of England's second innings wickets as Brown's men subsided for just 114 runs. Despite only mustering seven runs himself, the England captain blamed his batsmen for their lack of adventure in failing to achieve victory. Only Wardle, who smashed a quickfire 30 runs, was spared any criticism.

Luck favoured England at Lord's, though. After winning the toss England struck a breezy 311 with Ikin, Compton and Willie Watson (a Test debutant at Nottingham) scoring half-centuries. Overnight rain then turned the pitch into a spinners' paradise, allowing Tattersall and Wardle to clean up as they shared 16 wickets for less than 200 runs. After making South Africa follow on England won the game by ten wickets in less than three days.

Bedser was the star man in the next Test at Manchester, capturing 12 wickets for 112 runs, but England still faced a demanding victory target of 139 runs on a spiteful surface. After a three-hour delay for rain, openers Hutton and Ikin had an awkward hour to endure. McCarthy was distinctly hostile, but bowled much too short to exploit the helpful conditions. Still, Hutton and Ikin were made to suffer for their obduracy. Had McCarthy bowled to a fuller length, England might not have reached its modest victory target. On the final day, Hutton steered England to a nine-wicket victory, biffing the final ball to the boundary to take him to 98 not out.

McCarthy failed to take a single wicket in these bowler-friendly conditions, but that didn't stop tongues wagging. It wasn't his bruising hostility that was an issue so much as his apparently suspect action. The circumspect Brown admitted: "I personally had doubts as to the legitimacy of his action, but after all, he has passed the scrutiny of umpires in three Test series. It is only fair to mention that he is double-jointed in his right elbow, and this has given the impression that he sometimes threw the ball. On the other hand, he mostly made the ball come in off the wicket, which lent suspicions about his action." Not that Hutton was troubled, remarking that if McCarthy did throw, it was comforting to know that he could not move the ball away from the bat.

The highly respected English umpire Frank Chester did not suspect that McCarthy 'threw' his faster deliveries, he knew he did. He wanted to no-ball him in the first Test at Nottingham but dare not do this of his own accord, so he sought the prior support of Sir Pelham Warner and another senior MCC member. Warner refused to back him, cautioning: "These people are our guests."

According to Len Hutton, Chester was also threatened with removal from the Test panel if he 'called' McCarthy. Unsurprisingly, Chester backed down in order to protect his job, having no other to turn to. He must have been mortified to learn that the South Africans then claimed that McCarthy's action had been passed by England's leading umpire.

McCarthy did not escape unscathed, though. After becoming a Cambridge undergraduate, he was selected to play for the university side in the following summer. Doubts continued to be expressed about his action until finally umpire Paddy Corrall plucked up the courage to 'call' him in a match against Worcestershire. With the controversy mounting, McCarthy called 'time' on his first-class career, although he played for Dorset in the Minor Counties competition.

There seemed to be no agreed MCC procedure for dealing with such suspicions. Freddie Brown had concerns about the legitimacy of a Western Australian bowler's action during the winter tour. Having discussed the matter with Len Hutton, Brown decided he would take the matter up informally with the bowler himself. Unabashed, the bowler told Brown that he should have seen him in the previous year when his action was much worse. In the absence of decisive MCC leadership, it was small wonder that the throwing controversy intensified, thereafter, leading to the debacle of the 1958/59 Ashes tour.

The fourth Test against the South Africans was played on the easiest-paced wicket this country had produced in years. Freddie Brown described it as the dourest, dullest and most undistinguished game he had ever played in. Everyone seemed relieved when the final day's play was washed away by rain. That said, the game featured some memorable feats: Eric Rowan's painstaking innings of 236 runs, Roy McLean's brilliantly attractive 67, and the stunning debut of Peter May.

The *Wisden ESPN* profile describes Peter May thus: "In the 1950s PBH May – the initials were part of the style of the man – came to represent the beau ideal of English batsmanship and sportsmanship. He was tall and handsome with a batting style that was close to classical, and he was the hero of a generation of schoolboys. To his contemporaries at Charterhouse he was a heroic figure much earlier: from a very young age it was clear that he was going to play for England, and he glided towards greatness in an effortless-looking manner."

Peter May was a prodigy at Charterhouse, where he was coached by former England Test fast bowler George Geary. May was also a prolific run-getter at Cambridge for three years, amid a galaxy of batting brilliance never since equalled. He also made his debut in an exceptionally strong Surrey side in 1950.

May commented in his 1956 publication, *Peter May's Book of Cricket*: "I believe young cricketers should play on good wickets. I count myself fortunate. Most of my cricket at school and in the Services [National Service was retained until 1960] was played on pitches where you could play shots with confidence...Some critics have said that Fenner's makes batting too easy; I do not agree. Batting is never easy. Favourable batting conditions meant that the batsmen were confident and in form before the matches on the University tour; and it also meant that the bowlers had to strive for supreme accuracy so that, when they went off to bowl on more responsive pitches, their effectiveness was considerably increased."

During this period, the state of pitches in the county game was very variable, not helped, of course, by the fickle English weather. There were too many easy pickings for unremarkable bowlers. This did little to enhance the competitiveness of English cricket at either county or Test level.

BBC *Test Match Special* commentator Christopher Martin-Jenkins described May as: "Six foot tall, with broad and strong shoulders, he was exceptionally straight in defence, and quite a superb driver anywhere between cover and midwicket, but especially wide of mid-on and straight back past, or over, the bowler. He was an effortless timer of the ball and his approach to batting, as indeed to all his affairs, was disciplined and fastidious. Gentle, good-mannered and self-effacing in character, he always had a hard, almost ruthless streak as a cricketer – very much an amateur with a professional approach."

Yorkshire Post cricket correspondent Jim Kilburn wasn't easily drawn into eulogies, but he made an exception with Peter May. Frustrated with the interminably dull re-invention of 'leg theory', Kilburn saw in May a saviour from this sterile tactic. "He would finish it with that superb shot of his wide of mid-on," Kilburn purred.

At Leeds in July 1951, Peter May arrived at the crease with England 99-1, in reply to South Africa's huge total of 538. Yorkshireman Frank Lowson had just been dismissed for 58, but his partner, Len Hutton, looked well set and destined for his first ton of the series.

May recalled in *Peter May's Book of Cricket*: "There is an old adage in cricket, 'when in doubt, push out' [George Geary had drummed this into the young May]. By remembering that saying, I survived my first Test innings. I made a century (138), but it might easily have been nought... Headingley has no sight-screens and, as I went out to join Len Hutton, I was aware of the intensity of the light. It was a hot day and the sun, dancing on the white shirts and frocks of the basking crowd, produced a dazzling glare behind the bowler's arm.

"In view of the long wait in the pavilion and the fact that this was my first Test innings, you can imagine my feelings as I prepared to face the bowling. It was the last ball of the over from Athol Rowan, one of the best off-spinners of the post-war era. Up he came, over went his arm, and in that background I completely lost sight of the ball! 'When in doubt, push out' – my brain quickly flashed out the signal.

"Forward I pushed, instinctively down what I hoped was the right line. A moment later – it seemed at the time, an eternity – I felt the ball on the bat. Although Rowan's natural turn enabled it to snick the inside edge, I had the bat well forward to smother the spin, and the ball went along the ground, behind short leg, scuttling down Headingley's slope, to the boundary."

Freddie Brown thought that May looked the real deal. He considered May's technique admirable, and was pleased by his ability to hit the ball really hard. May recalled that Len Hutton had suggested that he should take a leg stump guard "as you'll know exactly where your stumps are and where you are placed in relation to them". During the early 1950s, seam bowlers often pitched their out-swingers on or just outside leg stump. May found that when he took a middle and leg guard he was left "feeling for the ball, playing across it, losing balance and generally making hazy contact". He thought that his leg stump guard helped him combat this tendency.

In discussing his technique May commented: "Having been blessed with strong wrists, I discovered that by turning my left – or top hand right round the handle of the bat, as I played forward defensively, with the back of the wrist facing me, I was best at killing the spinning ball...Fast bowling at the beginning of an innings presents a very different problem and there is a danger of being beaten by sheer pace. I usually stay as far as possible on my back foot so that I have an extra yard or so to see the ball.

"One stroke, which, although I have not discarded, I seldom use, is the hook...It contains too great an element of risk...I know a fast bowler loves to see someone trying to hook, for he feels that it is giving him an extra chance. Yet a bouncer is extremely tiring to bowl, and I am always glad to think that the bowler is taxing his strength when I bow my head.

"Powerful driving – along the ground and straight – is a profitable source of scoring. There is a substantial gap between the right-arm bowler, bowling over the wicket, as he finishes his delivery, and mid-on. Usually there is only one man to beat. Although it is a productive stroke the on-drive is difficult to learn and even more difficult to master. The batsman has to open himself for it. The trouble is that, in trying to hit straight and true, the legs so often get in the way. He has to learn to unstraddle himself, to put the front foot outside the line of flight and allow the bat to come through unchecked."

May's classical orthodoxy did not extend to his pick-up. He explained: "As I pick up my bat, my backswing starts in the direction of second slip. But when the bat comes down and forward it is straight enough. That is the essential."

In a BBC radio interview, given many years later, Sir Clyde Walcott recalled "Gubby" Allen once questioning the technique of Surrey opener Micky Stewart, who was said to pick his bat up the wrong way – that is, towards gully. Walcott felt that Allen's remark typified the pedantic English approach to cricket during the 1950s. Walcott said that when he played for the West Indies, he and his colleagues never bothered about how they picked up their bat as long as it came down the right way. May clearly agreed with this view.

The final Test against South Africa was a terrific contest, quite unlike the bore draw at Leeds. On a pitch taking spin from the start, Jim Laker bowled magnificently, taking ten wickets for 119 runs in 65 exacting overs. He was well supported by Alec Bedser who took 5-68 in 39.2 overs of nagging swing and seam bowling. Needless to say, this was a low-scoring match which England eventually won by four wickets.

Compton continued his rehabilitation with an impressive first innings knock of 73, the highest individual score of the game. Hutton was dismissed for the unusual offence of obstructing the field, having denied wicketkeeper Endean a clear catching opportunity by fending a ball, which he had already played, off his wicket. Brown's brave, beefy, biffing raised the siege, and took his side within sight of the finishing line, which Laker and his partner, Shackleton, ultimately crossed.

Despite losing the series 3-1 the South Africans had proved to be doughty opponents, enhanced by their voracious, athletic fielding. Just over a year later, their young, agile side, brilliantly led by Jack Cheetham, would give Australia an almighty shock Down Under. Cheetham's focus upon fitness training and intensive fielding drills presaged the approach of the modern cricket captain.

Having established a winning momentum, MCC considered that the winter tour to India, Pakistan and Ceylon merited only a second-string touring party. And once again their condescension was badly misplaced. Brown declared his unavailability, so yet another amateur replacement had to be sought.

Lancashire's Nigel Howard was finally chosen. He was the son of Major Rupert Howard, formerly the secretary of Lancashire County Cricket Club, and a manager of previous MCC touring sides. Despite boasting an unremarkable playing career – Howard had averaged under 25 runs per innings over his county career – he was deemed to have the right attributes to captain an MCC touring party.

In fairness, Howard adeptly handled the many social engagements of the tour, relieving his players of these arduous duties after they had spent exhausting days in the field. As Douglas Jardine found, an Indian tour entailed much 'hob-nobbing' with nobles and dignitaries. There were a few tigers to hunt as well. The days of the Raj might have been over, but certain imperial conventions and courtesies remained unchallenged.

As an MCC touring party embarked for India, in October 1951, a General Election was about to take place in Britain. A glum life of austerity had left the nation disaffected with Clement Attlee's "New Jerusalem". Although the export drive was working, rationing and restrictions had dragged on. Winston Churchill, Attlee's opponent, cleverly coined the phrase "queuetopia". It had electoral resonance, much like the 1979 slogan "Labour isn't working".

The result at the polls might have been different had the nationalisation of the steel industry not been mooted, had the Liberal vote not collapsed, and had the political character of London's inner city wards not been changed by large-scale migration to the fringe new towns, such as Stevenage and Harlow. Novelist John Fowles summed up the electorate's choice: "Now it is between Tory romance and Socialist practicality. The Tories offer nationalism, the Empire, freedom of enterprise and so on; the Socialists, increasing uniformity, the death of the *ancien régime* individual. I shall vote for the Welfare State."

As far as MCC members such as Jim Swanton were concerned, "Welfare State" was a derogatory term, at least in its application to cricket. It was used to signify sterile, safety-first, unadventurous, curmudgeonly defensive play. With county cricket attendances falling by almost a fifth since their post-war high of 2.2 million in 1947, MCC secretary Colonel Rait-Kerr was understandably concerned about the declining appeal of first-class cricket. Writing in the 1951 edition of *Wisden* he said: "Many people are highly critical of modern cricket and asking if all is well with it...Can the game survive the emphasis on security, first and last? County cricket club committees should encourage their captains and players in the belief that cricket must be eager, quick and full of action."

Swanton would surely have agreed. However, he was not the only cricket journalist to rail against the safety-first, 'welfare state' mentality that was thought to have infiltrated English cricket of the time. Neville Cardus seemed to be a kindred spirit. In 1952, Cardus wrote in an article entitled *A Call for Culture*: "The pressure of the spirit of the age hinders freedom and individuality. Life in this country is rationed. Can we blame Bloggs and Blankshire if in a four-hour innings he lets us know that his strokes are rationed?"

Even a decade later, West Indian writer CLR James was still using the term "Welfare Stater" pejoratively. Despite his Marxist sympathies, he used the term to denote an unhealthy obsession with defensive, safety-first play. Surely even Freddie Brown knew he could only biff heartily and happily for England if indemnified by a carefully-crafted ton from Hutton? There again, when facing yet another calamitous batting collapse, he might have reasoned he had nothing to lose by swinging the bat.

'JEWEL IN THE CROWN'

'Britannia Rag'

As documented in Ramachandra Guha's impressive book, *A Corner of a Foreign Field: The Indian History of a British Sport*, in the heyday of the British Empire the game of cricket enabled the colonialists to celebrate wistful home thoughts from abroad; it was intended to be a parochial, consolatory activity, a bold assertion of British superiority and exclusivity in a foreign field.

Consequently, select clubs were established in all of the major Indian cities, and some elsewhere; the membership of which remained a white British preserve until Indian independence in 1947. The clubs offered a refuge, a cosy watering hole, a location to mix with privileged, like-minded companions, a place to fly the flag.

The Indians were allowed to serve their imperial club members, to prepare their pitches, serve their drinks and food, but not to play for or against them. The Indians were considered too "lazy" or "feckless" to master the "noble art", at least those not of princely status, for Kumar Shri Ranjitsinhji became the first indigenous colonial player to represent England when he was selected to face Australia on 16th July 1896.

However, Ranjitsinhji, his nephew Duleepsinhji and the Nawab of Pataudi senior, who played briefly under Jardine during the 'Bodyline' tour, were 'noble' exceptions. While resident in England during the 1890s, Ranjitsinhji's wristy brilliance almost compelled his selection, but Lord Harris and his fellow MCC selectors were reluctant to choose him, possibly under influence from the British government. It was thought, at Westminster, that Ranjitsinhji's selection might establish an unwanted precedent, opening up the possibility of Indian involvement in British political life.

With regard to cricket played in the Indian subcontinent, the Parsis were the first Indians to penetrate the discriminative colonial circles. They were allowed to play the game of cricket with the colonialists once they mastered the game of imitation. They did this by becoming respectable merchants and civil servants, adopting Western dress, listening to or playing western music, and by demonstrating fluent use of the English tongue.

As with the semi-assimilated, mixed race or "coloured" members of Caribbean society, the Parsis considered themselves to be socially superior to other Indians. Once the Indian Hindus and Muslims picked up the game, initially outside the white club walls, the Parsis were reluctant to play them, just as the white British were, dismissing the Hindus as "slow learners" and young Muslims as preferring "marbles to bat and ball". Despite their efforts at maintaining this social exclusivity, invoking racial, religious or caste prejudices, the mass appeal of cricket would not be denied.

When Lord Harris, a future MCC president, was appointed as Governor of the Bombay Presidency in 1890, he was credited with widening its popularity, recognising that the emerging tensions, between the European rulers and their native subjects, could be dissipated through sport. This is a gloss. Native cricket was already well established in Bombay by the time of Harris's arrival.

And while Harris opened up competition, by sanctioning games between the rulers and the ruled, this competition was subject to segregated codes. Europeans could occasionally play cricket with Indians, but Harris thought that they should not "break bread" with them or share common facilities. That said, Harris insisted that the game could heal the intrinsic divisions within Indian society, stating that cricket is a "manly game open to the poor as well as rich...and by its simple merits can enlist the support and countenance of the wisest men of each religion and caste".

However, few Indians were fooled by his pompous claim. One Parsi writer saw the game then as no more than an "expression of conventional politeness when it is used in connection with teams formed of two entirely different nationalities". If the British imperialists thought that in pushing cricket as a political opiate, their hollow deceit would remain disguised, they were sorely mistaken. That knowledge, though, did nothing to suppress the game's appeal among the indigenous population.

Harris's arrival in India, in 1890, came 32 years after the Indian Mutiny, an army rebellion ignited by clumsy British attempts at modernisation, compounded by crass cultural ignorance. Hostility to British rule continued, resulting in the leading protesters forming the Indian National Congress in 1885. Imported Manchester cotton cloth was burnt as patriotic Indian entrepreneurs set up their own factories to compete with Lancashire's King Cotton. The road towards Indian independence began to map out.

As much as the Indian princely class was reviled by the Indian National Congress, not only for its dissolute living and merciless exploitation of the poor, but also because of its self-interested opposition to Indian democracy and independence, the Maharajahs and the Nawabs played an important role, too, in extending the game's appeal in India. They did this by rooting cricket firmly within Indian culture, building the stadia in which the game could be watched by many Indians, and by producing the early stars such as Ranjitsinhji.

History is not made by great men, but remarkable individuals, both men and women, continue to influence great events. Palwankar Baloo was one such individual. Baloo was the first member of the Dalit ("Untouchable") caste to become a famous cricketer. He graduated slowly from a humble groundsman to a net bowler, impressing with his left-arm spin; he could turn the ball sharply either way. Having proved his worth, he defied firmly-rooted caste discrimination in joining an All India side that toured Britain in 1911.

He was an outstanding success taking 114 first-class wickets at an average of 18 runs each. Boosted by his huge sporting prowess and popularity, he ultimately turned to politics. Alongside Gandhi, Baloo helped to bring an end to the stigma of 'untouchability', and, by the sheer weight of his achievements, on and off the field, helped puncture imperial presumptions of white superiority.

During the Prince of Wales's tour of India in the winter of 1905/06, a Hindu cricket team defeated a white European one. Cricket's colonial citadel had been scaled. While the Indian press discreetly suppressed the ensuing nationalist pride, parallels were drawn with the Japanese defeat of the Russian imperialists in Manchuria. One British Army officer warned: "While the British may appear to be as firmly in our Indian saddle as ever, it was as well that we should win and not lose whatever matches we play with the natives."

The military fiasco of the Boer War had left a huge scar. British victory had been achieved at a great cost of life and money. National prestige had been badly dented. It was unsurprising, therefore, that the British Army should be so nervous about the symbolic significance of this sporting defeat. If the supposed superiority of a ruling race, nation, empire or Reich could not be guaranteed on the sports field, then perhaps their presumption of supremacy was open to question. Was this not what Hitler and the Ku Klux Klan feared after the black American boxer, Joe Louis, had pummelled the white German champion, Max Schmeling, into humiliating defeat in 1938? Certainly, the gold medal triumphs of the black American athlete Jesse Owens had rammed that unpalatable message down their gulping throats at the Berlin Olympics, two years before. Sport is never that far apart from politics.

When Jardine's MCC touring party visited India in 1933/34, 21-year-old Lala Amarnath became the first Indian Test centurion. What's more, it was a belligerent, confident effort, achieved in less than two hours with 18 crashing boundaries. Not even the immaculate Hedley Verity could halt Amarnath's charge. Hailed as a national hero, he was garlanded by the Mayor of Bombay and rewarded by Hindu jewellers. In fact, gifts poured in from all quarters. Although England won the three-match series comfortably, Indian nationalist ambitions were stirred.

As with the All Indian touring party of 1911, the Indian side which faced Jardine's men comprised Muslims and Hindus. It seemed that cricket, like football and hockey, was helping unite an emerging nation. That was until the partitionist politics of Muhammad Ali Jinnah and his Muslim League tore that nascent unity apart. Up to that point, Hindu, Sikh and Muslim teams had played one another regularly in cricket tournaments organised in Bombay, Lahore, Karachi and Nagpur. The Bombay tournaments also featured white European and Parsi sides plus a team known as "The Rest", made up of Indian Christians, Buddhists and Jews. There was no evidence that these contests intensified Hindu–Muslim rivalry. On the contrary, their respective players and spectators exhibited strong mutual respect.

As long lasting as the Hindu–Muslim conflict has been, there have been times of calm, as in the 1920s, 1950s and 1960s, helped by measured, foresighted politics. Where public insecurities have brought about or fed off intemperate, excitable political posturing, those religious divisions have widened with combustible effect. Many bitter quarrels accompanied or followed India's partition in 1947. The fate of Kashmir has continued to be a major flashpoint, and so were the horrific episodes of ethnic cleansing, notably just before and after the partition of India.

Nevertheless, a Test cricket series, staged in India in 1952, was able to bring the largely Hindu Indians and the largely Muslim Pakistanis back into friendly competition. The British Empire did not have a monopolistic hold upon cricket's capacity to promulgate political, social, religious or caste harmony.

With Britain reliant upon the immense war efforts of its Commonwealth countries, the Indian National Congress had the leverage it needed to obtain full independence. Some Indian nationalists were eager to ditch cricket as an unwanted vestige of imperialist rule. India's then-Minister of Information and Broadcasting, BV Keskar, was one such individual. Keskar was strongly outspoken on the subject during the time of Howard's MCC tour in 1951/52. He exhorted the public to abandon interests which were alien to Indian culture and tainted by their time of servitude. His words cut no ice with millions of Indian fans, though, many of whom berated him in messages sent to the Indian radio stations. What Keskar failed to recognise was that cricket had become appropriated as an Indian sport, despite its colonial origins.

Keskar's purism seemed to smack of national insecurity, a rigid attempt to grasp the treasured uniqueness of Indian cultural heritage, and set aside foreign impositions in asserting a distinct Indian identity. However, many of his fellow Indians seemed more confident of their place and purpose, and of the prestige of their newly independent country. For example, there were no anxious or angry recriminations when India lost the fourth Test match against England in Kanpur, which put Nigel Howard's side one-up.

Nor were there febrile celebrations when India recorded their first ever Test victory over England at Madras, achieving parity with their former colonial masters. Unlike Lala Amarnath, the victorious Indian side was not garlanded or feted with jewellery. India's first Prime Minister, Jawaharlal Nehru, sent a congratulatory telegram, but did not lay on a lavish reception. The Indian press was appreciative, but quite restrained in assessing the significance of victory. One editorial stated simply: "This victory provides an important stimulus for the game in this country."

Nehru was confident about his position as head of the Indian state. He did not need a national sporting triumph to buttress his political credibility. His government was too busily engaged in building the dams and factories which would secure India's economic future. Symbolic victories, such as that at Madras, were welcome, but no longer necessary.

As a result of this series, England remained in third place in the world cricket hierarchy. Meanwhile, Australia confirmed that they were the unofficial 'world champions' after beating the West Indies emphatically, by four Tests to one, in the series Down Under. In marked contrast to England's timidity in contending with Caribbean power, the Aussies had gone for the jugular. They had subjugated the lethal fluency of the "Three Ws" with brutal, short-pitched, pace bowling and neutralised the wiles of Ramadhin and Valentine with refreshingly bold batting. At Melbourne, Ramadhin left the field in tears. It would take the West Indies a further 11 years to mount another challenge for the world's top spot.

As for England, their hold on third place was now quite precarious. Had it not been for some poor catching, India might have snatched this place from them. The status of English cricket had never sunk so low. Certainly, MCC could ill afford to leave players at home of the ability of Hutton, Compton, Edrich, May, Evans, Bailey, Bedser and Laker.

At Delhi in the first Test, England's frailty against top-class spin was exposed as their batsmen crawled to an inadequate total of 203. The beguiling leg breaks and googlies of the tall, spindly Sadashiv Shinde accounted for six English batsmen, while Vinoo Mankad's sharply-spun slow left-armers were too good for three others. Shinde had a tendency to lose length and direction when attacked, but, apart from Watkins who hit well with the spin, Howard's men were mostly crease-bound. After Shackleton disposed of stocky opener Roy, and Umrigar had been fortuitously run out, Merchant and Hazare took control, adding 211 runs for the third wicket.

In his autobiography, *A Spell at the Top*, Brian Statham recalled their partnership thus: "There are certain hazards [when touring India]. The water is undrinkable, the hotels poor, the food sloppy, wickets bad and cricket played under different rules. At least that is how India appeared to me. And yet it is a fascinating country. The biggest eye opener of all was the way they tackled the game.

"We had a perfect example in the first Test when India's skipper Hazare teamed up with Merchant in a 211-run partnership. Instead of the run-rate increasing as the pair grew in confidence and we wilted in the field under the burning sun, it became slower and slower. In one 90-minute period at the end of the day they managed only 30 runs. It became clear that they were not so much playing against England as against each other.

"When he had made 154, I bowled Merchant. It was the highest score made by an Indian batsman in a Test match against England at that time. [The Roman Catholic] Hazare carried on until he had exceeded Merchant's score and promptly declared. [The Hindu] Merchant's pride was hurt and we did not see him again in the series."

Actually, Merchant's shoulder was hurt more than his pride. A heavy fall in the field aggravated an old injury, forcing his immediate retirement from first-class cricket. However, Statham correctly recognised that Hazare and Merchant allowed their personal rivalry to supersede their commitment to their side. Their slow scoring rate, and delayed declaration, spared England's batsmen an awkward evening batting session, after spending a long, hot, dusty day in the field. Helped, too, by some hapless Indian catching, England mounted a stubborn second innings recovery led by Watkins (137 not out) and Donald Carr (76), who added 158 runs for the fourth wicket, ultimately saving the game comfortably.

Young batsman Tom Graveney returned to fitness in time for the second Test at Bombay. It was just as well because his patiently accumulated 175 runs helped England reach a first innings total of 456, less than 30 runs behind India's score. Once again Hazare contributed another big hundred (155), despite mis-hooking a short ball from Ridgway into his forehead.

Pankaj Roy put aside his failure at Delhi to reach a blistering ton (140) with 80 of his runs coming in boundaries. When India batted again, though, they were reduced quickly to 34-4 as Ridgway, Statham and Watkins got among the wickets. When India lost their seventh wicket, their second innings score was only 88, 117 ahead. However, Gopinath and Mankad made the game safe by adding 71 runs for the eighth wicket. The Glamorgan all-rounder Watkins was the pick of the English bowlers, taking three second innings wickets for just 20 runs. This was on top of another sterling display with the bat.

The third Test match at Calcutta was a bore draw par excellence. Twenty-seven-and-a-half hours of uninterrupted cricket produced a measly 1,041 runs and 25 wickets. The result was a foregone conclusion.

The fourth Test at Kanpur was played on a result wicket. The disappointing Don Kenyon was dropped and, with Lowson returning to open the batting, Robertson took over the number four slot to bolster a shaky middle order. Lancashire's left-arm spinner Malcolm Hilton came in for Leadbetter, who had failed to impress with his leg breaks. Hilton had the rare distinction of dismissing the great Don Bradman twice in a first-class fixture, but had not pushed on quite as expected.

However, Kanpur proved to be a triumphant occasion as he achieved match figures of 9-93 in 54.5 overs, helping county club-mate Roy Tattersall (eight wickets for 125 runs) to bowl England to an eight-wicket victory. India made the tactical mistake of selecting two leg-spinners, believing that the wicket would play quicker than it did. Having shot India out for 121 runs in their first innings, Lowson (26) and Watkins

(66) batted superbly on the sharply turning track to earn England a crucial 82-run lead. Although Umrigar (36) and Adhikari (60) added 58 for India's sixth wicket, the hosts could only manage 157 runs the second time around. Graveney's sublime, attacking innings of 48 not out saw England home in comfort.

However, India won emphatically at Madras by an innings and eight runs. Donald Carr, who had replaced Howard, both as a middle-order batsman and as captain, was one of few English batsmen to do himself justice in a poor first innings total of 266. India passed this total with ease, declaring at 457-9 with Umrigar 130 not out. Roy (111) had already battered the toothless English attack senseless. In England's second innings, only Watkins (48) and Robertson (56) showed any defiance against Mankad (4-53) and off-spinner Ghulam Ahmed (4-77). Five years after the Raj had ended Indian cricket had come of age.

Brian Statham, who had struggled to make any impact on the slow, low Indian wickets, added an amusing postscript to his disappointing series. He recalled in *A Spell at the Top*: "Some states in India were supposed to be 'dry'. It meant we could not take in our supply of beer and spirits. The only way round the regulation was for every member of the side to be registered as an alcoholic to get his ration of three bottles of spirits or a couple of dozen bottles of beer a month!"

By 1952, Western imperial rule was coming under increasing challenge from nationalist movements, intent upon shooting the past. A British Pathe news reporter announced: "In Vietnam the communist rebels are beginning to attack innocent French colonialists." There was little recognition, by Western reporters or their governments, that the Viet Minh resistance was fostered more by a pursuit of national unification than by ambitions of communist expansion.

This catastrophic error of judgement would result in over three million deaths after the United States became embroiled in the conflict. At least the British had the good sense to know that it was beaten in India, even if the musty mystique of the Raj seemed to inhabit Lord's for years after Indian independence was granted.

Elsewhere, British colonialism was facing severe challenges. Riots in Cairo left 17 British people murdered or burnt to death. King Farouk was forced to abdicate, leaving power in the hands of Egyptian General Neguib. As Neguib's right-hand man, Colonel Nasser saw his path to power. A spectre of Suez shimmered mirage-like on a desert horizon.

In Kenya, the Mau Mau insurgency was spreading among Kikuyu tribesmen. This secret society was pledged to drive white people from the

British colony by violent means, if necessary. On the other hand, peace broke out in the Gold Coast after Dr Kwame Nkrumah's campaign to end British colonial rule was given electoral endorsement, making him the first African Prime Minister south of the Sahara.

Meanwhile in South Africa, the apartheid laws were arousing strong protests from South African ethnic groups. After crossing race segregation barriers and openly defying the law requiring them to carry official passes, the protesters gave themselves up to the police and refused to ask for bail. About 150 demonstrators were taken to prison, most of them wearing gold, green and black armbands, the colours of the African National Congress.

Old orders were tried, tested and began to topple. And at Lord's a heresy was about to be committed. MCC decided to select its first professional captain of England. Unaccustomed to the winds of change in this neck of the woods, Lord Hawke must have turned in his grave.

'MEMORIES ARE MADE OF THIS':
1952 – 1956

"Remember lad, one day we'll have a fast bowler –
and I hope that day isn't too far off."
Len Hutton's words to Ray Lindwall, 1950.

"Noo, we 'aven't got mooch boolin. Got a chap called Tyson but you won't
'ave 'eard of him because he's 'ardly ever played."
Colin Cowdrey's account of Len Hutton's press conference, Australia
1954.

'THE AMATEUR CAN AFFORD TO LOSE'

'Indian Love Call'

During the 1950s, English first-class cricket remained in the firm grip of the upper and upper middle classes – the British establishment. It was they who wanted England to be captained by one of their own. It was they who supposed that professionals were more risk-averse and less disposed to lead. Len Hutton, who came from a lower middle-class/skilled working-class background, did not match their preferred class profile. The problem was that there seemed to be no eligible amateur candidates left. Howard's winter appointment had not been a success.

Consequently, Hutton became England's first professional captain more by default than design. He was certainly under no illusion that he was any more than a stop-gap. Not only was he required to secure the fragile England batting order, he was expected to captain the side with only a tepid vote of confidence, although he diplomatically insisted that "every MCC official gave him his complete support".

That said, some of MCC's dyed-in-the-wool traditionalists were not silenced by his appointment. Some touted David Sheppard of Cambridge University and Sussex as a rival claimant. Sheppard's four Test appearances had thus far yielded 98 runs at an average of 16 runs per innings while Hutton had scored 1,303 runs at an average of just under 70. Hutton was not only the best batsman in England he was the best in the world. Hutton's technical prowess and tactical knowledge was unrivalled, and yet Sheppard, an amateur player of immense promise, but unproven ability at Test level, was seen by some as a better bet.

The selectors who had chosen the 1950/51 MCC touring party were not convinced that Hutton was even the best *professional* candidate for the job since they appointed Denis Compton as Freddie Brown's deputy. The adventurous, cavalier Compton was regarded by MCC selectors as almost an 'amateur' in professional clothing, at least until his knee failed him. Hutton was considered, by many MCC members, as too cautious, too studious, too slow in his run-making despite his capacity to prop up his sinking side almost single-handedly. Moreover, Hutton's shrewd tactical brain had been eagerly picked by Freddie Brown on that Ashes tour. Compton's failing health and form eventually forced the selectors to switch horses, albeit reluctantly.

Not that Hutton had any quarrel with Compton's appointment as vice-captain. He recognised that he could not compete with Compton's popularity and debonair style of play. He held no grudge, admiring Compton's zest and flair greatly. Hutton also dismissed the view that Compton's appointment had been nepotistic or indicative of any southern bias. Instead, he decided that Brown had looked for a personality closer to his own.

Thirty years after the event, Len Hutton remained diplomatic on the subject, while acknowledging that it might have been a mistake to "shackle the free-ranging Compton to the responsibilities of management". By that time, Hutton had seen the downside of Ian Botham's appointment as England's captain.

Once appointed as England's captain, Hutton remarked: "I was not naive enough to believe I would not come under the closest scrutiny, and maybe provoke a backlash from the inflexible traditionalists. I could see their point of view and, in the interests of England's Test side, I hoped they would see mine, for [given the emergence of young talent such as May, Statham and Trueman] I was plainly better placed than any of the previous post-war captains to get results against the strongest opposition."

However, Hutton remained deferential towards the selectors, Yardley, Brown, Wyatt and Ames, observing: "As I considered myself a stop-gap, I was at a disadvantage among selectors with amateur backgrounds and distinguished playing records...I felt rather like a head boy called to a meeting of house masters and, as there seemed to be no shortage of sense,

I was mainly content to rely upon their judgement." Hutton must have known that his playing record was considerably better than any one of the selectors. However, he knew when it was advisable to 'bend the knee'.

According to Anthony Sampson's *Anatomy of Britain* the UK was riddled with class snobbery during the 1950s. It was noticeable that since making his record-breaking innings of 364 at the Oval in 1938, Len Hutton had suppressed his natural dialect. The video footage of his 1938 interview depicts a delighted young man at ease with his broad Yorkshire accent. And yet 15 years later, the Pathe News record captures captain Hutton making his Ashes victory speech with a pastiche of 'Oxford' pronunciation. Hutton was not the only British sporting leader in the 1950s who felt compelled to 'toff it up' at public or formal occasions.

World Cup-winning England football boss Sir Alf Ramsey felt obliged to re-invent himself, too. He came from a working-class background. He had a taste for jellied eels and the simple life. And yet he knew he had to smarten up his act if he was to make his name as a successful football club manager. It was not enough that he'd had a glittering international playing career. Like John Major, he encased himself in an elocution straitjacket. He needed to be credible within the social circles he was expected to inhabit.

At Ipswich, this included the club 'aristocracy', the Cobbolds. The trouble was, when Ramsey tried to 'toff it up' he sounded like Harold Steptoe. Ramsey's diction was so formal, so clipped, so contrived, that when he used the f-word it had a startling effect as if the Queen decided to sport a Mohican hairstyle. He was not the only club manager to feel constrained in this way. Take the stilted, florid prose adopted by other football managers of the period such as Burnley's Harry Potts. These were the strained attempts of working-class men to prove themselves in an elitist climate. With educational snobbery still rife, they felt obliged to present themselves in refined tones. When alone with their teams, they were much more relaxed and informal. In public, they were constantly on guard.

In 1955, when Len Hutton retired as England's captain, and when Alf Ramsey became the manager of Ipswich Town, the national press was having a field day with Professor Alan Ross's study of 'U' – that is to say, 'upper-class' – and 'non-U' linguistic conventions. Reactions ranged from the outraged to the amused. It was almost as if Nancy Mitford, the aristocratic novelist, had her tongue in her chic when she pontificated upon 'U' etiquette, insisting that it was 'non-U' to refer to the lavatory as the 'toilet'.

John Betjeman commented drolly upon the issue in his poem, *How to Get on in Society*. He smirked at the notion that tea drinkers who preferred their milk in first were betraying their lower class origins. The stultifying class distinctions, that these conventions signified, were less of a laughing matter, though. These served to inhibit the greater freedom of opportunity and social mobility that was beginning to emerge, by the mid 1950s, for British people from less privileged backgrounds.

It was not clear whether Evelyn Waugh was speaking in jest when he accused the 1944 Butler Education Act of opening up British universities to a "new wave of philistinism". It was academic, though, as very few working class students gained university places before the late 1950s. Novelist Malcolm Bradbury recognised that those who did largely attended the red-brick institutions such as Leicester. Bradbury commented: "Leicester did not offer glittering prizes: what it offered was sober futures in low or middle management or school teaching."

It wasn't just the exceptionally privileged who looked down their noses at those classes deemed to be socially inferior. Take the stolidly middle-class Philip Larkin, for example. He cast his jaundiced eye upon working class life in his poem *The Whitsun Weddings*, which recalls a rail journey spent in the company of various newly-weds. Here, he recounts "an uncle shouting smut", broad-belted fathers who have "never known success so huge and farcical", and "mothers loud and fat".

He describes permed and "pomaded" women in their "parodies of fashions", their "lemons and mauves"; their "heels and veils"; and their "jewellery substitutes". This much-anthologised poem is rightly admired for its atmospheric and observational qualities, but his descriptions of working class life seem snidely snobbish. With class conceit so rife in 1950s Britain, England's first professional captain was minded to watch his 'Ps and Qs' as closely as Lindwall's subtle shades of pace.

If the appointment of a professional England captain represented a social revolution, it wasn't one that Hutton felt inclined to crow about. He felt no compulsion to ruffle feathers. Unlike Freddie Trueman, his frisky young Yorkshire fast bowler, Hutton remained respectful and reticent. When asked about the place of the amateur in English cricket, he replied that there had been many amateur players and captains who had made a "magnificent contribution to the game both at a national and county level".

Hutton insisted that most professionals could provide examples of the "invaluable advice and encouragement given to them by their captains, early in their careers, and I am no exception". He added: "I am sure such figures as Lord Hawke and Lord Harris did much to set standards which the game will be ill-advised to despise and ridicule as old-fashioned nonsense." For someone who was succumbing to arthritis, Hutton remained remarkably quick on his feet.

Cricket correspondent and broadcaster, John Arlott, observed in an article for the *1953 Playfair Cricket Annual*: "[Hutton] was an ideal man for the post; a very complete professional, calm, thoughtful, much respected by his fellow players, both amateur and professional. It will seem amazing to younger readers that a number of spectators – not all of them of great age – were heard voicing regret and even anger at the appointment. If the point of the professional captain was to be made, there was no better time and no better man to make it."

Hutton's first assignment was to defeat the Indian tourists. This seemed to be a more challenging task than in 1946 for the Indians, under Vijay Hazare, proved to be England's equals during the previous winter tour. However, the Indians crumpled against the guile of Bedser and the pace of newcomer Freddie Trueman. Hutton recalled: "Hazare, an accomplished batsman and former pro with Rawtenstall and Royton, had a side which became disjointed and demolished by Trueman's speed. They couldn't cope with Bedser either." Trueman took 29 Indian wickets at 13.31 each in the four-match series, while Bedser captured 20 at an average of 13.95.

In the first Test at Leeds, Hazare won the toss and chose to bat on a benign strip. Much to Trueman's disappointment he was asked to bowl up the slope. Deprived of his favoured end, "Fiery Fred" struggled for rhythm, accuracy and pace so Hutton relieved him quickly, bringing on Worcestershire's leg-spinner, Roley Jenkins, instead. However, once Alec Bedser had bowled Gaekwad for nine, Hutton recalled Trueman to the attack.

Trueman remarked in his autobiography *As It Was*: "[New batsman] Polly Umrigar was a super batsman...but he didn't like pace. The previously unruffled Umrigar looked uncomfortable at the very first ball I bowled. Minutes later, he jabbed at a delivery and edged it [to] Godfrey Evans...I had claimed my first ever wicket at Test level. I didn't run up to Umrigar and wave a fist at him. I didn't do a lap of honour. Nor did my team-mates run to me arms aloft expecting a high-five.

"And I didn't look over to the members' enclosure and place a finger to my pursed lips. That wasn't the way it was back then. I simply nodded in [Umrigar's] direction and he reciprocated. Outside I was calm and collected, but inside my emotions were roller-coasting; excitement coursed through my veins and I was consumed with pride. I knew I had arrived."

With Jenkins also claiming Roy's wicket, India was reduced to 40-3, but then Hazare (89) and Manjrekar (133) mounted a brilliant recovery before Trueman and Bedser struck back in the final overs, leaving India 272-6 at the close. Overnight rain made the Headingley wicket a more awkward proposition on day two, allowing Laker to mop up the tail for only 21 more runs.

India's off-spinner, Ghulam Ahmed, then bowled superbly to dismiss Hutton, Simpson and Compton cheaply as England lost four wickets in reaching 92. Had Vinoo Mankad not been contracted to play for Haslingden in the Lancashire League, India might have established a substantial first innings lead. He, at least, would have bottled up one end while Ghulam Ahmed applied the pressure at the other. As it was, fellow spinner Shinde leaked 71 runs from his 22 overs allowing Graveney (71), Watkins (48), Evans (66) and Jenkins (38) to enable their side to jump jail, and gain a 41-run first innings advantage.

Within 15 minutes of starting their second innings, India was reeling at 0-4. This time Hutton gave Trueman the use of the slope at the Kirkstall Lane End, and he seized the opportunity eagerly, charging in with snorting hostility. Roy attempted to hook his second ball, a rank long-hop, from well outside the off stump, but could only lob a catch to Compton at second slip. The startled Hazare reacted by promoting his wicketkeeper, Mantri, presumably so that Trueman's pace might be dulled before he risked exposing himself.

Hazare was not a great leader. Although pleasant, he was reticent by nature, risking little. Here, his timidity availed him not. Trueman gave Mantri a fearful working over, but it was Gaekwad who was next to depart after Bedser produced a brute of a delivery that found the splice of his bat, and Laker took a simple catch at gully. It was the only delivery which misbehaved that day.

Smelling blood, Trueman roared in for his second over. His first delivery was extremely quick, far too quick for Mantri whose middle stump was sent cartwheeling. The wonderfully wristy Manjrekar replaced Mantri, rather than his captain, Hazare. Twenty-year-old Manjrekar was still a novice at Test match level, notwithstanding his dazzling century in the first innings. He seemed reluctant to accept his promotion as he muttered to the passing Mantri, "I've been made the sacrificial goat." The pressure placed upon the young man proved too much, as he essayed a loose cover drive at his first ball which clipped an inside edge before ricocheting onto his leg stump. Trueman was on a hat-trick.

Hutton responded by creating a 'Carmody field' with eight close catchers almost encircling the beleaguered Hazare. At last Hutton had someone with Lindwall's firepower, if not yet his finesse. Trueman's first ball to Hazare was a yorker, but fractionally outside the Indian's off stump. It screamed past the edge of Hazare's tentatively proffered bat and his stumps by the narrowest of margins, leaving the packed crowd to emit a loud gasp.

The bemused Umrigar did not stay long, either, providing the bowler Jenkins with a return catch, with the Indian total on 26. Although Hazare (56) and Phadkar (64) then resisted stoutly, lifting India to 136-6 at the close, this was not before Trueman had shattered Hazare's wicket with another straight, express delivery. Jenkins and Bedser mopped up the remaining Indian batsmen, on the Monday morning, for the addition of just 29 runs. England then sauntered to a seven-wicket victory with Simpson contributing a painstaking 51 runs. Hutton failed again, though, having made only ten, matching his first innings score.

Although the belatedly-recruited Mankad made his presence felt in the second Test at Lord's, scoring 72 and 184 and taking five wickets for 196 runs in 73 overs, his side took another fearful beating, losing by eight wickets. In England's huge first innings total of 537 runs, Hutton scored a patient 150; Evans smashed a rapid 104 and May (74) and Graveney (73) added polished half-centuries. Despite Evans' pyrotechnics, England's largely watchful effort took 206 overs to complete, but it helped them establish a first innings lead of 302 runs.

Despite a magnificent innings from Mankad (184), during which he shared a 211-run partnership with Hazare (49), England was set a victory target of 77 runs. This was accomplished easily by eight wickets. Trueman took two further four-wicket hauls at Lord's, demonstrating again not only his striking prowess, but his impressive stamina. Trueman completed 52 overs during this match. Only Bedser with 69 overs worked harder.

Although Hutton had achieved the perfect start to his captaincy, some MCC members continued to carp about his choice of methods. For example, Freddie Brown commented in *Cricket Musketeer*: "There is no doubt that Hutton did a very fine job and batted with all his usual mastery to quell any notions that leadership impaired his skill in this respect...but I was at a loss to understand his approach when we wanted 77 in the last innings in 80 minutes to win the match. Mankad and Ghulam Ahmed bowled very accurately to defensive fields, but Hutton and Simpson made no effort to win the game that night...it would have served us right if the heavens had opened next day and washed all chances of victory away."

Hutton read the situation differently. He retorted: "Of course I was not 'satisfied' to let the match go into a fifth day, but my critics seemed not to understand how well the Indian spinners bowled." Hutton always sought to win, but only stepped on the gas when the prospect of defeat seemed remote – 'Catenaccio' thinking.

While some MCC members and cricket journalists saw Hutton as too defensive and unadventurous, his players took a very different view. For example, Brian Statham said in his 1969 autobiography *A Spell at the Top*: "I played under nine different Test captains and the best, in my judgement, was Sir Len Hutton [Hutton was knighted in 1956]. I select him not just because he never lost a series for England, but because he was very shrewd, knowledgeable and professional [by 1969, it was a term that had been freed of its pejorative implications]. Leonard knew exactly what he wanted, where he was going, and who he was going to use to get there. He entered every Test match with a single objective...to win the match. Nobody in the dressing room was left in doubt what Leonard expected of them."

While this is de rigueur today, in 1952 it was generally considered to be 'bad form' for an English first-class cricket captain to instruct his players on how they should play. For example, cricket correspondent Peter West expressed the view in the *1953 Playfair Cricket Annual*: "Only in exceptional circumstances should a captain have to tell his men what policy to adopt...a batsman of Test calibre should have the experience and the skill to adjust his methods as best he can to meet his side's particular needs...the matter should rest with the individual batsmen."

While Gower took this view in his time as England's captain during the 1980s, arguably to his and England's cost, Bradman and Jardine had no truck with it. They had no qualms about instructing their sides how they should bat, bowl or field. And they were winners.

Once on top, Hutton was ruthless in administering the *coup de grace*. In characteristically damp, chilly, gusty conditions at Old Trafford, the Indians were simply blown away by Trueman's pace and Bedser's craft. They were bowled out twice in under a day on a green, lifting wicket for scores of 58 and 82. The carnage was completed in less than 60 overs. Trueman took eight wickets for 31 runs in the first innings while Bedser took five for 27 in the second. Once again, Hutton led from the front scoring a brilliant 104 on a difficult track against good bowling. May (69) and Evans (71) supported him well as England posted a winning total of 347-9 declared.

It had taken them over two days of rain-interrupted graft to achieve this platform. It was rarely pretty, but certainly effective. After six years of playing often uncompetitive Test cricket, Hutton was developing a team capable of challenging Australia, by ability and mental strength. He commented: "India, admittedly, cut a pitiful figure, and as one of our bowlers said it was the first time he had bowled at the stumps without a batsman in his range of vision. There was a tendency for them to retreat in the direction of square leg, and one batsman ran in, hardly took time to take guard, and ran out again. I never saw anything like it at Test level, but it was a heartening fact that England had a fast bowler to demoralise opponents."

That Old Trafford Test match saw the introduction of Surrey spin twin Tony Lock, whom Hutton described as an "aggressive player, an immense asset to every side he played for, never giving up and fighting to the last ditch. As a close fielder he was peerless, outstandingly brave, and he had the ideal temperament." Lock was controversial, too, for he seemed to throw his faster deliveries.

According to Alan Hill, author of *Tony Lock: Aggressive Master of Spin*, after spending the previous winter practising in Croydon's indoor school, Lock abandoned his orthodox, flighted slow left-arm deliveries in favour of a more sharply spun, quicker style. To some extent, his remodelled action was the product of bowling under a low-slung roof. It wasn't just because Lock was cramped for room, though, that his new, quicker, more aggressive style emerged.

He found that by "digging" the ball into the wicket at increased pace it turned more. This made him a much greater threat. It also gave him the means of competing with his senior spin partner and great rival Jim Laker, who had previously been the more prolific wicket-taker. Alec Bedser reckoned that Lock had also become tired of taking the punishment that his slower style invited. His more hostile approach forced his opponents to play him more cautiously.

John Arlott was startled at the makeover, after finding that Lock could turn the ball sharply on the most placid pitches, with his faster deliveries whistling through at alarming speed. Just days after taking four Indian wickets in the Manchester Test, Lock was called three times for throwing by umpire Fred Price, but, while other umpires, and some players, had grave reservations about the legitimacy of Lock's quicker ball, nothing was done.

MCC selectors "Gubby" Allen and Les Ames deemed Lock's action "peculiar", but not illegal. Once he had been picked for England, the trial by innuendo stuttered to a halt – at least, for the time being. Hutton was entirely unabashed when questioned on the subject, stating: "Yes [Lock's] action is peculiar, but he'll win the Ashes for us next year."

The final Test at the Oval threatened to be a carbon copy of the Manchester debacle. Sheppard made his debut Test century; Hutton added 86 and Ikin 53, as England racked up 326-6 declared, although it took them 154 overs. Demoralised India sought to contain the England run rate by bowling wide outside the off stump to defensive fields. It was ascetic stuff.

India had the ill fortune to bat late on the second day, in murky light, and how Trueman made them pay. After 25 minutes of wretched defence, India was 6-5. The tourists eventually struggled to 98 all out with Hazare top-scoring with 38, but then the weather closed in, saving them from a further hiding. Trueman and Bedser had an equal share of the first innings spoils.

Had it not been for the poor weather at the Oval, Hutton would have achieved a clean sweep in his first series in charge. Once again he led from the front with a batting average of marginally under 80 runs per innings against fine spin bowling. His management of the bowling, his field placing and his aggressive out-cricket was widely commended, as was the vast improvement in England's fielding, notably the close catching.

And yet while dutifully praising Hutton's positive contributions, the *1953 Playfair Cricket Annual* editor Peter West focused more on the negative aspects of his captaincy stating, "Hutton takes very few risks, and nearly all of his innings are put together slowly. His average time for a Test hundred is four hours...heaven knows, we do not really mind how long he takes to make a hundred against Australia, so long as he makes it. But the complaint is that the sight of the maestro on the defensive has an enervating effect on colleagues less able to play a waiting game and to choose the moment to go over to the offensive.

"All I will say here is that a batsman like Simpson, Sheppard, May and Graveney must have been affected, consciously or not, by Hutton's slow tempo last summer, and that in the case of at least three of them they did not always look so good or so effective as they might have done."

It could be argued of course that it was often the poor shot selection of Hutton's colleagues which required him to bat with such grim application. Marshall McLuhan wrote in *Medium is the Massage*: "The amateur can afford to lose. The expert is the man who stays put." How apt was that observation to Hutton's situation.

As badly as India batted against England's pace attack – they would perform much better against West Indian bouncers, in the Caribbean, during the following winter – their spin bowlers, Ghulam Ahmed and Vinoo Mankad, posed a constant threat while giving almost nothing away. Freddie Brown remarked that Ahmed was one of the best off-break bowlers the English players had ever faced. He was said to possess all the attributes of a class performer: spin, flight and variation of pace.

As for Mankad, Peter West commented in the *1953 Playfair Cricket Annual*: "As a batsman he has a wonderful eye and wrist and a spirit of adventure...His bowling lacks the spin of Valentine – which is not to say he cannot make ample use of a turning wicket – but his other attributes rank very high: persistence, accuracy, flight, unceasing craft and guile. On a wicket offering him no help, he will bowl perhaps eight balls out of ten wide of the off stump – and be ready with a tigerish leap into the covers to run out any batsman hopeful of an easy single."

After his scintillating success against the Indians, Freddie Trueman was the toast of the nation. At last England had a tearaway fast bowler who could trade blows with Lindwall and Miller, someone who could return fire with fire. He became the prizefighter who was expected to knock the blocks off the Aussies when they arrived in the following spring. It was left to journalist and former Yorkshire and England fast bowler Bill Bowes to put Trueman's achievements into perspective.

Bowes wrote in the *1953 Playfair Cricket Annual*: "Perhaps it is unfair to say that all our hopes are centred upon this Yorkshire fast bowler, now 22 years old. We have promising young batsmen in Peter May, David Sheppard and Tom Graveney. The England XI at Manchester last year proved themselves to be one of the best fielding combinations we have seen in years [the selections of Lock, Trueman, Watkins, Ikin and Sheppard improved, immeasurably, the quality of England's close catching]. But Trueman is the mainspring of our hopes.

"When this stocky, powerful Maltby miner-lad first came to the Yorkshire nets some five years ago, I warmed to the thought that here was another Larwood...There was the same breadth of shoulder, strength of back and legs and the prospect of the same controlled vitality...To cultivate fast bowling means continual squeezing for that extra half-yard of pace. Once obtained it can be found again. The rarity becomes regular, and with care so that it shall not be overdone, the pressure is then increased for more pace still. Run-up, feet, wrist, arm and body have to be co-ordinated into a final action that produces speed and yet more speed. Length and direction, those other great assets of successful bowling, have many times to be forgotten.

"Norman Yardley, the Yorkshire captain, used him judiciously in short spells [as did Hutton], and even in first-class games, the erratic deliveries were forgiven provided they had speed...Trueman returned figures better than any ever produced by another fast bowler in Test cricket. He claimed victims by virtue of speed and there were occasions when opposing batsmen retreated before his onslaught. It was all very cheering. Nevertheless, there were occasions when Trueman obviously slowed down in his later spells of bowling.

"Full physical development is not usual in a fast bowler until he is 23. Trueman has not the necessary experience to bowl a series of 'rest overs', achieving surprise and balancing effort by only occasional deliveries at express speed...By the end of the 1954 season I believe he will have learned how and when to hold a little bit of strength in reserve and will not need to be 'nursed' by a kindly captain."

While Trueman's star was rising, Denis Compton's appeared to be waning after he had requested his release from the Manchester and Oval Tests on grounds of poor form. Freddie Brown was not impressed stating: "It was a strange step for a cricketer to write a letter like this...If it had been for business reasons it would have been a different matter. It did not set a good precedent, and I do not think that our decision to leave him out of the side for the Test match at Manchester was influenced in any way by the receipt of his letter."

Brown seemed miffed that Compton, a professional cricketer, had the presumption to make a decision that Brown believed only an MCC selection committee should make. On the other hand, as Brown intimated, amateur captains frequently excused themselves from MCC's tours on 'business grounds'. This had become an established precedent.

While doubts circulated as to whether Denis Compton had played his final Test for England, his Middlesex buddy, Bill Edrich, sturdily rebuffed the notion. He argued that Compton was as great a cricketer then as he had ever been, pointing out that he had played some magnificent innings for Middlesex during the previous season. Edrich claimed that Compton, who was then 35 years old, was one the very best players of really fast bowling. He also dismissed all doubts about the fitness of Compton's knee as it had not only survived the strain of the previous cricket season, it had also withstood Compton's dashes around the squash court.

THE NEW ELIZABETHAN AGE

'Faith Can Move Mountains'

The year 1953 marked the beginning of a new Elizabethan Age. The popularity of the Royal family had grown significantly since George VI's accession in 1936. Their exposure to the Blitz enhanced their public stature as did their experience of other wartime privations.

Consequently, when Princess Elizabeth succeeded her deceased father in 1952, she was overwhelmed by a tide of goodwill. An estimated 27 million people watched her Coronation on TV in June 1953. The euphoric occasion was talked up by Winston Churchill and the press as heralding a glorious new Elizabethan era, characterised by pumping patriotic pride, revived economic vitality, freedom from want and austerity, and greater home comforts and leisure options.

The conquest of Everest by a Commonwealth team came bang on time. So did Roger Bannister's sub-four-minute mile. Randolph Turpin raised the profile of the plucky Brit by winning back the world middleweight title. Despite intensification of the nuclear arms race, with the Soviets developing an H-bomb, the Korean War finally came to an end. And to cap it all, car and TV ownership grew as these items became more affordable for working people, while the hated meat rationing petered out, albeit unofficially. The question remained whether the England cricket team could add to the national feel-good factor by taking back the Ashes after a 20-year wait?

Central to the new Elizabethan myth were the supposedly exceptional qualities of the British people – brave, humane, resourceful, determined, fair-minded, but tough. The nation's valiant, lone stand against another armada, a Luftwaffe one, was seen to epitomise those qualities. During the mid 1950s, British courage in the face of overwhelming odds was celebrated by a series of war films, showcasing outstanding bravery with stiff upper-lipped or jaunty conviction. Films such as *Cockleshell Heroes*, *The Desert Rats*, *Reach for the Sky* and *Battle of the River Plate* could be seen in this light.

Even more solemn and subdued representations of heroism, as in *The Dambusters* and *The Cruel Sea,* emphasised the gallantry of this small island. As cartoonist David Low put it, in his depiction of "Tommy", shaking his fist at waves of oncoming bombers, it had been a case of "very well, alone". So, with a heady mood of jingoism about, the Magical Magyars' humiliation of the England football team, at Wembley in November 1953, came as an unwelcome surprise. The horrific crash of a prized de Havilland Comet jet airliner was much more appalling, though.

With no MCC tour arranged for the winter of 1952/53, focus shifted to the exploits of England's main rivals: Australia and the West Indies. While the West Indian team struggled to overcome their Indian visitors, the Australians were unexpectedly held to a 2-2 home draw by the South Africans.

Jackie McGlew, then an inexperienced Test opening batsman, recalled in his biography *Cricket for South Africa*: "We were the team that no one wanted. We had no pretensions as to class, and in fact we were told in advance that we hadn't any. If a number of the critics in South Africa and Australia had their way, we would have never sailed for the Antipodes in 1952." The South African captain, Jack Cheetham, announced: "We have come to learn."

The Australian press was bemused by Cheetham's training drills. Instead of focusing upon net practice, Cheetham organised strenuous fitness exercises, and long, challenging fielding routines. McGlew remembered: "There were hours upon tedious hours spent in the sun perfecting our fielding, catching, returning to the wicket...Hours broken only by a break for lunch which sometimes we took to the practice fields with us, and during which those who came to watch thought what extraordinary methods these were of preparing for stern trials of strength. Some of them said so. But we proved our point."

McGlew added: "We set considerable store by fitness, too, and to this end we incorporated in our training schedule a roster of exercises...There were conferences with individual players, too, in which field-settings for bowlers were discussed, batting fads and fancies studied, and the best possible distribution of our fielding resources...I doubt whether any captain had a team more loyal, more firmly decided to give him of their very best, than Jack Cheetham had on this tour.

"It was not an easy task. Players such as Cheetham, McLean, Tayfield, Endean, Waite and myself – and we were not alone – had obviously become members of the team of whom considerable performances were required in the major matches. This was imperative, despite the fact that we could not be regarded at this stage as fully-fledged Test cricketers. We lacked a background of well-versed international players."

Cheetham reasoned that a team without batting stars might still average 250 per innings in the Test matches, but a team without bowlers would be caned unless they fielded superbly. And as far as the batting was concerned, he impressed upon each member of his side that they should eradicate all risky shots, and sell their wickets as dearly as possible. McGlew got the point, taking eight hours in scoring 182 runs in the opening first-class game against Western Australia.

The Australian critics called it wrongly. South Africa batted long and adhesively, bowled meanly, fielded tigerishly, and caught brilliantly. Fine fielding transformed their limited bowling attack into a worthy one, and helped make Tayfield's slow-medium off spin extraordinary – he took 30 Test wickets at 28 runs each. Only on the faster surface at Sydney were the South Africans greatly disturbed by Lindwall and Miller.

Twice South Africa came from behind to draw the series. South African journalist and broadcaster Charles Fortune proclaimed: "This was South Africa's finest hour."

Despite Peter West's assertion that "most cricketers believe that we will never beat the Australians by a negative approach", the moral drawn from this South African success was that the Australians could be beaten by patient, disciplined batting from top to bottom, and by maintaining tight, probing bowling to shrewdly-positioned, predatory and agile fields. Except for the scintillating Neil Harvey, the Australian batsmen were unnerved by the pressure applied by the South Africans, notably Tayfield who caught as brilliantly as he bowled.

Cheetham proved to be an astute and inspirational captain, who had successfully welded an inexperienced group into a formidably competitive team. His place as leader of his side had become unrivalled, and yet his English counterpart, Len Hutton, had no such security of tenure. In fact, he had no guarantee of the English captaincy beyond the opening Ashes Test in 1953.

It had been a traditional practice of MCC selectors to decide the England captain, for home series, on a Test-by-Test basis. Such a fragmentary approach carried the risk of undermining team cohesion, and upsetting tactical planning, but the chairman of the selectors, Freddie Brown, pompously dismissed all criticisms, stating: "I do not think there was any precedent [for appointing Hutton as captain for the whole series]."

In his book *Test Match Diary 1953*, John Arlott reminded his readers that this Ashes series had parallels with that of 1926. He wrote: "Immediately after the 1914-18 war, as in 1946/47, we sent a team to Australia which was soundly beaten. Then – 1921 and 1948 – the Australian touring side overwhelmingly defeated us by the employment of two outstanding fast-bowlers – Gregory and Macdonald, and then Lindwall and Miller. The following MCC tour of Australia – Gilligan's team and Brown's – lost the rubber but succeeded in gaining the first post-war win over Australia. In 1926 we won the rubber: history's reputed repetition, we have encouraged ourselves to believe, should bring us the Ashes back in 1953."

It is unlikely that Len Hutton indulged in such speculation, any more than he allowed his head to be turned by criticisms of the Australian touring party. One newspaper went so far as to say this was the worst Australian touring side since 1912. Another claimed that Jack Hill, the Victorian spin bowler, had burst out laughing when he was told he'd been chosen.

Hutton was guided by results not frivolous gossip. As he prepared for the first Test at Nottingham, he was well aware that the Australian tourists had won seven and drawn five of their opening 12 first-class matches. Six of their victories had been by an innings and completed in two days. Of their five draws, three were moral victories. This was not the form of pushovers. It was the kind of form that Bradman's "Invincibles" had shown five years before.

However, there were cracks in the Aussie armoury. Miller and

Harvey had batted expansively, and well, but the others had not been as impressive. There was a question hanging over who should open with Morris. McDonald's vulnerability against the new ball had been exploited ruthlessly by the county seamers. Hole had filled in (as it were), but seemed too loose with his shot selection. The limpet-like Hassett had looked a better option, although his promotion threatened to expose an untested middle order.

As for the bowlers, South African reports of Lindwall's demise were exaggerated. He seemed as fast and controlled as ever, possessing even more subtle variations of pace and swing than on his previous tour. Because the Australian pace and spin bowlers had enjoyed so much success against the county sides, Miller had been freed to concentrate on his batting. The injured Johnston had also been given more time to recover from a knee injury which he sustained in a warm-up charity game at East Molesey. Ultimately this injury would curtail his first-class career.

The Australian team for the first Test at a murky Trent Bridge was: Morris, Hole, Hassett, Harvey, Miller, Benaud, Davidson, wicketkeeper Tallon, Lindwall, Hill and Johnston. Their team comprised four specialist batsmen, three all-rounders and three specialist bowlers one of whom, Lindwall, had a Test hundred to his name.

Meanwhile, England felt compelled to exclude Sheppard, Watson, Watkins and Trueman on grounds of form, Ikin and Lock because of injury and Appleyard, because of persistent illness. Freddie Brown explained that Sheppard, a recent contender for the English captaincy, had been excluded also because "with his high backlift we never felt confident of his power against the quick bowlers".

Brown's doubts about Sheppard's technique had not diminished. The team chosen to represent England was therefore: Hutton, Worcestershire's Don Kenyon, Simpson, Compton, Graveney, May, Bailey, Evans, Wardle, Bedser and Tattersall. This seemed a cautious selection, with Hutton's side comprising six specialist batsmen, an all-rounder (Bailey), who would share the new ball with Bedser, and two spinners, one of whom (Tattersall) could bowl seam-up, and the other (Wardle) who could adopt a containing role. That said, there was inordinate pressure placed upon Bedser's broad shoulders. Once again he was the main strike bowler and the willing workhorse.

Typically, Bedser yanked England back into the game after Australia had threatened to break loose, at 237 for the loss of only three wickets. Bedser disposed of centurion Hassett, with a wonderful leg cutter, and then, with some assistance from Wardle (one for 55) and Bailey (two for 75), he shot out the rest for a further 12 runs, finishing with figures of seven for 55 from 38.3 overs. The English bowling had been so tight, and the Australian batting so cautious, that the tourists' innings of 249 had consumed just over 140 overs, at a run-rate of 1.8 per over.

England's batting effort, late on the second day, was little better. In fact, it was as dismal as the misty, grey haze which engulfed Nottingham. Although the playing surface was sound enough, as Hassett (115), Morris (67) and Miller (55) had shown, the atmospheric conditions were ideally suited to Lindwall's swing bowling. Hassett responded by giving him a ring of eight close catchers to accompany wicketkeeper Tallon: four slips and a gully, a leg-slip and two short legs, one backward. Only the fleet-footed Harvey, at cover, patrolled the outfield.

England's top order was blown away rapidly. Kenyon was completely bewildered by Lindwall's late out-swing, and it was almost a mercy when he was snaffled by Hill, at leg-slip, having involuntarily jabbed at a very fast, full-pitched delivery on his leg stump.

Kenyon had been picked on account of his good county form, with his fluent century against the tourists at New Road advancing his case. But the Aussie quick bowlers were renowned for keeping their powder dry in these preliminary games. Brown had hoped that Kenyon, with his wide range of shots, might enable England to put 40 or 45 runs on the board in the first hour of play, thereby establishing an early momentum, and breaking the stranglehold that Lindwall often applied.

Even against the highly attacking fields that the Australians employed, this was a difficult strategy to bring off, not only because of the quality of the Aussie pace bowling, but because of the technical limitations of the English batsmen, Hutton and Bailey excepted. It was for this reason that Hutton wanted the unruffled and battle-hardened Washbrook to be his opening partner. Hutton observed many years later: "No matter how experienced a batsman might be, he likes to have some assurance from his partner, and there were times when my partners were so overcome by the occasion that they were half-out before they took guard." After Washbrook's failures in Australia, the selectors would not hear of the idea.

Next up was Reg Simpson, the conquering hero at Melbourne in 1951.

He was reputedly a fine player of swing bowling, but he lasted just two balls. His first delivery from Lindwall beat him for pace; the second caught him in front of his stumps, shouldering arms, having misread the late in-dipper as an out-swinger. At 17-2, England was once again in the mire.

Things became worse. Compton marched in, thrashed Lindwall's second ball to gully, where Morris took an astonishing catch, and promptly trudged off. Although Graveney helped Hutton to steady the ship, playing attractively in scoring 22 runs, he perished with the total score at 76. Catastrophically, Hutton (43) and May (9) followed quickly, leaving England in a parlous position at 92-6 at the close of day two. Hill had proved no laughing matter. He had taken two for 24 in 14 overs, dismissing May and Graveney with his brisk, flat leg-spinners and top-spinners, and astounding his detractors with a prodigious leg break that beat Graveney's bat, the stumps and wicketkeeper Tallon, before scuttling to the third man boundary for four byes.

Saturday dawned as grey and grim as the preceding two days. Evans began the proceedings with a joyous, clattering hook for four in Lindwall's second over. Thereafter, he and Bailey poked and prodded their way to 106 before the England wicketkeeper edged first-change bowler Davidson to Tallon. Bailey departed 15 runs later, having unaccountably abandoned his front foot catechism. He was adjudged lbw going back to Hill's top-spinner. Although Wardle played boldly, doing his best to farm the strike, Ray Lindwall dismissed both of his partners, Bedser and Tattersall, with the new ball, and England was all out for a paltry score of 144 runs.

With England facing a customary crisis, the trusty Alec Bedser came once again to their aid. Between lunch and tea, Bedser shattered the Australian batting, reducing them to 106-8. After Morris and Hole had begun at the gallop, capitalising on some loose bowling from Bailey, Bedser bowled Hole through the gate for five runs with a late in-swinger (28-1). The apparently imperturbable Hassett followed quickly, after Bedser had made a ball on leg stump jump viciously, flick the shoulder of the bat, and find Hutton's safe hands at short leg (44-2).

Bedser then cramped the adventurous Harvey with a nagging leg stump line of attack. Tiring of this, Harvey hooked injudiciously at a ball which grew big on him and was caught brilliantly, by Graveney at short leg, for just two runs (36-3). Miller began in an attacking vein, but, having recognised the associated risks, quickly reverted to stolid defence.

So dogged was he in defence that he was slow to spot Bedser's full toss, guiding this meekly to Kenyon at mid-wicket (64-4).

Benaud did not stay long, either, as he was deceived by a leg-cutter that bowled him between his legs for a duck (68-5). Meanwhile, Morris progressed to his fifty, only six runs of which had come off Bedser's bowling. Bedser was finally rested after an unbroken spell, lasting an hour and 40 minutes. In his 14 overs Bedser had taken five wickets for 24 runs.

Upon replacing Bedser, Tattersall immediately bowled Morris with a sharp off break (81-6). Having misheard his captain's instruction of "to give the light a go" as "to give it a go", new batsman, Don "Deafy" Tallon, encouraged his batting partner, Davidson, to join him in some bold, rustic hitting.

Davidson soon holed out at deep midwicket off Tattersall for six runs (92-7), while Tallon's lofted hook off the same bowler found Simpson fine of square (106-8). Bedser then wrapped up the Australian innings shortly after tea for 123, leaving England 229 runs to win. During this match, Bedser had taken 14 wickets, in almost 56 overs, conceding just 99 runs.

Hutton and Kenyon began their pursuit of victory confidently until Kenyon smacked a full toss from Hill straight to Hassett at short mid-on (26-1). Nevertheless, England completed a dark, but most satisfactory, day at 42-1. Then the heavens opened on Sunday evening with the deluge lasting for 24 hours. In that time Nottingham absorbed 1.15 inches of rain, preventing any play before 4.30pm on the final day. Hutton and Simpson took no risks, lifting the England score to 120-1 before time was called.

Lindwall was surprised at Hutton's reluctance to chase the winning target. He commented in his autobiography *Flying Stumps*: "I cannot help thinking England wasted a good chance. With the bowlers so handicapped, they had everything to gain with no appreciable risk of defeat." The normally cavalier Freddie Brown took a different view, though, stating: "To score 187 runs in two hours on a pudding of a pitch with a sodden and very slow outfield would have been asking for real trouble. We should have been on a hiding to nothing."

Three changes were made in the England side, for the second Test, at sunny Lord's. Freddie Brown was persuaded to come out of Test retirement – he still captained Northamptonshire – to replace Simpson

Double international Willie Watson came in for Peter May and Statham was preferred to Tattersall.

Brown explained that May had lost confidence after several morale-sapping encounters with Ray Lindwall, including one traumatic over in the Surrey game at the Oval in which the Aussie fast bowler had beaten him with each delivery, some of which had cut in while others had moved away. The Australians had been very wary of May's ability, particularly captain, Lindsay Hassett. According to Richie Benaud, Hassett was intent upon destroying May's self-belief before the Test series began. So successful was this strategy that, after Nottingham, May did not play in another Test match before the Oval decider.

With regard to his own selection, Brown wrote in *Cricket Musketeer*: "We wanted a leg-break bowler at Lord's, where the slope is an advantage to the type and where the wicket was likely to be of assistance to slow bowlers as the match progressed. I could be used as a dual purpose bowler, bowling seamers against the left-handers, the hope being that if need be I could apply the brakes by shutting up one end. Moreover, Lord's has always been my lucky ground." Brown professed that, "after a long discussion", Hutton had asked him to play, but admitted that it was his wife who finally persuaded him to have "one final fling".

In his *Test Match Diary 1953,* John Arlott wrote that Brown's selection was a "backward step", adding: "At 42, a man needs to be something of a genius to be an effective Test player, and Brown is only a good county player... Moreover, the presence of the chairman of the selectors in the dressing room must, inevitably, have some effect upon the relations between the players and a captain who is being chosen from Test to Test.

"Surely Hutton has done enough to be appointed captain for the series... It seems a grudging attitude, emphasised, in many minds, by the fact that Hutton is a professional. I have heard many suggestions...that if Brown comes off at Lord's, he will take over the captaincy...Grimmest of all, Brown could not command a place in the Test team on the Australian tour of 1932/33 when he was at the peak of his powers as a leg-break bowler and forcing bat. Moreover, he has announced that he will retire from first-class cricket at the end of this season. It simply does not make sense that a player retires when he is of genuine Test status."

An incredulous Ray Lindwall remarked in his autobiography *Flying Stumps*: "Hutton was so much in the habit of addressing [Brown] as

'Skipper' that he could not break it. Throughout the match such gems of dialogue would be heard as: 'Would you like to take a turn at the top end, Skipper?' and 'well bowled Skipper, have a break now, will you?'

"The rest of the team followed Hutton's example with the strange result that they called the captain 'Len' and one of their team-mates 'Skipper'... Some of the distinctions existing in England between amateur and professional are a source of bewilderment to Australians, accustomed to the free interchange of Christian names... Even the youngest player always addressed Bradman as 'Don' or 'Braddles', and Ian Craig would no more think of calling Lindsay Hassett as anything but Lindsay than Lindsay himself would expect him to do."

Australia also made two changes to their line-up, bringing in the more experienced leg-spinner Doug Ring for Jack Hill and Gil Langley replaced veteran wicketkeeper Don Tallon. Hassett decided, too, that he should partner Morris at the top of the Australian batting order.

Thursday 25th June was a sumptuous day; a beaming sun blazed down from an almost cloudless sky with a gently caressing breeze to moderate the heat. After the glowering greyness of Nottingham, it was not before time. Hutton lost the toss while his team lost the plot, dropping eight catches as Australia made 346 with Hassett scoring his second century of the series (104), Harvey adding a restrained 59, and Davidson contributing a bludgeoning 77.

Buttressed by Wardle's four important scalps (Miller, Hole, Benaud and Davidson), Bedser's five-wicket haul once gain dragged England back into contention, after Australia seemed to be scorching ahead at 190 for the loss of Morris. Although an exhilarating 168-run unbroken partnership between Hutton and Graveney took England to 177-1 in reply at the end of the second day, Hutton could only ruminate gloomily upon his succession of dropped catches.

He told John Arlott: "I have played in over 60 Tests and I have dropped more catches today than in all those other games put together." He was being unduly hard on himself. Not only had he produced a splendid innings of 83 not out, his command of his bowling and fielders had been estimable, successfully arresting Australia's momentum, and helping create the pressure that enabled Bedser and Wardle to winkle out the tourists on a perfect pitch.

However, Lindwall was at a loss to understand why Hutton and Graveney had stepped off the gas, in the final hour of play, rather than ramming home their advantage against a tiring attack. Certainly, Graveney was left to rue his lack of ambition as Lindwall yorked him the following morning without any addition to his overnight score of 78. Graveney's early exit exposed the incoming batsman, Compton, to the new ball.

Although Compton (57) helped Hutton (145) raise England's score by a further 102 runs, thereafter, the advantage they had patiently gained was frittered away as seven wickets fell for a mere 93 runs. England had achieved a first innings score of 372 – a 26-run lead. On a wicket offering him little assistance, Lindwall took his second five-wicket return of the series. The day closed with Australia back in front, having scored 96 for the loss of Hassett, controversially 'caught' by Evans on the leg side off Statham. The ball seemed to have brushed Hassett's hip, not his bat.

On Monday there was a decisive shift in fortunes, or so it seemed. Australia posted a second innings score of 368 featuring a faultless 109 from Miller, a muted 89 from Morris and a savage 50 from Lindwall who chanced his luck. This meant that England needed 343 runs to win in approximately seven hours. However, in the final 53 minutes of play, Lindwall ripped out both openers: Hutton for five runs and Kenyon for two while Johnston knocked over Graveney, also for two. England was left reeling at 20-3. It might have been worse. Lindwall, at leg-slip, failed to pouch a chance given by Watson in the final over bowled by Ring. His rare error would have a crucial bearing on what happened on the final day.

That final day featured one of the finest rearguard actions ever staged by an English Test side, particularly one that had shown itself to be serially fallible against world-class bowling. The English heroes were Willie Watson (109) and an exhausted Trevor Bailey (71) who added 163 for the fifth wicket when all seemed lost.

Bailey recalled in his autobiography, *Wickets, Catches and the Odd Run*: "When I joined Willie my sole objective was still to be there at lunch. [We decided] I would take as much of the leg spin as possible, because the rough was making things very difficult outside his off stump for my left-handed partner."

At lunch, Bailey wolfed down most of Watson's meal in addition to his own – nerves affected the batting partners in opposite ways. Bailey continued: "Afterwards, much to our surprise and delight, Johnston and Davidson shared the attack which gave us the opportunity to become re-accustomed to pace bowling before the all-out [new ball] assault began just before three o'clock...It was noticeable [then] that the crowd and the tension had increased.

"At no stage did we ever consider going for the win...but we gratefully accepted any runs that were available. Willie was a very fine runner between the wickets which meant we picked up plenty of singles [which took up extra time as the field had to change over, disturbing the Australians' line of attack]...Willie completed a splendid [maiden Test] century and was eventually caught off Doug Ring, whom we considered the most dangerous bowler, and probably should have been used more. At six o'clock I attempted a cover slash off Benaud, in the circumstances a stupid shot, and was caught out for 71."

By then, England was almost safe. Len Hutton added in his autobiography *Fifty Years in Cricket*: "While it is true that the pitch became progressively slower, the demands on Willie, or Billy as he was known in the North, and Trevor were abnormal. Their discipline and concentration had to be verging on the inhuman. At tea, one of players looked at Billy, and voiced all our thoughts: 'I'm lost in admiration. He's batted all this time knowing that if he makes one mistake, just one tiny error of judgement, we have had it. And he's still at it.'"

Other important supporting roles were played by a measured Denis Compton (33), and a harum-scarum Freddie Brown (28) whose batting alarmed an anxious John Arlott. Arlott commented in his *Test Match Diary 1953*: "Brown mis-hit in a quite terrifying fashion. He hit five fours but they didn't matter and one would have changed them all for a single maiden over played off the middle of the bat."

Brown explained: "When I found the spinners were operating against me with an attacking field, I worked out that if I hit it over the heads of the in-fielders it would take them a bit of time to go and fetch the ball...I thought there was everything to lose in playing pawky; I might have been out very quickly because it is not my natural game...I must say I was absolutely staggered when Lindwall continued to graze in the field."

As at Nottingham, Lindwall thought that England had missed the boat by not going for victory on the placid Lord's wicket. He recalled in his autobiography: "Neither of England's two heroes attempted to

119

hit anything but rank long-hops and full-tosses. They just blocked half-volleys. The fact that Hassett took off his slow bowlers, whenever they looked in danger of being punished, should have been a clear indication that Australia did not share the view that the task facing England was too big to be achieved, and the final score [282-7] indicated how near they came to winning...The wicket was of no use to fast bowlers. The ball seldom rose waist high and it went through very slowly. On the other hand, the spin bowlers could make it turn [but they] were below their best."

Nevertheless, Hassett persisted with them, believing they gave him a greater chance of victory, not only with the degree of turn they achieved, but because of the more intense pressure they applied by bowling their overs two or three minutes quicker than the pace men. That said, the England tail-enders were as relieved to be spared a late onslaught from Lindwall as he was disappointed to be ignored.

The Australian team took some stick on the back pages for failing to press home their advantage with their former Test batsman Sidney Barnes leading the charge, accusing the team of carousing in a London nightclub on the penultimate evening. In his autobiography, Ray Lindwall retorted angrily: "We enjoyed a pleasant hour or two at the Café de Paris but I doubt if any member of the team went to bed that night later than he would have done in the ordinary way [and as for Hassett who was accused by Barnes of exercising insufficient discipline] he is the best leader of men under whom I played."

Actually, that was not the whole truth. Keith Miller recalled that before eating at the Café de Paris the team had watched a performance of *Guys and Dolls* at the Coliseum and had then attended a backstage party. The Australian manager was forced into issuing an explanatory statement, in which he confirmed that "he was personally satisfied that everyone was in bed by 1am"! Perhaps he might have been a bit more media savvy in his press release.

As the third Test at Manchester approached, it was learnt that Hutton might not play, having been treated for fibrositis. The 'forgotten man' Cyril Washbrook was put on standby duty. With a chiding comment, obviously aimed at MCC, John Arlott wrote: "Perhaps a jolt like this was needed to make us appreciate Hutton, whose importance to the side was something we were beginning to accept as an automatic asset after such a long run of his rescue and backbone innings. The fact is that, without Hutton – or Bedser – England does not look like a Test team."

Unsurprisingly, Kenyon was dropped after four failures, and 'reprobate' Bill Edrich returned deservedly to take his place. There were few English cricketers of the time as combative and gutsy as Edrich. Besides, his post-war Test batting average was almost 50. His eagerness to party, though, was not to everyone's taste.

Just before his death in 1986, Edrich told the *Guardian* journalist Frank Keating about an escapade in a Scarborough hotel during the town's cricket festival in September 1953. Edrich recalled that he awoke in a hotel room, which he mistakenly presumed to be his own. He was positioned at the foot of the bed still dressed in his best bib and tucker. Unbeknown to him, he had been sharing the same bed as Norman Yardley, his former England skipper, and Yardley's wife.

Apparently, in a half-sleepy state, Mrs Yardley had been rubbing Edrich's ear mistaking him for the family dog, which customarily slept at the foot of their bed at home. Once the Yardleys realised the unbelievable truth, they were incandescent with rage. Edrich, who had been booked into the adjoining room, was told dire consequences would follow. Not that this seemed to bother him one jot as he nonchalantly blasted a joyous 133 for Yardley's team of 'Gentlemen' later that day. Hutton was in need an opening partner, adept at clambering out of holes. Edrich seemed to be just the man.

Brown was not retained at Old Trafford. Although he took four wickets at Lord's, these perhaps flattered him. His batting against the classy Australian pace bowlers was not really good enough, either. Consequently, off-spinner Jim Laker was recalled alongside Reg Simpson, with Brian Statham, who was innocuous on the mellow Lord's surface, also making way. So England reverted to a four-man bowling attack, with Bailey once again partnering Bedser with the new ball.

Having been dissatisfied with the performances of his two leg-spinners, Benaud and Ring, at Lord's, Hassett replaced them with Jack Hill and a debutant specialist batsman, Jim de Courcy. With Bill Johnston struggling with his leg injury, all-rounder Ron Archer was drafted in to help with new-ball duties.

Once again Manchester was damp and dismal. Consequently, it took Australia over two days to reach their first innings total of 318.

This represented a considerable revival, as Hassett's side were perilously placed at 48-3 soon after winning the toss. Had Evans not unaccountably dropped Harvey off Bailey, with the score at 52, they might not have recovered. Bridling at Harvey's fortunate escape so early in his innings, Bedser remarked with typical saltiness: "Neil you don't need a boat to return home. With your luck you could walk."

Despite playing sketchily at first, Harvey (122) led a magnificent fightback, adding 173 runs with his increasingly confident batting partner Hole (66). Although the docile wicket had helped their occupation of the crease, it was not conducive to shotmaking.

With Laker incapacitated by a pulled leg muscle and Wardle hampered by a wet ball, Bedser was required to bowl 45 overs during the Australian first innings, representing almost 40 per cent of the workload. Once again he did the business, taking five wickets for 115 runs, while Wardle chipped in with three quick wickets at the end of the innings after the ball began to lift ominously and turn sharply off a length.

Hutton and Edrich began determinedly against Lindwall and Archer. The roller had done its work, providing a temporary reprieve from the worsening conditions. However, as soon as Hassett turned to Hill, after only six overs of pace, batting became considerably more difficult. Once again Hill belied his maligned reputation by delivering a sizzling leg break. Edrich played for the top-spinner, but was not far enough forward to counter the turn. The ever-reliable Hole snaffled the edged chance at slip.

At Edrich's departure, England had mustered only 19 runs. Graveney began fluently, but just as he was getting into his stride he played an expansive drive at, what he believed to be, Miller's offbreak. It wasn't, and de Courcy took an easy catch at mid-off. England was then 32-2 and Graveney, like Edrich, had departed for a single-figure score.

With the wicket becoming increasingly venomous, Compton joined Hutton. Hill's bowling was particularly threatening, producing both steepling bounce and sharp turn. Hutton and Compton resisted with estimable resolution and technique, though. Hutton was a batting maestro on poor wickets, but, here, Compton matched him, abandoning his characteristically cavalier swishes to leg in favour of strict, straight orthodoxy.

Only once was Compton tempted to desert his born-again asceticism. He swivelled to hook Archer's head-high bouncer, hitting the ball high and fine for six, but immediately reproached himself as his shot barely cleared the leaping de Courcy. Having toiled dutifully for two-and-a-half hours against extremely testing bowling, in difficult conditions, disaster struck within sight of the close. First Compton departed (45) having been caught at the wicket off Archer, and then, almost immediately, Lindwall trapped Hutton lbw (66) with the score still on 126.

It mattered not. Monday was another day of steady rain, ruling out play for the day. Then yet more rain delayed the resumption of play on Tuesday. England's only concern at that point was to avoid the follow-on, realising that if they had to bat again this would expose them to a difficult rearguard action on a suspect strip. After several heart-stopping moments, Bailey and Simpson averted danger by taking the score to 209-6 at tea.

Thereafter, Evans celebrated by smashing 44 runs in 47 minutes, and England's innings ended with 276 runs on the board. None of the long-suffering spectators could have imagined what would happen next as the Australians disintegrated in losing eight wickets for 35 runs before the close. Wardle took four wickets for just seven runs. Australian Alan Davidson dismissed this fiasco as "partly explained by the fact that no result was possible, and our players did not try very hard".

While Australia might have switched off, having felt in no danger of defeat, their collapse handed Hutton's side a huge psychological advantage. Hutton realised then that, while Bedser offered him the best protection against defeat, the Australians' vulnerability against spin offered him the best prospect of victory, particularly if he could catch them again on a turning surface.

With that in mind, the fit-again Tony Lock replaced the unfortunate Wardle. As much as Hutton valued Wardle, he knew that Lock's devastating faster ball and greater bite carried Ashes-winning menace. Besides, Lock was a supremely agile close catcher, arguably the best in the country. Hutton had been intensely frustrated that Lock had been sidelined with a sore spinning finger, the product of his heavy workload for Surrey.

'England expects', but the Surrey captain, Stuart Surridge, expected more. Some doubted whether Lock was yet fit enough to play in a four-man attack, particularly if Australia batted well and the weather remained fine. After Laker's indisposition at Old Trafford, Arlott considered Lock's inclusion to be particularly risky. With Laker fully recovered there were no further changes to the England XI.

As for Lindsay Hassett, the late trauma at Manchester left him more risk averse. Instead of persisting with Jack Hill, who had troubled the English top order there, all-rounder Richie Benaud was recalled, presumably to solidify the batting. Of course, Australia only needed to draw the series in order to retain the Ashes. Hassett's luck held as he won the toss for the fourth time in succession.

Hutton tried to bluff him into batting, by feigning frustration, even hurling the 'offending' coin in the direction of the crowd. Hassett was too wily to fall for such theatrical gestures, and promptly invited Hutton to bat on a still damp wicket. Hassett had no wish to face Bedser on that greenish surface.

England began disastrously as Lindwall yorked Hutton with an in-swinger before he had scored. Hutton's middle and leg stumps were spread-eagled. Lindwall celebrated with a delighted leap, both arms thrust upward in triumph. Hutton recalled in *Fifty Years in Cricket*: "There was no sight screen at the football stand end in those days. I never saw the ball that yorked me. Not to my surprise, I read that I made a rather crude jab with my bat some distance from my pad."

Lindwall remarked in *Flying Stumps*: "Len Hutton must come next to Bradman for skill allied to certainty. The shock of bowling him out second ball was as big to me as to anyone in the ground... I know of few batsmen who are less perturbed than Len when they cannot find many scoring opportunities...Bowling against him is almost a hopeless task."

After Edrich had played resolutely for 80 minutes before being lbw to Miller (10), Compton promptly prodded Lindwall's slower off-cutter to Davidson at fine short leg to depart for a duck. Despite an elegant half-century from Graveney (55), and a brief, defiant knock of 24 runs from Watson, England subsided dismally to 142-7 by the close. Simpson had been forced to retire hurt, having been struck on the arm by a sharply rising ball from Miller. Bailey and Watson also exited painfully, leaving doubt as to whether they would be fit to field.

Bailey commented in *Wickets, Catches and the Odd Run*: "Watson was lbw to a direct hit on his foot. And I was not only run out but also, in my frantic dive for safety, landed so heavily on my left knee that it came up like a balloon...This was rather serious as it was plainly a seamer's wicket, and without me, our attack consisted of Alec and two spinners." England had spent most of this day of sunshine and showers in turgid defence.

With the run-rate barely reaching 1.5 per over, the large Leeds crowd watched the day's play mostly in glum silence.

It took Australia just 13 more overs to dismiss England for a wholly inadequate total of 167 runs. Lindwall took five for 54 in 35 overs of probing swing, principally assisted by Miller who settled for medium-paced seamers. He achieved astounding economy, too, in taking two for 39 runs, in 28 overs.

Morris and Hassett then began the Australian reply at 12.30pm under leaden skies and a threat of rain. Simpson was deemed unfit to field, although Watson and Bailey bravely defied their injuries, and joined their team-mates on the verdant Headingley outfield. Bailey even took the new ball albeit bowling at reduced pace from a shortened run.

Once again "Atlas" Bedser had to carry the England attack, and once again he performed heroically, taking six wickets for 95 runs in almost 29 overs to hold Australia to 266, a 99-run lead. Despite his painful knee, Bailey provided sterling support taking three wickets for 71 runs in 22 overs of highly accurate medium-paced bowling.

As at Manchester, Hutton's men were frustrated by Harvey (71) and Hole (53), whose sparkling strokeplay was interspersed with customary streakiness. Hutton was particularly maddened by the Aussies' bright last-wicket partnership of 48 runs, between young Ron Archer (31 not out) and Gil Langley (17). It was ended by Bedser's 217th Test wicket – a new world record. Fortunately, Bedser's final strike came so late in the day that England was spared batting until the following morning.

Bailey recalled in *Wickets, Catches and the Odd Run*: "If we had held our catches we would have reduced their total by about a hundred runs, nonetheless I was well satisfied with my three wickets in 22 overs as I was still in some pain. During the day Bill Edrich was twice hit on his thumb while in the slips and went to hospital, but fortunately discovered that it was only badly bruised."

Hutton and Edrich began England's second innings brightly and confidently, scoring at almost three runs per over against Lindwall and Miller before first-change Archer managed to get a delivery to lift spitefully off a length, inducing Hutton to snick the ball to Langley (25). Lindwall observed in *Flying Stumps*: "If Len has a weakness it is in playing at balls rising above his off stump but I think any bowler who concentrates his forces in the slips and tries to trap Hutton there is making a mistake.

Possibly Len's innings will finish with a catch in the slips but more than likely he will add another century to his list beforehand."

Frustratingly, Hutton had just persuaded the umpires to allow play to continue with rain starting to fall steadily. Hutton had been anxious not to lose momentum, with the opening pair having just raised England's first opening partnership of 50 runs or more in the series. The rain then set in, closing play for the day with England positioned at 62-1, still 37 runs in arrears.

Monday began with a threat of thunderstorms, but with the promise of peace in Korea. As John Arlott observed, this momentous event put the Ashes conflict into a salutary perspective. Not that this was any consolation to Tom Graveney, as Lindwall promptly bowled him through the gate with no change in the score. In came Denis Compton, on a pair, to join his close friend, Bill Edrich. They proceeded to bat with grave care until a thunderstorm curtailed play shortly after noon.

Resuming just after 2pm, the pair continued their partnership in a similar vein, doubling the score with a mixture of watchful defence and slashing cuts and pulls. Having put 139 runs on the board, Edrich slashed once too often at Lindwall, and de Courcy took a stinging catch at third slip (64). Watson (15) then kept Compton company as they lifted the total slowly to 167, whereupon Watson perished to a ferociously rearing delivery from Miller who was bowling at full pace. The injured Simpson departed, first ball, to a similar sizzling effort, leaving Bailey to deny a hat-trick. Bailey survived and England ended the penultimate day at 177-5 off 99 overs, only 80 runs on.

Compton was unable to resume his innings on Tuesday morning. During the previous day, he had taken a blow on the hand in fending off a fierce delivery from Miller, and the resultant swelling left him unable to grip the bat. He thus became England's fifth casualty.

Consequently, Evans joined Bailey at the start of play, and played initially with restraint, but reverted all too quickly to type, and began swishing recklessly. It wasn't long before he was dismissed, for just one run, having failed to spot Miller's slower ball, and holed out to Lindwall. England was then 182-6, and in grave danger of capitulating. An unexpected hero emerged to replace the impetuous Evans. Despite making two Test half-centuries, including a fiercely-struck effort against Bradman's "Invincibles", Laker's batting skills cut little ice with his partner.

Bailey remarked in *Wickets, Catches and the Odd Run*: "I need not have worried because it was one of Jim's not-all-that-frequent good days with the bat when he either hit the ball in the middle or missed it entirely. Having existed for about 15 minutes [playing Lindwall and Miller with studious ease], Jim began to play some very handsome strokes while I, uncertain about Compton's hand, dropped anchor."

Although Benaud achieved sharp turn and Davidson disconcerting movement off the seam, Laker treated both bowlers with disdain, repeatedly thumping the ball to the boundary. Fortune favoured the brave as England reached 235-6 at lunch, 136 runs ahead.

Although Bailey played defensively, he was far from passive. He persistently needled the Australians with his superciliousness and his blatant delaying tactics. Time and again he moved aside with an imperious halting gesture, just as the bowler was starting his run, in order to make some minor glove adjustment. His *piece de resistance*, though, was his ludicrous appeal against the light in blazing sunshine.

Having noticed that the Australians were attempting to squeeze in a further over before the lunch interval, Bailey beckoned Laker towards him, announcing: "It's a lovely day and we haven't a chance of an appeal against the light. But I can't say I feel like another over before lunch." Bailey proceeded to submit his appeal, compelling the umpires to confer. This meant that there was no time to complete a further over. The Australians had already dubbed Bailey as "Sir Laurence" (after Olivier) because of his theatrical antics, but this wheeze took the biscuit. Miller did not even wait for the umpires to confer. Knowing that he had been outfoxed, Miller immediately removed the bails, and presented these to the umpires before wandering off the field with his team-mates.

In an unattributed press interview, Test match umpire Dai Davies recalled: "[The Australians] would always let Bailey have a short-pitched ball to start with. Trevor would duck and come up again chewing, and then a very superior smile would come over his face. He had beaten them at the nerve-war in the middle and he knew it."

Australian pressman and former Test batsman Jack Fingleton reckoned that Bailey flouted a "superiority complex" in front of his "colonial" opponents. The normally good-natured Miller was so incensed by Bailey's behaviour that as he left the field at the end of the England innings, he turned angrily on an elderly heckler, who had the temerity to shout at him: "You bloody great Australian prawn."

Laker departed shortly after lunch to another lifter, this time from Davidson who had reverted to bowling his slow cutters. Laker had contributed a vital, well-struck 48 runs. At this point Compton returned, having had an injection to numb the pain in his hand. He was patently ill-at-ease, though, particularly against Lindwall's booming swing.

Having survived two ferocious appeals for 'catches' taken at slip and by the wicketkeeper, Compton was adjudged lbw to Lindwall after adding just one run to his total (61). The Australians were peeved at umpire Frank Chester for granting Compton two reprieves, meaning that he remained at the wicket for a match-saving 25 minutes.

Lock was equally adhesive, helping raise the score to 259 before executing an ugly and imprudent hook off Miller which gave Morris a simple catch. Bailey was the last man out at 275. He had batted for four hours and 20 minutes for his 38, helping set Australia an improbable winning target of 177 runs at 90 per hour.

With Len Hutton believing the winning target was beyond the Australians' capabilities, he decided to attack from the outset hoping to bring about a Manchester-like collapse. Hutton asked Bedser and Lock to open the attack. The ball was leaping around alarmingly, but neither Bedser nor Lock bowled well enough to exploit the conditions. With Lock unable to find his length or direction, the Australians shot out of the blocks. Although Lock did manage to produce a sharp turner to bowl Hassett with the score at 27, there was no stopping the Australian assault.

Morris and Harvey proceeded to cart the wayward England attack to all parts of the ground. Morris was stumped off Laker for 38, with the Australian score at 58, but Harvey and Hole carried on regardless, keeping up with the clock until Bailey applied the brake. By this time Bedser had removed the dangerous Harvey (34) with Australia on 111-3. Realising he could not win the game, Hutton brought on Bailey to save it by bowling wide down the leg-side to a packed on-side field. Hole (33) perished at 117, in a last-ditch attempt to confound the stalling tactics, but, thereafter, the game petered out into a tame draw as Australia finished on 147-4.

Observer cricket correspondent Alan Ross described Bailey's Test batting repertoire as "limited to three strokes: the forward defensive, the late cut and the swing to leg with the ratio in favour of the first about one hundred

Bradman's Invincibles at Worcester, May 1948. Back: Ian Johnson, Arthur Morris, Ernie Toshack, Keith Miller, Don Tallon (wicketkeeper), Ray Lindwall, Neil Harvey. Front: Bill Brown, Lindsay Hassett, Don Bradman (captain), Colin McCool, Sidney Barnes.

World champions elect: Ashes-winning Australian team at Adelaide, January 1959. Back: Les Favell, Ken Mackay, Norman O'Neill, Keith Slater (12th man), Gordon Rorke, Alan Davidson, Wally Grout (wicketkeeper). Front: Ray Lindwall, Colin McDonald, Richie Benaud (captain), Neil Harvey, Jimmy Burke.

Ashes-winning England team at the Oval, August 1953. Back: Trevor Bailey, Peter May, Tom Graveney, Sandy Tait (masseur) Jim Laker, Tony Lock, Johnny Wardle (12th man), Freddie Trueman. Front: Bill Edrich, Alec Bedser, Len Hutton (captain), Denis Compton, Godfrey Evans (wicketkeeper).

Australian hit men: Ray Lindwall (left) and Keith Miller. Both received an MBE.

Bent arms: Sonny Ramadhin bowling during the West Indian tour of England 1957 (left), Tony Lock bowling in a Surrey county championship game in 1953 (right).

Ian Meckiff of Australia bowling at Colin Cowdrey during the infamous Ashes series of 1958-59.

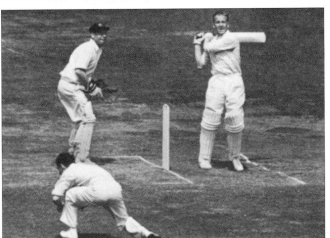

To the rescue (1): Willie Watson's match-saving century at Lord's 1953.

To the rescue (2): Cyril Washbrook's match-winning 98 at Leeds 1956. He later received a CBE.

Blowing up a storm (1): Frank Tyson at home and abroad. (Right) Tyson dismisses Keith Miller, caught Edrich, at Melbourne with supposedly his 'fastest delivery' as Australia are blown away for 111 in their second innings to lose by 128 runs, giving England a 2-1 lead in the 1954-55 Ashes series.

Blowing up a storm (2): the Manchester dust bowl of 1956. The Suez Crisis intensifies as the Australians stumble to Ashes defeat at Old Trafford on a wicket that Neville Cardus described as 'patriotically prepared'. It proved pitch perfect for Jim Laker, though. England's off-spinner took a record nineteen wickets in the match.

The amateur cricketer, priest, bishop and life peer, David Sheppard, who seemed destined to replace Hutton as captain on the Ashes tour of 1954-55 until the MCC selectors had a late change of mind.

Rival captains: (Right) England's first professional captain, Len Hutton (later Sir Len) with Australia's skipper, Lindsay Hassett MBE before the Old Trafford Test match of 1953. Hutton refused the MCC's request that he should become an amateur before being awarded the England captaincy.

MCC 'Gentlemen' (1): Sir George 'Gubby' Allen, a former England captain, chairman of the selectors and MCC president.

MCC 'Gentlemen' (2): Charles Lyttelton, 10th Viscount Cobham, MCC president in 1954. He and Col. R.S. Rait-Kerr, CBE, DSO, MC, the MCC secretary between 1937 and 1952, advocated more attractive cricket but the poor state of many English wickets did little to encourage this.

MCC 'Gentlemen' (3): Before the annual fixture against the professional 'Players'. Amateur 'Gentlemen': (Back) Doug Insole (Essex), David Sheppard (Sussex), Wilf Wooller (Glamorgan), Peter May (Surrey), Don Brennan (wicketkeeper, Yorkshire), Robin Marlar (Sussex). Front: Reg Simpson (Nottinghamshire), Trevor Bailey (Essex), Freddie Brown (captain, Northamptonshire), Bill Edrich (Middlesex), Charles Palmer (Leicestershire).

MCC selectors choosing the Ashes winning team of 1953: (Left to right): R.E.S. Wyatt, L.E.G. Ames, N.W.D. Yardley and F.R. Brown. All had their initials listed before their surname to denote their amateur status.

Peter Heine, South Africa's volatile fast bowler, nicknamed 'the Bloody Dutchman' by the bruised 1956-57 MCC tourists.

Hugh Tayfield, South Africa's naggingly accurate off-spinner, nicknamed 'Toey' because of his habit of tapping the toe of his boots before each delivery.

Jim Laker who took 19 Australian Test wickets at Old Trafford in 1956 to help England retain the Ashes. Less happy times lay ahead, though, on the controversial 1958-59 MCC tour of Australia. Having rowed with captain, May, before the ship set sail, and also with manager, Brown, while Down Under, Laker suffered with an arthritic spinning finger which forced his withdrawal from the crucial Adelaide Test match. He also unsuccessfully sought temporary amateur status for the duration of the tour having discovered that he would be better off, financially!

The 'Springboks' of 1956-57. Back: Taylor, Keith, Goddard, Heine, Adcock, Watkins, Funston. Front: Tayfield, Endean, McGlew, Viljoen (manager) Van Ryneveld (captain), Waite (wicketkeeper), McLean.

A force for change: West Indies in 1957. (Back) Gilchrist, Pairaudeau, Weekes, Hall, Sobers, Kanhai. (Front) Atkinson, Worrell (later becoming West Indies' first regular black captain), Goddard, Ramadhin, Smith.

to one". It was as if Bailey, supposedly bred as a bold, swashbuckling amateur, had converted to Stafford Cripps' 'welfare state' asceticism. He was certainly no laughing cavalier. As was the case with Jardine, Bailey's aim was always to win the Test match, and if not the match, then the series. In the immediate post-war period, the English side was not only short of Test class players, it was also short of mentally strong competitors – Bailey was an exception, as were Hutton, Edrich, Compton and Bedser.

Bailey paved the way for a different kind of Test-playing amateur. He was followed by Peter May and Colin Cowdrey, both of whom possessed similar mental discipline and application. They, too, played in a manner inspired by Hutton. It was perhaps a crucial legacy of Len Hutton's leadership that the term 'professional' became re-framed as a virtue rather than as a sin or subordinate status. He inspired his Test side to play winning cricket. And if that had to be achieved by curmudgeonly tactics, or even by blatant gamesmanship, then so be it.

Not that gamesmanship was necessarily offensive to MCC's grandees. Even the chairman of the selectors, Freddie Brown, the self-styled "Cricket Musketeer", felt moved to praise Bailey's match-saving bowling at Leeds despite this disturbing Brown's 'amateur', 'good of the game' principles.

Brown wrote in the *Cricket Musketeer* book: "Of course what saved Hutton's and England's bacon was the decision to call up Trevor Bailey to bowl defensively wide of the leg stump. It is by no means an easy thing to do – certainly not for a man who by this time was functioning on one and a half knees and who had already put up another tremendous performance as a batsman earlier in the day – but Bailey did his duty with the greatest of precision. I do not pretend to like the method by which England saved the match, but there was nothing new about it." Four years later, new regulations were introduced, limiting the number of leg-side fielders, thereby curtailing these 'spoiling' tactics.

While Freddie Brown was renowned for his advocacy of gung-ho, attacking principles, he not only endorsed Bailey's negative tactics, he also criticised Godfrey Evans' undisciplined batting, stating: "He must concentrate more and realise that by so doing he can make some very useful contributions."

These apparent contradictions seemed reconciled by Brown's view of due process. Hutton's captaincy for a home Test series was determined on a match-by-match basis because this had been time-honoured procedure, and he saw no precedent for doing otherwise. Similarly, Brown criticised Compton's self-withdrawal from the Test side because he considered this to offend existing protocol. On the other hand, Bailey's controversial match-saving tactics were deemed acceptable because Brown recognised that this practice was not unprecedented.

MCC seemed to be an organisation driven by tradition, but in a rapidly changing world their adherence to fixed, tried and tested solutions proved insufficient. As Joe Mercer, the wily former football manager, once said: "Tradition can be a wonderful friend but a dangerous enemy."

After the Test match at Leeds was drawn, Brown declared: "It was win or bust now...there could be no playing for safety." Arguably England's fastest bowler, Freddie Trueman, was recalled as was Peter May who had just rediscovered his best form. Certainly, the England side chosen to play at the Oval was the most attacking one selected during this series, comprising five specialist batsmen – a risk given that England had only once scored more than 300 runs in seven attempts – and five bowlers. The England team was: Hutton, Edrich, May, Compton, Graveney, Bailey, Evans, Laker, Lock, Bedser and Trueman.

Australia made one change, replacing Benaud – dismissed as a "festival player" by Hutton – with Bill Johnston whose knee problem had improved. Six days were allocated to the Test match so that a positive result might be achieved. However, unless bad weather intervened yet again, it seemed unlikely that six days would be needed with both sides displaying so much frailty in their batting.

On Saturday 15th August, Hassett went nap by winning the toss for the fifth time in a row. He was well aware that the Oval wicket tended to be dry and dusty, offering much assistance to Laker and Lock, particularly in the latter stages of the game. So, despite the threat posed by Bedser in the steamy conditions, Hassett decided to bat first. Bedser began with an attacking field of two slips, a gully and three short legs, but as soon as Hassett had glanced Bedser for four, Hutton directed Bailey to guard the long-leg boundary. With less specialist batsmen at his disposal, Hutton was unprepared to give any runs away.

Trueman began at the Pavilion End, and should have had Morris caught by Compton at leg-slip in his first over. With the score at 32, however, Bedser righted Compton's wrong by producing an off-cutter which jagged back from outside the off stump to trap Morris in front of his stumps, and not playing a shot. The Australian total had increased by only ten when Bailey produced a viciously late in-swinger to dismiss Miller, lbw for one run. Hassett remained imperturbable, though, reaching his half-century, just before lunch, when Australia was 98-2. So far, Australia was marginally in front. The lunchtime rain enlivened the wicket, though, and it was not long before Bedser and Trueman had the tourists in a heap of trouble.

First to go was Hassett (53), who feathered Bedser's in-swinger to a triumphant Evans (107-3). Trueman's pace was discomforting Harvey, forcing him uncharacteristically onto the back foot. The left-hander perished trying to lift the siege. A poorly-executed hook shot sent the ball soaring in the direction of midwicket. Hutton caught it brilliantly over his shoulder (107-4).

Jim de Courcy was due in next, but his appearance was briefly delayed by rain. Once he and Hole re-appeared in blinding sunshine, de Courcy blasted a no-ball from Bedser to the long-on boundary. However, de Courcy was only to add one more run before Trueman's perfect out-swinger induced him to fish outside his off stump, and edge a catch to Evans (118-5). For the new batsman, Archer, Hutton provided Trueman with no fewer than six slips! Talk about payback time.

Archer was not intimidated, and neither was Hole. Together, they went on to the offensive. Consequently Trueman was replaced by Bailey. He was no more effective, so was quickly substituted by Lock. It was to no avail. The runs still came quickly. Forty-two were added at almost a run per minute. Therefore, Hutton returned to Trueman whose rest period had amounted to less than 20 minutes. Trueman showed no sign of fatigue, in the sticky heat, as he bounded in once more off a curving run, a dishevelled, glowering bundle of bustling belligerence. He was a thinking one, too.

Rather than attempting to blast Hole out, he tempted him with a full-pitched out-swinger. Hole tried to thrash the ball through cover, with an angled bat, but only succeeded in presenting Evans with his third catch of the innings (160-6). Hutton immediately brought Bedser on for Lock to bowl at the new batsman, Davidson. Bedser removed Archer instead, caught and bowled, for ten (160-7). The Australian innings was in ruins, and Bedser had captured his 39th wicket of the series, surpassing Maurice Tate's record total for an Ashes series.

Realising that they needed to take the initiative before the new ball arrived, Lindwall and Davidson attacked the England spinners vigorously, adding 47 runs in double quick time. With England unnerved by the Australian assault, Davidson was dropped at slip off Bailey immediately after the tea interval. The score was then 178-7. The batsmen were able to add a further 29 runs before a snorter from Laker induced Davidson to jab involuntarily at the lifting ball, leaving Edrich to grasp the chance with remarkable agility (207-8). Lindwall should have followed soon after, but Graveney dropped a swirling catch in the covers.

Much to England's disappointment, the new ball did not bring about the Australians' demise. With the pitch having dried, it became placid once more, so while Lindwall thumped productively, Langley blocked determinedly. It was Lock who finally removed the latter with Edrich taking another sharp catch at slip (245-9).

By now, the England bowlers were flagging in the enervating conditions. This allowed Lindwall to take the Australian total to a respectable 275, and his own contribution to 62, before he edged Trueman to Evans. Hassett was elated as much as Hutton was disappointed. At least, England's captain managed to complete the final two overs unscathed as England closed the day at 1-0.

Monday's play followed a similar course in that England seemed well on top during the early afternoon, with Hutton and May batting serenely at 137-1. This strong position was soon lost as six wickets went down for the addition of only 98 runs. Once Hutton (82), and May (39) were dismissed only Bailey (35 not out) seemed capable of averting yet another batting disaster, although Evans stayed longer than his initial carving shots suggested.

England's specialist batsmen allowed themselves to be bogged down by the Australians' relentlessly accurate seam bowling. Even Hole managed to tie Compton down with his innocuous floaters. It was small wonder that Hutton looked so exhausted and grave at the close of play.

What a difference a day made! Just when it seemed that England might concede a first innings deficit, its tail wagged with unexpected vigour. First Trueman (10), and then Bedser (22 not out) helped Bailey lift his score to 64 thereby taking the England first innings total to 306 – a small lead of 31.

Hutton's mood was transformed. With the wicket showing signs of wear, and the dry, dusty surface almost certainly conducive to spin, he knew he had the upper hand. After only cursory use of Bedser and Trueman, Hutton turned to Laker and Lock, and by mid-afternoon the Australians were tottering at 61-5. Hassett, who had previously played pace bowling competently, was all at sea against Laker. He was lbw after a particularly torrid over, in which he was pressed unhappily onto the back foot. Laker's sixth delivery dismissed him (23-1). It was an ignominious end to Hassett's magnificent Test career in which he averaged over 46 runs per innings.

Hole was promoted with the intention of smiting the Surrey spin twins out of the attack. Hutton was too canny for that stratagem to work, and Laker duly had Hole lbw after the Australian also played back against the biting ball (59-2). Lock's quicker delivery then rapidly punctured Harvey's jauntiness, bowling the left-hander for just one run (60-3). Miller played tentatively forward to Laker, but failed to smother the turn. The resulting edge flew to Trueman who grasped the opportunity at backward short leg (61-4). The previously untroubled Morris followed immediately after being adjudged lbw to Lock (61-5). Four wickets had fallen, in 16 balls, for only two runs.

A recovery of sorts was mounted led by Ron Archer (49) and Alan Davidson (21) who hit out boldly, particularly against Laker, but with an hour gone of the final session, the Australians were all out for 162. Lock had taken five wickets for 45 runs and Laker four for 75. It had been a rout. The pitch had not been to blame. The ball had gripped, but not turned so viciously as to account for the scale of the Australian collapse. Freddie Brown reckoned that a good county side would have made 230 on this track. After the gloomy conditions at Nottingham, Manchester and Leeds, the Oval light had been much better. But having been destroyed here by spin, a spectre of 1956 drifted across the Australians' vision.

England needed just 132 to win, on a turning wicket, against a side who had not selected a specialist spinner. By the close, that target had been reduced by 38 runs, but with one wicket down, Hutton having departed after a foolish run-out. Holding their nerve, though, the English batsmen waltzed to an easy eight-wicket victory. It was fitting that Edrich should top-score with 55 runs, and Compton should sweep the winning boundary. Both men deserved their moments in the sun after bravely defying the Australians' might over the previous seven years.

After a dreadful summer, the new Elizabethan age had been blessed finally with radiant sunshine. The exultant British supporters poured onto the still luscious Oval turf, gathering in their thousands in front of the pavilion. A visibly relieved Len Hutton and a philosophical Lindsay Hassett exchanged pleasantries. They both waved and smiled. Hutton, suitably vindicated, reflected privately: "The pinpricking criticisms of my supposed caution from predictable quarters did not seem too important."

Hassett then made a droll speech, pretending also to throw his blazer into the crowd as a gesture of mock disgust. Both men then retreated to quaff copious quantities of champagne. Away from the public gaze, though, Hassett was less diplomatic. Having been congratulated by MCC's Walter Robins on his amusing speech, Hassett responded: "Yes. I think it was pretty good considering Lockie threw us out." In six years time, the accusers would become the accused.

'A HIGH WIND IN JAMAICA'

'Ebb Tide'

With MCC about to select a side to tour the West Indies, during the winter of 1953/54, the subject of immigration was vexing the Conservative British government. A bill was mooted to curb further entries, particularly those of Afro-Caribbeans. Meanwhile, proposed measures for eradicating racial discrimination were set aside. It was hardly a message of welcome to Britain's Commonwealth brethren.

According to Bob Carter, Clive Harris and Shirley Joshi of the University of Warwick Centre of Research in Ethnic Relations, black people were seen then to be threatening an essentially [white] British way of life. In their joint paper, entitled *The 1951-55 Conservative Government and the Racialisation of Black Immigration*, the authors argued, that by 1952, both Labour and Conservative governments had instituted covert, and sometimes illegal, means of discouraging legitimate black immigration. These measures did not reduce the number of black British passport holders entering the UK, though. Consequently, by the early 1950s, some government departments were favouring restrictive legislation.

While Len Hutton was leading a heroic series recovery in Kingston, Jamaica, in April 1954, the British government had decided that black immigration was largely to blame for the nation's rising social problems. Seeking the facts to support their presuppositions, the national figures for unemployment, welfare benefit take-up, homelessness, crime and miscegenation were scoured to supply the necessary evidence.

Because black Caribbean people were caricatured as unreliable workers or work-shy, government officials believed that they placed an unacceptable strain on public finances. With many black immigrants congregating in areas of acute housing shortages, such as London, Liverpool and the Midlands, they were castigated for creating "new Harlems". They were blamed, too, for disfiguring neighbourhoods by allegedly peddling drugs or living off immoral earnings.

According to Carter et al, the facts did not confirm the government's prejudices. Some of those in local positions of authority disassociated themselves from the blind discrimination of national politicians. For example, the Chief Constable of Middlesbrough noted in 1952 that: "...on the whole, the coloured population are as well behaved as many local citizens".

Two years later, just as a draft new Immigration Bill was being prepared, a *Times* home affairs correspondent observed: "Everywhere they have appeared, the police and magistrates are ready to say that the West Indians make no trouble, which is more than some are ready to say of Irish workers." But this contrary evidence made no impact upon the national government which seemed intent upon curbing black immigration.

Admittedly, West Indian immigration rose dramatically in 1954 with 10,000 people entering the UK, a five-fold increase on levels in previous years. While Betty Boothroyd at the Board of Trade acknowledged this, she maintained that "overall immigration from coloured empire countries has not increased in any dramatic way". "It is interesting," noted one civil servant, wryly, "that the police estimate of the number of coloured people now in the United Kingdom gives a total of less than 25,000 Colonials, as against our unofficial estimate of 50,000 to 60,000."

While legitimate West Indian immigrants were being shunned and obstructed by an increasingly hard-nosed Conservative government, Len Hutton's team did little to raise the nation's popularity in the Caribbean. West Indian writer CLR James wrote in *Beyond a Boundary*: "The 1953/54 MCC team was actively disliked. This was not due merely to unsportsmanlike behaviour by individuals. There is evidence to show that the team had given the impression that it was not merely playing cricket, but was out to establish the prestige of Britain and, by that, of the local whites."

Sir Clyde Walcott thought the tour was even stormier than the 1932/33 'Bodyline' series. In a much later BBC interview, he reckoned that half of Hutton's team would have been fined or suspended if modern day disciplinary standards had been applied. The tour was mired by controversy from beginning to end. There was a bottle-throwing riot in British Guiana,

Tony Lock was no-balled for throwing, umpires' decisions were contested and the alleged misbehaviour of Hutton's players drew adverse comment from blacks and whites. Hutton and his MCC tour manager, Charles Palmer, were criticised for exercising insufficient control.

Hutton reckoned that the tour left him "physically and mentally drained", probably foreshortening his playing career by two years. He blamed the political vortex in which his team was expected to play. Reacting to anti-colonial forces elsewhere in the world, the Caribbean winds of change threatened to yank the furiously fluttering union jack from its mast. An upsurge of West Indian nationalism alarmed the white colonialists whose long-standing political, economic and social supremacy became threatened. Some of them impressed upon Len Hutton's players the importance of putting the black Caribbean 'upstarts' in their place.

According to Alex Bannister, author of *Cricket Cauldron*, there were many West Indian whites who were indignant that England should be led by a professional. With their gripes mounting in reaction to the flagging fortunes of Hutton's side, and regarding his alleged failure to keep his players in check, some of them joined forces with the carping press who accused Hutton of tactical weakness after the first two Tests were lost emphatically.

As in the dying days of the Raj, the diehard colonialists feared sporting defeat, by those deemed to be inferior, because this questioned their presumption of political, social and racial supremacy. With Caribbean pro-independence sentiments gathering strength, their nervousness escalated. Meanwhile, US politicians and intelligence staff kept a close eye on events lest the native anti-colonialist factions became hijacked by communists, as was feared in British Guiana in 1953, and realised in Cuba in 1959. Senator McCarthy's communist 'witch hunts' were then at their zenith, allegorised by Arthur Miller's play, *The Crucible*.

Not that the Caribbean tensions rested entirely upon a simple black versus colonial white dimension, because inter-island jealousies severely complicated the issue. It was the insular nature of island identities and politics which caused the short-lived West Indian Federation to founder, having been set up by Britain in 1958 as a self-governing union, spanning ten former island colonies. Colour prejudices existed also between the Afro-Caribbean blacks, Caribbean Indians and those of mixed race.

When Frank Worrell was appointed as the first regular black captain of the West Indies side, in 1960, it was proof of his inspired leadership and charismatic statesmanship that he managed to weld these disparate, and sometimes discordant elements into an integrated and winning team.

The fact that the 1953/54 series was dubbed the 'unofficial championship of the world' hardly helped contain the febrile mood. Hutton recalled that on the eve of the team's departure, Sir Walter Monckton, a British diplomat, briefed the squad on the political situation they would face in the Caribbean. Hutton remarked in *Fifty Years in Cricket*: "Excellent as far as it went, but it did not tell us how sensitive the situation could be."

In his 2004 autobiography *As it Was*, Freddie Trueman maintained that it was the then Colonial Secretary, Lennox-Boyd, who addressed the team on the eve of their departure not Monckton, telling them that the Caribbean political situation was a "tinder box" and that the players were "not to do or say anything that might inflame it... [They] were to be diplomats at all times". Apparently, Trueman retorted that: "He should like to be paid like one."

As Brian Statham confirmed in his autobiography *A Spell at the Top*, Trueman was "possibly a little too boisterous at times, a little indiscreet, but so are many cricketers making their first tour abroad. But all the stories I have heard about Freddie and his so-called wild behaviour have been grossly exaggerated...The most famous of all was when he was alleged to have remarked to a High Commissioner during a dinner in Barbados 'pass the salt, Gunga Din'. This is completely untrue."

Statham recalled that it was Tom Graveney, not Trueman, who, politely, took a woman to task for criticising the behaviour and performance of the English players on only hearsay evidence. However, the woman, who was a close friend of the Governor of Barbados, complained that a tall, dark-haired cricketer had insulted her, and Trueman immediately became the prime suspect.

As Statham conceded, though, Trueman did sometimes speak out of turn, as at a Barbados yacht club dance. This only increased his burgeoning notoriety. On one occasion Trueman and his room-mate, Tony Lock, were asked by Hutton to meet an English woman who complained about their allegedly offensive behaviour while they had shared a hotel lift. Having successfully appeased their irate accuser, Hutton complimented Trueman on his handling of the situation, stating: "I thought you took that pretty well", to which Trueman retorted: "So do I, considering it wasn't us!"

Although exonerated in this instance, Trueman was incensed that he was the only member of the touring party not to receive a good conduct bonus. He had a point. It wasn't as if everyone else had behaved impeccably. For example, Tom Graveney had angrily thrown the ball to the ground when a West Indian Test umpire had rejected his appeal for, what seemed to be, an indisputable catch.

Trueman's sharp tongue and sharper bowling courted hostility, though, especially when he bowled venomously short. This earned him the reputation of "Mr Bumper Man". When he broke the arm of Jamaican hero "Masa" George Headley with a bouncer, he received a torrent of abuse, unsurprisingly so, since the local people had just raised £1,000 to bring Headley back to his native island.

One incensed West Indian player called Trueman a "white English bastard", which produced an angry confrontation between the two in the middle. Hutton was accused of not doing enough to curb the short-pitched stuff, particularly from Trueman, but Frank King, the one genuine fast bowler on the West Indian side, was equally culpable, often bowling as many as three bumpers per over. Shorn of potency because of the serial flatness of the Caribbean tracks, it was unsurprising that the fast bowlers should resort to bouncers.

Hutton confirmed in his autobiography that he regretted taking Trueman on the tour. He wrote in *Fifty Years of Cricket*: "The absence of Bedser [who was exhausted by the summer's exertions, and withdrawn at his county's request] threw Trueman into an adventure for which he was not properly prepared." After helping England draw this irascible series, Trueman would not play in another Test match under Hutton, only returning in 1955 when May took over the captaincy.

Many years later, Trueman publicly confronted Hutton, blaming his former captain for curtailing his Test career while he was in his prime as a fast bowler. This seemed unfair. Many MCC members had already made up their mind about Trueman, irrespective of what Hutton thought or said. One remarked to Yorkshire coach Bill Bowes: "My word, this Trueman's a bad-tempered devil, isn't he? What a troublemaker he is, and totally uncontrollable." To his credit, Bowes summarily dismissed the criticism as ill-informed.

Journalist Jim Swanton expressed regret that Hutton did not have a more disciplinarian manager to support him, pointing out that: "Len was a superb technician and had plenty of instinctive dignity, but he was by nature inclined to be shy, withdrawn, introspective, not the sort to wear authority easily. Nor was he physically robust as he approached his 14th, and most difficult Test series inside eight years." Hutton was also approaching his 38th birthday.

Troubles accompanied Hutton until the very end of the series. The Caribbean wickets might have been flat, but the political climate, like the heat, was very sticky indeed. Upon returning to Jamaica for the crucial final Test, Hutton found that the pavilion staff had ripped up their complimentary passes in front of an astonished Denis Compton. Worse still, Hutton was accused by Alex Bustamante, the Jamaican Chief Minister, of deliberately snubbing him. As Hutton trudged wearily off the field for the tea break, on the third day, having just made an unbeaten double century, he failed to hear Bustamante's congratulations.

The Chief Minister was so affronted that he pursued Hutton into the dressing room, berating him for his rudeness. Exhausted by the Kingston heat, and bewildered by Bustamante's accusation, Hutton's concentration became so badly disturbed that he lost his wicket immediately upon the resumption of play – bowled Bustamante, it seemed.

Nevertheless, Hutton moved quickly to defuse the situation by writing a letter of apology to the Chief Minister. It was a wise move because Bustamante was a colossus in Jamaican politics, later proclaimed to be a national hero of Jamaica, alongside Norman Manley and the black liberationist Marcus Garvey, for the leading role he played in bravely defying colonial rule, helping establish universal suffrage, and agitating successfully for Jamaican independence in 1962.

During the height of the anti-colonial struggle, Bustamante was imprisoned for his political activities. Like Nelson Mandela, he graduated from agitator to statesman, becoming Jamaica's first independent Prime Minister, and holding office until 1967. Given the intensity of the political struggles in which Bustamante was immersed, his heightened sensitivity at Hutton's apparent snub is perhaps understandable.

Although Walcott understood Hutton's preoccupied state of mind, at Kingston, better than Bustamante, he was less sympathetic when Hutton wrote in his 1956 book *Just My Story*: "The gradual exclusion of white folk is a bad thing for the future of West Indian cricket." If this represented Hutton's honest opinion at that time, it was hardly a helpful one.

In the mid 1950s, black West Indian cricketers were still engaged in a tussle for racial equality. Their clamour for the appointment of a regular black West Indian captain had yet to be satisfied, despite the best efforts of advocates such as CLR James. Players such as Walcott, Worrell and Weekes were still striving to combat the racial prejudice endemic in Caribbean cricket, although, encouragingly, a higher quota of black players appeared in the West Indian side of 1953/54 compared with the touring party of 1950, half of whom were white, at least according to Walcott. Whether Hutton was as protective of white interests, then, as Walcott claimed, is unclear. What is clearer is that Hutton had his work cut out on the 1953/54 tour in trying to pick his way through so many conflicting factions.

Hutton was reproached for discouraging fraternisation with the West Indian players, although he denied this in his biography *Fifty Years in Cricket*, maintaining that he sought only to protect his players from the excessive number of social functions, and the strong Caribbean liquor. However, vice-captain Trevor Bailey admitted, in his book *Wickets, Catches and the Odd Run*, that his team did not endear themselves to their hosts by their "slightly arrogant and distinctly intolerant attitude [concerning the calibre of] accommodation provided and some of the arrangements".

Hutton was also criticised by West Indian players and officials for his derogatory opinion of Caribbean umpires, compounded by his alleged lack of restraint, when some of his players questioned their decisions. According to the tour manager, Charles Palmer, there were eight highly contentious decisions which went against England, whereas the West Indies seemed to suffer only two.

Because of intense local rivalries, each island claimed the right to nominate their own officials to stand in their home Tests. This practice ensured neither quality of officiating nor consistency of standards, and the dubious decisions which resulted sometimes led to friction. The choice of players was also subject to island politics. For example, Jamaican George Headley was selected in the first Test at Kingston although his current form and advanced age hardly warranted his inclusion.

Throughout this tour Hutton was assailed on all sides. With bad news travelling fast, he must have felt he was on borrowed time. Once again MCC thoughts were turning to Sheppard as a possible replacement. The pressure placed upon Hutton must have been almost intolerable. With so much preying upon his mind, it was small wonder that he should have seemed remote at times, and that his health – both physical and emotional – should have suffered.

And yet Hutton scored almost 700 priceless runs during this Test series, achieving an incredible average score of 96.7, and producing match-winning innings at Georgetown (169), and, at Kingston, in the final Test (205). As proof of his pre-eminence in the English batting averages, Compton came next with 49.7 runs per innings. These were gritty performances by men afflicted by depleting disability. However, Hutton's Caribbean experience exhausted him so much that he was never the same batsman again. As proof of this, during the next 12 months, Hutton averaged 6.33 in the two Tests he played against Pakistan, 24.44 in the Ashes series in Australia, and 22.33 in his last two Tests against New Zealand.

Despite the huge criticism that Hutton received during this ill-starred series, Denis Compton said that, without Hutton's sublime batting and his brave leadership, England would have lost this rubber. Compton recalled in his book *End of an Innings* how Hutton refused to leave the field at Georgetown when the bottle throwing began. Compton believed that the riot had been triggered by a large loss of bets when the crowd's hero, Cliff McWatt, was run out.

Although a ground official asked Hutton and his team to leave the field, Hutton coolly defied him and the thousands of angry demonstrators, replying: "No, I want a couple of wickets before the close." In a later BBC interview Compton concluded, "This was so typical of Len."

England did well to win in Georgetown, British Guiana, having lost the first two Tests so abjectly. The opening Test match had been lost unexpectedly on the final afternoon when a cataclysmic collapse resulted in seven English wickets falling for just eight runs. Then, Walcott's savage innings of 220 runs in the second Test at Bridgetown, made in just six-and-a-half-hours, gave the West Indies a decisive first innings advantage of 202 runs. While Ramadhin and Valentine continued to mesmerise most of the English batsmen, Hutton's battery of pace bowlers made little impression upon the powerful home batting line-up.

At Georgetown, however, Hutton's luck changed. Having won the toss for the first time in eight Tests, his superb knock of 169 guided England to a match-winning total of 435. When the West Indies replied, Statham made early inroads. Laker and Lock then mopped up the rest, dismissing their hosts for only 251 runs. After enforcing the follow-on, Hutton once again deployed his bowlers skilfully, and the home side could manage just 256 at the second time of asking, losing eventually by nine wickets.

England's victory was all the more impressive because the local political situation in British Guiana was still very tense. With strikes and unrest accompanying the victory of the Jagan's People's Progressive Party in the April 1953 elections, the British government despatched a military force to the flood-infested country to restore order, and stem a perceived communist threat. As the United States looked on anxiously, the local constitution was suspended, leaving the British governor and his appointed officials to rule for the next three years, using emergency powers.

A bore draw followed on an all-too-perfect strip in Trinidad, in which England negated a West Indian first innings score of 681-8 declared with 537 runs of their own. Hutton's side surpassed themselves in the final Test at Kingston, though, winning once again by nine wickets. Bailey bowled superbly on a flat track to skittle the West Indies for 139, taking seven wickets for 34, before Hutton's stupendous double century took England to 414 in reply. Despite scoring another impressive century, Walcott (116) was unable to avert defeat. By the skin of his teeth, or the width of his bat, Hutton had preserved England's status as unofficial world champions.

As for the West Indies, their star was falling, despite the emergence of a brilliant 17-year-old all-rounder named Garfield Sobers. A year later, the Australians would thrash them 3-0 on their home turf, racking up a succession of mammoth totals. Unlike the MCC tourists of 1953/54, the Australians were well-liked wherever they played, but they did not have to carry the heavy imperial baggage around with them, that weighed down Len Hutton's side.

Caribbean poet Edward Kamau Braithwaite summed up the West Indian malaise, in the conclusion to his 1954 poem 'Rites': "But I say it once an' I say it agen: when things goin' good, you cahn touch we; but leh murder start an' ol man, you cahn fine a man to hole up de side."

Braithwaite's poem vividly recreates one of the pivotal contests of the series, between Clyde Walcott's flashing blade and Jim Laker's crafty spin. Despite being dismissed four times by Laker, during this series, Walcott had the better of the contest, scoring 698 runs with three tons and an average of 87.25. Laker took 15 wickets in the four Tests, though, playing a leading role in England's two victories. Overall, Laker had a good Test record against Walcott, dismissing him 11 times, more than any other Test bowler achieved. Walcott liked Laker and his dry sense of humour. He considered him to be a great bowler with excellent control, plenty of spin and a good delivery which drifted straight on.

Walcott's opinion of Laker's spin partner, Tony Lock, was less favourable, though, on account of Lock's suspect action. After Lock was called in the first Test, Hutton intervened, compelling Lock to cease using his faster ball. While the West Indian match officials equivocated, Walcott was convinced that Lock's bowling was illegal. According to rare film footage of the series, MCC tour manager Charles Palmer agreed. However, Lord's took no further action. It would be another five years before MCC yanked its head out of the sand.

Lock would eventually repent, and remedy his defective action on his own accord. In the meantime, Ramadhin was permitted to 'hurl' his mesmerising spinners with impunity. In a cooler political climate, the next MCC tour to the Caribbean in 1959/60 was a much more relaxed and friendly affair, allowing a redeemed Trueman to achieve both success and popularity.

'THAT'S ALL RIGHT MAMA'

'Friends and Neighbours'

By 1954, British food rationing had been consigned to history. A trade surplus signalled a strengthening UK economy. With young people having more disposable income, a vibrant youth culture emerged. Encouraged by a full-scale US invasion of pulsating, adrenaline-driven, rabble-rousing rock 'n' roll, generational lines were quickly drawn.

The days of *Family Favourites* and other generic family entertainment were numbered. Adolescence became inserted between childhood and adulthood. Defining their distinct identity, British teenagers set out what was 'cool' and what was 'square'. Their struggle for recognition proved to be a rancorous affair in the conservative climate of 1950s Britain. The once toffish 'Teddy Boy' look became resurrected as a badge of working class rebellion.

And boy did it find its target. With the new 'rip it up' rock 'n' roll music providing a defiant beat, the sneering 'Teds' promptly aroused a moral panic. Reacting to the youthful provocation, the *Daily Mail* described rock 'n' roll as "tribal", "jungle" music perhaps representing "the Negros' revenge".

While the mums and dads remained entranced by Frank Sinatra, Dean Martin, Nat King Cole, Perry Como and Doris Day, their teenage sons and daughters were clamouring for Bill Haley, Elvis, Gene Vincent, Jerry

'THAT'S ALL RIGHT MAMA'

Lee Lewis and Little Richard. The divide applied to British imitators, also. Filed under adult 'easy listening' were Frankie Vaughan, Dickie Valentine, Michael Holliday, Alma Cogan and Ruby Murray, while the teenage market embraced 'safer' British versions of the American rockers including Tommy Steele, Lonnie Donegan, and Cliff Richard.

Screenings of the 1955 film *Blackboard Jungle*, featuring Bill Haley's song 'Rock Around the Clock', prompted exuberant, anarchic and sometimes violent reactions from the teenage audiences. This was the genesis of the 1950s 'Youthquake', emphasising that the spectre of teenage folk devilry started long before the Sex Pistols. The teenagers had their preferred eating houses, too, as the Wimpy chain opened for business in 1954, having been licensed for business by that most British of institutions, Lyons Corner House. US-style hamburgers, Knickerbocker Glories and milk shakes began to supplant sausage and chips, suet puddings, and lemonade or tea as the teenage food and beverages of choice.

Just one year after the 1953 Coronation festival, with its celebration of British patriotic pride, alarm was registered at the potentially harmful impact of American cultural imperialism. Briefly, attention focused upon the perversion of young minds by American comics, which featured lurid tales of grave robbers, monsters and flesh eaters. As improbable as it now sounds, a Comics Campaign Council was created, and, in conjunction with the National Union of Teachers, it lobbied successfully for legal restraint of such material. Their efforts resulted in the passing of the 1955 Children & Young Persons (Harmful Publications) Act.

At the heart of this censorship was a middle-class desire to preserve what was vaguely defined as a uniquely British way of life, with its restrained notions of propriety. Not that American cultural influence was uniformly condemned – quite the contrary. For in drab, dour, depleted post-war Britain, American jazz and swing restored vibrancy to dismal lives, while US films offered colourful escapes with panoramic shots of sweeping prairies, rugged mountains and exotic island paradises. So did the intoxicating brushes with Hollywood glamour. British people began to experience what freedom from want, smog and stodge should feel, smell and taste like. After so many years of self-denial the allure was all the more powerful.

The popularity of English first-class cricket began to recede further, pushed aside by brighter alternatives. A Do-It-Yourself craze took hold, encompassing both home improvements and skiffle music. Britain became less a nation of spectators. Average gates at English Football

League grounds were down by 7% on the 1946/47 high point. Cinema admissions were falling too, but not as fast as attendances at England's county grounds. By 1956, county cricket attendances were over a million less than in 1947, a massive drop of 47%.

Many teenagers dismissed cricket as irrelevant or 'square'. The stuffy image perpetrated by MCC, and its county brethren, did little to discourage their view. During the tea interval, at one county ground, an impromptu game was broken up by the stewards. As they did so, a pompous tannoy announcer declared: "There are ten reasons why you should not play cricket on the outfield. The first is that committee says so. The other nine do not matter." The languishing first-class game could ill afford to indulge such imperious disdain.

The interminable saga concerning the England captaincy vividly illustrated MCC's distrust of change. Although Len Hutton had successfully captained the national side for two years – having won back the Ashes and fronted a heroic recovery in the Caribbean – many MCC members still believed that the England cricket team should be led by an amateur, on grounds of disposition, personality, playing style and social background. During that spring Hutton's captaincy was reconsidered, and not solely because of his failing health. Many thought that David Sheppard would prove to be a better leader.

Jim Swanton, for one, backed Sheppard, believing that no one else had the qualities for the post. The *Observer*'s cricket correspondent Alan Ross agreed, writing in his 1955 Ashes journal *Australia 55*: "Sheppard had captained Sussex with remarkable skill...He was one of the best close to the wicket fieldsmen in the country, and he seemed as likely to make runs going in first as anyone else...[Hutton's] captaincy has lacked, to my mind, the qualities of character and determination that distinguish his batsmanship...[In] the 1953 Tests, he let good positions slip away without appearing able to do much about it.

"He started out... with defensive fields, as if preferring to save a possible four and miss a wicket than take the right risks. His native caution showed itself again in his reluctance to use his slow bowlers when Bedser and Bailey were under fire...Nor again, had Hutton struck one as a captain greatly encouraging to his bowlers...Hutton's own batting, too, seemed to have a depressing effect on those that followed him."

It is difficult to understand the clamour for Sheppard's candidacy, even with lofty hindsight. Sheppard had not played in a Test match for two years. As confirmed by Freddie Brown, he had failed badly in Australia, during the 1950/51 series, and not been exposed to bowling of the highest class since. It was one thing to batter the largely sub-standard county bowling attacks, as Sheppard had done successfully during the summer of 1953, but quite another to collar the likes of Lindwall, Miller and Johnston Down Under.

Moreover, Sheppard was embarking upon a career in holy orders, having recently begun ordination training at Ridley Hall. Conceivably, the nagging doubt at the back of MCC minds concerned Hutton's ability to keep his players in order. The petulant outbursts, by the likes of Graveney, at poor umpiring decisions had offended their standards of sportsmanship and decorum.

Nevertheless, it seemed as if MCC officials had a good idea about how the British public might regard their doubts, for they attempted to hold their debate secretly at the home of their secretary, Ronnie Aird. But it did not take the press long to rumble what was going on. Soon, the issue was being openly debated on the back pages of every British newspaper.

With the cat out of the bag, Sheppard was placed in an invidious position. He consented to lead the England side in two of the four Tests against Pakistan while Hutton was recovering from mental and physical fatigue. However, he was deeply unsure about leading an MCC touring party to Australia and New Zealand. Not only did this mean postponing his Anglican ministry training, it also meant openly contesting Hutton, whom he considered to be a highly respected friend. Having taken the advice of other friends, and his college principal, Sheppard finally took the plunge, and declared he was available for selection Down Under, but only if offered the captaincy.

It appeared that those who advanced Sheppard's claim, not only demeaned Hutton's huge contribution to England's success, but also that of Trevor Bailey, his able deputy on the Caribbean tour. Hutton considered Bailey to be "a strong leader with many ideas". Although the 'amateur' Bailey had the right profile, having had a public school and Oxbridge education, he had defied MCC rules in publishing articles about the Caribbean tour before the regulatory two-year period had elapsed. He was therefore stripped of the vice-captaincy.

The sanction seemed excessive and counter-productive. Having narrowly won back the Ashes after a 19-year wait, it should have been clear to MCC's selection committee that England had little hope of retaining them without deploying its battle-hardened troops, and its shrewdest leaders. After all, was this not the profile of Bradman's "Invincibles"? With England's batting line-up prone to inexplicable collapses, there seemed little room for a batsman, like Sheppard, who had proved to be technically deficient during his toughest examination thus far, on the quicker wickets of Australia.

With great magnanimity, Hutton urged Sheppard to take the post if it was offered. Sheppard mistook Hutton's generosity of spirit for a loss of appetite. Once the MCC selectors had a change of heart, and invited Hutton to lead the Ashes party, it was clear that Hutton's keenness for the job was undaunted. Selector Walter Robins explained to Sheppard that he thought they had been unfair to Hutton in not recognising the difficulty of his position in the West Indies. This suggested that MCC's doubts about Hutton's captaincy focused upon his suitability, rather than his physical or emotional fitness.

Jim Swanton, who was considered close to senior MCC members, suggested as much, commenting that Sheppard's exclusion was "a loss indeed at a time when character and integrity of conduct were never more needed both on and off the field." Hutton's new vice-captain, Peter May, had no doubt about the calibre of Hutton's leadership, though, remarking to Geoffrey Howard, MCC's 1954/55 tour manager: "What a good job we've got Len out here because David would never have done it."

Without doubt, MCC's selectors reached the right decision, but the manner in which they arrived there seemed questionable. It is unclear what part, if any, Hutton played in their deliberations. The implication, from Robins' account to Sheppard, was that it was only late in these protracted proceedings that the criticisms of Hutton's captaincy were put into their proper perspective.

Hutton had been left to ponder his fate as he watched a rival, less qualified candidate being courted for his post. Fortunately, he had learnt to keep his own counsel, and to exercise "discrimination in his reading habits and to suffer the fool gladly", as he elegantly put it, in his book *Fifty Years in Cricket.*

Yorkshire Post correspondent Jim Kilburn wrote: "[Hutton] always seemed to feel himself on trial...He was persistently anxious not to tread on corns." It can only be speculated what the outcome might have been had the press not got wind of what was afoot. As Jim Laker would find, when he encountered angry reactions to his grumpy, but compelling book, *Over to Me,* while cricket's administrators felt free to express unaccountable views and bias that could prejudice a professional's career, that player had less right to question such arbitrary and discriminative treatment, and no right to do so in public. Fortunately, the press was less inhibited. They, at least, compelled a degree of accountability that Hutton could not.

In the drenched summer of 1954, a team from Pakistan arrived to play its first Test series with England. The Imperial Cricket Conference had only admitted it to the Test-playing fraternity two years previously. As Len Hutton observed, many of its players were "as green as the colour of their caps". But the very fact that they were playing Test cricket was indicative of the healing capacity of international cricket.

Pakistan and India had fought their first war over the disputed Kashmir region during the winter of 1947/48. A Pakistani invasion was repelled by the Indian Army, reinforced by the local Muslim population. Following an Indian appeal to the United Nations that Pakistan had violated its sovereign territory, the UN brokered a peace deal that was still in place when the two countries contested their first Test series between October and December 1952.

The fact that this series took place at all was testament to the supreme statesmanship of the Indian premier, Jawaharlal Nehru. He set aside the Kashmir conflict, and the horrific Partition process, in which 12.5 million were violently displaced, and up to one million killed, amid scenes of widespread 'ethnic cleansing', rape and destruction, to extend the hand of friendship to his Muslim neighbours, offering a Test series on Indian soil.

The Pakistani touring team included two players who had previously represented an All Indian side. Their captain was Abdul Hafeez Kardar, an aristocratic Oxford Blue, who would later become a Pakistani politician. He was a haughty advocate of his Muslim state, insisting that, while touring India, he was only prepared to visit places of Muslim historic interest.

Nevertheless, the reception he and his players received from Indian civic authorities was courteous, cordial and free of religious bigotry. Both the Indian and Pakistani press expressed the hope that the series would mark a sea change in relations between the estranged nations. Meanwhile, affluent Pakistanis travelled down by boat from Karachi to watch the Bombay Test, in a manner which harked back to the days of the Pentangular tournaments.

Even Kardar's hard heart was melted by the warmth of the Indian reception. When Vinoo Mankad achieved, what was then, the fastest Test double of 1,000 runs and 100 wickets in only 23 Test matches, Kardar arranged a celebratory party. Also, in response to a welcoming address at a club for Indian Muslims, Kardar said, through sport, the two separate countries had become closer, expressing the wish that the Indian team visit Pakistan soon as confirmation of their rediscovered friendship.

India won that inaugural series 2-1, but the Pakistani team acquitted themselves well. Several of their players caught the eye, including the diminutive 17-year-old opener, Hanif Mohammad, who scored a disciplined half-century in his first Test innings. He also scored a century in each innings against North Zone, becoming the youngest first-class player to do this.

His opening partner Nazar Mohammad did well, too, scoring his country's first Test hundred in the second Test at Lucknow, as did Waqar Hassan, who averaged 44 runs per innings. Seamer Fazal Mahmood took 20 wickets at 25.6 runs each, employing the in-swinger and leg-cutter expertly, in the manner of Alec Bedser. However, apart from Kardar, few members of the Pakistani side had experience of playing in England. It was expected that they would struggle.

The first Test at Lord's was almost a complete washout. After heavy rain had wiped out the first three days, Hutton put Pakistan in to bat on a soggy, unresponsive track. In the two hours and 35 minutes played on the fourth day, Pakistan crawled to 50-3 with the almost strokeless Hanif becalmed, but unbeaten on 11 runs.

On the final day, play started on time, and Hutton went in pursuit of an improbable victory. He started well with Statham and Wardle routing the remaining Pakistani batsmen for just 37 more runs. However, in a commendable effort to throw the bat, the English batting order came unstuck against fine defensive bowling from Fazal Mahmood (4-54) and Khan Mohammad (5-61), who operated unchanged for 31 overs.

This left England with little more than 30 overs to bowl out Pakistan again, and knock off a small victory target. Although Bailey removed the off stump of newly-capped Alimuddin for a duck, Hanif and Waqar Husan then added 71 runs in relative comfort, displaying a variety of attractive shots. When Waqar was dismissed for 53, with the Pakistan score at 123, the game was called off.

Hutton, who had been dismissed for a seven-ball duck, was clearly in need of rest and recuperation, and took a month-long sabbatical on health grounds. Sheppard took over at Nottingham. He was fortunate to have Bedser fit again, but his luck with the toss was no better than Hutton's. Kardar decided to bat on a true surface, and although Statham proved too quick for Alimuddin, Hanif and Waqar proceeded to bat with the confidence they displayed at Lord's. After an hour, though, Sheppard turned to Test debutant Bob Appleyard and Pakistan was soon in the mire.

Appleyard, the 30-year-old Yorkshireman, had missed the previous two seasons having contracted tuberculosis. While in hospital he lost the upper half of his left lung and almost lost his life as well. Appleyard was a tough cookie, as underlined some years later when he won a legal battle with Robert Maxwell for unfair dismissal. Having worked hard to recover his strength and fitness – he had to learn to walk again – he set about recovering his bowling.

And what an array of talents this man possessed! He could bowl fast-medium swingers, seamers or off-spinners with almost the same action. In the summer of 1951, the year before his illness was diagnosed, he took 200 wickets at 14 runs each. He later added off-and leg-cutters to his impressive armoury, making him a lethal English version of the Australian Bill Johnston.

At Nottingham, Appleyard demolished the Pakistani top order, taking four wickets for six runs in 26 balls. Although the tourists made a partial recovery after lunch, led by their captain Kardar (28), they were all out before tea for a paltry total of 157 runs. Appleyard took five wickets for 51 runs, bewildering the Pakistanis with his repertoire of seam, spin, flight and pace. After three hours of Test cricket, he had placed one foot on the boat to Australia.

Helped by Fazal's pulled leg muscle, and a catalogue of missed chances, England cruised past Pakistan's score to post a massive total of 558-6 declared with Compton scoring 278, Simpson 101 and Graveney 84. Having opened the innings with Simpson, Sheppard made 37 in a 98-run opening partnership.

Facing a deficit of 401, the Pakistani openers Hanif and Alimuddin decided to counter-attack aggressively, scoring 43 runs in the first half-hour with a brilliant array of savage cuts and hooks. After Hanif had departed for a belligerent 51, Pakistan's fortunes slumped, though, and only Kardar (69), Fazal (36) and wicketkeeper Imtiaz Ahmed (33) offered much resistance. England won by an innings and 129 runs. The gulf between the two sides seemed enormous.

The third Test at Manchester seemed to be heading the same way before incessant rain washed out all but ten-and-three-quarter hours of play. With Simpson and Appleyard ruled out through injury, Glamorgan off-spinner Jim McConnon and Sussex batsman Jim Parks were given their first England caps.

Sheppard was fortunate to win the toss, and in the best batting conditions of the match, England made 293-6 at the end of the first day. Although Sheppard was bowled by Fazal for only 13 runs, Compton (93) and Graveney (65) ensured England achieved a dominant position. Pakistan played competitively, though, bowling and fielding with greater discipline, reliability and thought than at Trent Bridge. But forced to bat on a spiteful rain-affected wicket, they were undone as some deliveries shot up off a length while others squatted. With the English spinners also turning the ball sharply, Pakistan lost 14 wickets for 155 runs on the third day before the rain spared them further humiliation.

Rain also affected the final Test at the Oval. Nevertheless, with Hutton returning in place of Sheppard, and Simpson replacing Parks, few, if any, could have anticipated the result. The selectors seemed so certain of victory that they decided to drop Bailey and Bedser, so they could have a closer look at the lightning fast Frank Tyson, and the Surrey opening bowler Peter Loader. This left England with five specialist batsmen. Given Evans' unpredictability with the bat, the tail began at number six. This complacent and risky team selection backfired badly.

All seemed well at the end of a rain-interrupted first day. Pakistan had been dismissed for 133 after Kardar had chosen to bat first. It might have been much worse, as Pakistan was in huge trouble at 51-7 shortly before tea. On a placid strip, Tyson had bowled Alimuddin for ten and Maqsood Ahmed first ball, also having Imtiaz caught at the wicket for 23. Then Kardar (36) led another recovery, assisted by tail-enders Shuja-ud-din (16), Zulfiqar Ahmed (16) and Mahmood Hussain (23). Pakistan eventually struggled past 100.

When England batted, Simpson fell almost immediately for two. Then, with a cloudburst leaving much of the Oval under water, England had to bat in very difficult conditions on day two. Fazal and Mahmood Hussain made the ball fizz around and leap sharply off a length. With batting becoming a lottery, the English batsmen tried to hit their way out of trouble, but to no avail. Hutton was caught at the wicket off Fazal for 14, and May scraped together 26 runs before falling to the same bowler.

Six English batsmen failed to make double figures. Only Compton, who rode his luck in scoring 53 runs, managed to stay at the crease for longer than two hours. England conceded a lead of three runs on the first innings. It was a fitting way for Pakistan to celebrate their Independence Day. Fazal, who bowled unchanged, took six wickets for 53 runs off 30 overs while Mahmood Hussain took the other four wickets for 58 runs off 21.3 overs.

The pitch appeared to be drying when Pakistan batted for a second time. Sensing that the conditions might be more conducive to spin, Hutton turned to Wardle and McConnon. While McConnon was merely steady, Wardle began to exact disconcerting turn. By the close of the third day, the tourists were 63-4.

The fourth day began disastrously for the tourists, as they lost a further four wickets for the addition of just 19 runs. But then Wazir Mohammad (42) and Zulfiqar Ahmed (34) put together a stubborn partnership of 58 runs. After Wardle dismissed the latter, Mahmood Hussain propped up one end while Wazir added a further 24 runs to the Pakistani total.

Wazir spent two-and-three-quarter hours over his unbeaten 42, setting England a 168-run victory target. Wardle bowled magnificently, taking seven wickets for 56 runs off 35 testing overs, but lacked the support of his spin partner McConnon, who dislocated his finger in a fielding accident.

As if still smarting from Brown's criticisms two years before, Hutton ordered his batsmen to strike out for victory that evening. Although Hutton was soon caught at the wicket off Fazal (5) when the total had reached 15, Simpson and May batted imperiously, adding 51 runs in 40 minutes for the second wicket. Their aggressive policy seemed justified. Even when off-spinner Zulfiqar briefly arrested the charge, by catching Simpson off his own bowling, Compton slipped into gear quickly, helping May to raise the hundred with only two wickets down.

When May departed at 109, having scored a brilliant 53 runs, Hutton promoted Evans in an attempt to maintain the momentum. Fazal quickly disposed of him, though, for just three runs. Then Shuja-ud-din trapped Graveney lbw for a duck with his left-arm spin. England had collapsed to 116-5. Worse still, Compton departed shortly before the close for 29, having snicked Fazal to Imtiaz behind the stumps. England closed on 125-6, needing 43 more with all recognised batsmen gone, and McConnon suffering with a dislocated finger.

Even ultra-caution could not save the remaining English batsmen. Pakistan wrapped up victory after only 55 minutes' play, on the final day. Incredibly, Pakistan had levelled the series with a 24-run win. Fazal took two more wickets to finish with six for 46 off 30 overs and 12 for 99 for the match. Hutton lamented the omission of Bedser, but Bailey's absence had been equally crucial.

'REAPING THE WILD WIND'

'Shake, Rattle and Roll'

Hutton's 1954/55 Ashes touring party contained a number of surprises, the biggest of which was the selection of the Oxford University captain Colin Cowdrey. On his own admission, Cowdrey had not enjoyed an auspicious season in 1954 although he was hardly helped by the profusion of rain-affected wickets on which he was expected to bat. However, he had performed well enough to be chosen as twelfth man for the final Test against the Pakistanis. Besides, he had done very well in the previous summer, leading both the Oxford University averages at 51 runs per innings and the Kent County Cricket Club averages at almost 32.

The selectors recognised that the 21-year-old possessed a rare talent. Cowdrey was so composed at the crease, so classical in executing his shots, and so exquisite in his timing and placement that he seemed to caress the ball to the boundary with effortless, elegant ease. The undoubted quality of his batting had managed to impress even the sternest of critics, like Yorkshire's Brian Sellars.

In 1950, the selectors were premature in picking the Cambridge pair Sheppard and Dewes, but they were spot-on in choosing young Cowdrey. Although he had yet to play for England, he had already scored a pair of half-centuries against Lindwall and Miller when representing the 'Gentlemen of England' in 1953. Admittedly, this was a festival game, and the Australians' thoughts might have been focused upon their impending return voyage, but Cowdrey's classy technique and calm temperament had been outstanding. If Cowdrey was an inspired selection, so was that of Frank Tyson, the tall, lean, but muscular Northamptonshire speedster.

Len Hutton recalled in his autobiography *Fifty Years in Cricket*: "My introduction [to Tyson] had been in a one-day match at Redcar [while Tyson was qualifying for Northamptonshire]... A raw-boned lad with a rather cumbersome action charged in from an over-long run. In his first over he produced a full toss which thudded against my pads before I could use my bat in defence – and that hadn't happened to me for a long time.

"That evening I wrote to Gubby Allen to tell him I had seen a genuine fast bowler... [After Tyson appeared for Northants, against the Indians in 1952, the county's captain] Freddie Brown declared he had not seen faster bowling since Larwood...I could not have had more cheering news. A further advantage was that Tyson was able to escape the trumpeting on publicity. He was the ace that England was able to hold back."

Hutton was clearly disappointed not to have Laker, Lock and Trueman at his disposal, though. Trueman was omitted by a single vote. Given Trueman's excellent first-class bowling record in 1954 (134 wickets at 15 runs each), he should have been an automatic selection. The ramifications of the stormy Caribbean tour continued to trouble MCC, though. Therefore, Surrey's Peter Loader took his place. Loader had performed well in helping his county to a further County Championship, but he did not have Trueman's hostility or guile.

There was doubt, too, about the legitimacy of Loader's bouncer and slower ball, whereas Trueman's arm remained perfectly straight at whatever speed he bowled. Neil Harvey was not the only Australian to be perplexed by the omission of "Fiery Fred". Lock's absence was more understandable, given the Caribbean hullabaloo about his 'jerky' action. Hutton was bewildered, though, as to why the unproven Glamorgan off-spinner Jim McConnon had been selected instead of Jim Laker who had helped bowl England to Ashes glory in 1953. South Africa's Hugh Tayfield had already exposed the myth that the Test wickets Down Under were off-spinners' graveyards, and Laker was easily England's best exponent of off spin.

These omissions meant that Hutton had six novices in his squad: Cowdrey, Tyson, McConnon, Loader, Northants wicketkeeper Keith Andrew and Yorkshire batsman Vic Wilson, who was chosen as cover for the ailing Compton. Five of these six tourists had not played any Test cricket, while the sixth, McConnon, had only two Tests and four wickets to his name.

All six were told by Hutton that they were likely to be 'secondary' players on this tour. To have a third of his players marked out as fringe performers seemed excessive for such a challenging assignment. It was uncertain whether Compton would make it, either. While Hutton and the rest of his party set sail, Compton had to undergo further knee surgery. It was hoped that he would join them later, making up for lost time by travelling by air.

Compton aside, Hutton was left with five battle-hardened warriors in Edrich, Bailey, Evans, Wardle and Bedser, plus the blossoming brilliance of May, and the more mercurial talents of Simpson and Graveney. As for the rest, stealthy Brian Statham had graduated as a front-line opening bowler, and Bob Appleyard had demonstrated his skill and versatility in his one Test appearance, but there must have been doubts about Appleyard's health and fitness following his prolonged illness. The harsh heat of an Australian summer would allow him few hiding places.

Not that Ashes victory seemed to be MCC's greatest priority. At the eve-of-departure dinner at Lord's, MCC president Lord Cobham reminded Hutton and his squad that it was more important not to disgrace the name of English cricket, even at the cost of the series. Clearly, the Caribbean scars were still inflamed. Lord Cobham emphasised that an MCC tour was an ambassadorial duty, helping to maintain the unity of the Commonwealth.

In his article, *The D'Oliveira Affair: Forty Years On,* sports writer Rob Steen suggested that Lord Cobham's determination to maintain sporting links with South Africa ultimately led him into some very choppy waters, notably during the D'Oliveira Affair of 1968. Steen reported that Lord Cobham had seemed so keen to keep alive the prospects of the planned MCC tour of South Africa in 1968/69 that he initially drew a veil over the South African Prime Minister's refusal to accept D'Oliveira's selection. Arthur Coy of the South Africa Cricket Association described Lord Cobham as determined to "do almost anything to see that the tour is on". Steen thought that Lord Cobham had not formally reported Dr Vorster's refusal to admit D'Oliveira to the appropriate MCC committee, as he hoped to avoid a political backlash at home, while exploring the possibility of a negotiated settlement. According to Steen, Lord Cobham's adviser in this matter was "Gubby" Allen who, like Lord Cobham, had been a former MCC president.

As for the 1954/55 Ashes tour, Lord Cobham's cautionary injunction had placed Len Hutton in a double bind. Hutton knew that as far as most English supporters were concerned, the tour would only be regarded as a success if he returned with the Ashes. And yet in order to ensure victory he knew his team had to play 'rough' cricket, as he put it, which might cause disquiet among senior MCC members such as Lord Cobham. Hutton had already sensed Sir Pelham Warner's discomfort as he put his case for a battery of fast bowlers. The spectre of 'Bodyline' seemed to trouble Warner more than the splenetic series of 1953/54.

While on the *Orsava*, Frank Tyson saw what he described as "a spare, stooped old man, dressed immaculately in a pin-stripe suit" telling the young Colin Cowdrey: "When you reach Australia, just remember one thing – hate the bastards!" He spoke with such vehemence that Tyson asked MCC baggage master George Duckworth who the elderly person was. As a 'Bodyline' veteran, Duckworth had no difficulty in identifying him. "*That* was Douglas Jardine," he replied.

Having impressed Hutton with a polished knock of 66 not out, in the heat and humidity of Colombo, Colin Cowdrey had put himself in the frame for Test selection. Hutton immediately recognised that the young batsman had "match temperament", and might yet make the cut. Hutton confided in Cowdrey that he should prepare himself for some "rough" cricket ahead. Irrespective of Lord Cobham's parting injunction, Hutton left Cowdrey in no doubt what their primary objective was. Hutton might have lacked Jardine's haughty, bristling abrasiveness, but he had his mental tenacity.

According to Peter May's biographer, Alan Hill, Hutton was essentially a shy man who "masked his shyness beneath an enigmatic smile". He was most at ease in his own company and "the sudden, brilliant gleam of his striking blue eyes meant you had intruded upon his private thoughts". Nevertheless, beneath Hutton's natural reserve was his driving ambition. As Hill observed: "Despite their vastly different backgrounds, he and Peter May were kinsmen in manner and temperament." Peter May had been chosen as Hutton's vice-captain, ahead of the more experienced Bailey and Edrich, but May's appointment did not imply any softening of the side's approach. While en route to Australia, Hutton thought it prudent to clarify this matter with May, advising his deputy about his mental preparation.

May told Hill: "[Hutton said to me] 'I want to tell you how to get on in Australia...You walk slowly to the wicket. Mind you, at your pace and in no rush. Then you look around and get used to the light. It's pretty sharp out there. At the wicket, you take guard. Take a little stroll and give the bowler a glare, just to show you're not frightened of him. Then you check your guard and have another look round to inspect the field.'...

May waited attentively for the final telling conversational thrust. 'What next?' he asked. Len said: 'You just keep buggering on.'"

Hutton was a dab hand at mind games. At his inaugural press conference in Australia, Hutton's deftness had Colin Cowdrey spellbound. "It was all underplayed," recalled Cowdrey. Hutton explained to the pressmen, who were expecting bluster and bravado, "Noo, we 'aven't got mooch bowling. Got a chap called Tyson, but you won't 'ave 'eard of him because he's 'ardly ever played. Ah, yes, Lock and Laker. Aye, good boolers, but we 'ad to leave them behind [no explanation]. Batsmen? Well we 'aven't got any batsmen really. We've got these youngsters, May and Cowdrey, but we haven't got any batsmen." Then wearily: "What it comes to is that we're startin' all over again. We've got a lot to learn from you." In keeping his powder bone dry, Hutton took the wind out of the sails of the Australian press.

As if to emphasise his art of understatement, Hutton's side made an inauspicious start. Other than Hutton, Compton, who made a century shortly after his belated arrival, and Cowdrey, who made a pair of tons against a strong New South Wales side, MCC's batsmen were unimpressive in the preliminary games. The bowling was below par, too. An attack of shingles left Bedser as a pale shadow of his normal self, and the spinners achieved little against the stronger state teams.

This was the prelude to Hutton's perplexing selection of four fast bowlers, and no spinners, for the first Test at Brisbane. Hutton compounded his unorthodoxy by asking the Australians to bat first. The pitch seemed perfect. Australian all-rounder Alan Davidson thought that Hutton had been kidded by press misinformation. It was said that the Gabba strip might be favourable to pace bowling. Hutton seemed inclined to believe this.

Certainly, the ball had moved around and lifted in the early stages of the preceding MCC game against Queensland. Hutton seemed to think that his quartet of pace bowlers – Bedser, Statham, Tyson and Bailey – might make quick inroads. However, Cowdrey thought Hutton's decisions were often premeditated. His invitation to Australia, to bat first seemed a case in point. The bald facts were, that helped by some shocking English fielding – 12 catches were dropped – Australia amassed 601-8 declared, with Morris (153) and Harvey (162) making big hundreds, having enjoyed outrageous fortune.

With Compton absent hurt, after breaking a bone in his hand while fielding, England batted abysmally. Cowdrey made an accomplished 40 runs in his first Test, May made 44 while Edrich (88) and Bailey (82) exhibited commendable defiance, too, but England was beaten by an innings and 154 runs.

Many years later, in a BBC *Test Match Special* broadcast, Trevor Bailey remarked: "We made the mistake – which is now considered a very good thing – of going into the match with four fast bowlers. I thought it absolutely mad at the time...Compton could bowl a little [but] it was... a completely unbalanced attack and we paid the penalty. Today [in the heyday of Holding, Marshall, Roberts and Garner] we would say it was a beautiful attack."

Cowdrey and May retained their places for the second Test at Sydney, having batted impressively against Victoria in the intervening state game, but, with Bedser still debilitated, Appleyard was selected in his place. Graveney also came in for Compton, whose broken finger had yet to mend. Hutton decided, too, that Bailey would be a more robust opening partner than Simpson, who was replaced by another spinner, Wardle. As for the Australians, they were without Johnson, their injured captain and lead off-spinner. Miller was unfit, also. Morris assumed the Australian captaincy.

In heavy, overcast conditions, Morris won the toss and put England into bat on a green top. With Davidson adopting his quicker style, Morris had at his disposal a quartet of pace bowlers of greater menace than England's foursome at Brisbane. Bailey was yorked by Lindwall for a duck and May fell for five, having played loosely at Archer's in-swinging half-volley. Somehow, Graveney clung on with Hutton until lunch with England placed unsteadily at 34-2. The post-lunch session was equally attritional with Lindwall continuing his cameo of high-class swing bowling. It took England 150 minutes to reach their half-century.

Shortly afterwards, Hutton departed having flicked Johnston's in-swinger to leg-slip. It seemed a certain boundary until Davidson swooped to pull off an astounding catch. Hutton had made a patient 30 runs. Graveney (21) followed him almost immediately, edging a wide delivery from Johnston to Favell at third slip. England was in a mess at 63-4. Cowdrey and Edrich were the last remaining specialist batsmen. Once Edrich was dismissed with the total at 86, Cowdrey was compelled to play more expansively. However, in trying to force Davidson he perished also.

Shortly after tea, England was reduced to 111-9. Only a cavalier display from Wardle, which was well supported by Statham, lifted England's first innings score to 154 all out. Australia began confidently in the evening gloom, with Morris and Favell posting 18 untroubled runs, before Bailey produced a sharp, lifting ball on Morris's leg stump that the Aussie captain could only glove to Hutton at leg-slip.

The following morning was as grey as the preceding day, but this did nothing to inhibit the free strokeplay of Favell and Burke, who rapidly took the Australian score to 64, before Bailey removed Favell, inducing the South Australian to edge his out-swinger to Graveney at slip. Nevertheless, with Harvey playing a subdued supporting role to Burke, Australia was strongly placed at lunch having made 100-2. As Hutton led his side back on to the field, he turned to the literary Tyson and urged, "Frank, England hath need of thee!" Tyson had thus far managed 1-160 at Brisbane and two wild, unproductive overs at Sydney. It had been an unprepossessing start, but Tyson's moment of destiny had arrived.

In his autobiography, *A Typhoon Called Tyson*, he explained: "To bowl quickly is to revel in the glad animal action; to thrill in physical prowess, and to enjoy a certain sneaking feeling of superiority over the other mortals who play the game. No batsman likes quick bowling, and this knowledge gives one a sense of omnipotence." Here, at Sydney, he would walk or, more aptly, launch the talk.

In his autobiography, the lyrically-minded speedster described the thrill of bowling at over 90mph: "With a feeling of uncertainty, I scar the ground with a little shuffle, and then away, long and loping, counting mechanically, yet rhythmically, the nine strides of my approach. My body bows, head forward, preparing to rise, reaching, clawing for height before bringing the ball banging down on the batsman. I feel my legs tense, my head is on one side and the wickets are in my sights. There is a sudden shock, shaking me to the skull, as the stiff left leg crashes into unsympathetic turf, and my whole body flings itself after the ball, as if in malediction towards the batsman.

"The batsman seems to be stooping in an effort to pick up the flight of the ball earlier. Or could it be that he is cowering slightly, anticipating the ball, fearful of its speed and doubtful about my intentions? There is the breathless moment of the batsman's quicksilver duck; the moment of truth as the ball finds the edge of the bat, and the slips snatch their prey off the very ground."

In this short post-lunch spell Tyson reduced his run, achieving searing speed without losing control as he bowled to a fuller length. He continually made the ball lift and break viciously back from the off. Without any addition to the lunchtime score, Harvey could not evade a Tyson thunderbolt that kicked sharply. Helplessly, he diverted the ball to Cowdrey at gully. Four runs later Bailey dismissed Burke for 44 runs.

And only 18 runs had been added when Tyson proved far too quick for Graeme Hole, knocking back his leg stump with a full delivery that had flashed between the Australian's bat and pads. Hole's high, circular backlift left him vulnerable to Tyson's extreme speed. Benaud seemed equally deficient against high pace. Tyson subjected Benaud to a torrid assault which the all-rounder was extremely fortunate to survive. With Bailey beating the bat with monotonous regularity, Australia remained under the cosh. Amazingly, Benaud and his batting partner, Archer, survived until tea. The afternoon session had produced just 41 runs and three wickets (141-5). This was taut, compelling cricket.

Immediately after the tea interval, Statham produced a nippy off-cutter that kept low. It was too good for Benaud's flimsy defence, and caught him in front of his stumps (141-6). With his pace men needing a rest before the arrival of the second new ball, Hutton introduced Appleyard into the attack. Sensing his opportunity to lift the siege, Archer hit high, long and hard to good effect.

Inspired by Archer's success, Davidson followed suit. England's inadequate first innings score was passed in a flurry of furious shots, but, with the score at 193, Davidson chanced his arm once too often, swishing across the line to a spearing delivery from Statham, and lost his leg stump. Twenty runs later, Archer's destructive innings also came to a close, one short of his fifty, as the returning Tyson made the new ball lift unexpectedly and the Queensland all-rounder jabbed to third slip where Hutton pouched the singeing chance with aplomb.

By this time Lindwall was into his stride, but at 224 he mistimed his swing at Tyson's weary bouncer, and gloved the ball to wicketkeeper Evans. Hutton had no wish to bat out the final minutes, in indifferent light, so he ordered Tyson to bowl wide down the leg-side to the last man, Johnston, who was merely a bemused spectator. In the final ten minutes, though, Bailey produced a swinging delivery which clattered into Langley's off and middle stumps. Australia had reached a first innings total of 228 – a potentially match-winning lead of 74 runs.

The third day threatened to be a reprise of the first. Bailey poked, prodded and plodded for 40 minutes before edging Archer's out-swinger to wicketkeeper Langley (18-1). The arrival of May, though, stirred the funereal momentum. Playing forcefully off his legs, May punctured Archer's clamping control, encouraging Hutton to follow his lead. With the bashful sun finally appearing, the England half-century was raised with a succession of neat glances and firm drives.

Alas, Hutton then poked hesitantly at a wide half-volley from

Johnston, and was caught by the leaping Benaud at gully (55-2). Graveney did not last long. Having fished imprudently at his first ball, he edged Johnston's next delivery, bowled across him, to Langley (55-3). In belatedly sparkling weather, England lunched gloomily.

And yet Cowdrey and May batted with such fluency, in the post-lunch session, that any sense of crisis soon dissipated. While Cowdrey stroked the ball around the ground, May peppered the area between square leg and mid-on with a series of cracking shots. Lindwall and Johnston were made to look innocuous by their sunny lack of inhibition.

Benaud was introduced to bowl a long containing spell, with the field set well back, but the timing and placement of May's and Cowdrey's shots proved too good for such restraining measures. Time and again, the ball fizzed assuredly over the verdant Sydney outfield, as the young batsmen collected their runs with almost nonchalant composure.

During a later BBC *Test Match Special* broadcast Trevor Bailey said of May: "[He] was a high quality player, not a genius, but a very fine player. Correct and sound, he didn't hook [neither did Hutton, who didn't pull either, following his arm injury]. But he played well off the back foot... May's greatness was that he could score runs off the good ball with safe shots...It's the great player who hits the good ball either off front or back foot for four runs, with a straight-bat shot, without taking a chance."

However, with the close of play in sight, the advancing Cowdrey smote Benaud's googly long and high, but with insufficient sweetness to clear Archer at long-off. He had scored 54 runs in a glorious partnership of 116 with May. There was no letting up, though. The incoming Edrich immediately set about the tiring Australian attack, pulling and driving with muscular power. Not to be outdone May drove Johnston wide of mid-on and then to the left of mid-off with spanking disdain. Thirty-three runs were gathered at the gallop before Morris's wilting troops were granted a grateful respite.

On the fourth day the sun departed, leaving Sydney under heavy cloud once more, with shrouds of drizzle wafting across the partially obscured Botany Bay. In conditions more helpful for swing bowling, Lindwall, Johnston and Davidson placed a clamp on England's scoring rate. May completed his century, by flicking Lindwall through the short-leg cordon for two, but added only four more before he was yorked, having been surprised by Lindwall's sudden burst of pace (222-5). Once again, England's long, drooping tail was exposed. Lindwall enticed the new batsman, Tyson, by offering him a series of full-pitched deliveries that the Northants pace man played confidently.

However, in the dim morning light, Lindwall's well-disguised bouncer undid him. Picking up its speed and trajectory far too late, Tyson turned his back on the viciously climbing ball that smashed into the back of his skull. Tyson crashed to the ground, arms flailing, as if shot by a sniper. Apparently concussed, he was eventually helped to his feet, and uneasily led, wobbly-legged, from the field by a pair of ambulance men. It seemed as if Tyson had played his last part in this game, and possibly the series, for it was feared that this sickening blow might have fractured his skull. Not so.

With England's innings subsiding dismally after lunch, a wan, but glowering Tyson strode to the crease. He proceeded to batter a brace of bellicose boundaries before being bowled by his assailant. It was a hugely brave, if pointless, gesture for England had collapsed from a position of potential strength at 222-4 to a probable losing one at 250-9. They were only 176 runs ahead. But, once again Hutton was indebted to a sparky last-wicket partnership. While Appleyard pushed forward with purpose, Statham deflected and drove acquisitively. Together, the pair added 46 vital runs, helping set the Australians a more robust winning target of 223 runs.

Tyson's mood remained ugly as he seized the new ball. Hell-bent upon revenge he hurled himself into the action, helped by a stiffening wind at his back. Although made odds-on to win this low-scoring match, the Australians began their final innings in jittery fashion. Despite Tyson's lightning speed, it was Statham who mostly discomforted the openers, Morris and Favell. In fact, Favell was desperately lucky to survive his first over having narrowly survived a ferocious lbw appeal and edged another ball through Edrich's outstretched fingertips, at slip.

The pressure seemed to afflict Morris more, though, as after a composed start against Tyson, he proceeded to play Statham chaotically as if his well-honed technique had suddenly deserted him. The Lancastrian received his just desserts when, with only 27 runs on the board, Morris was adjudged lbw, having swung wildly across the line of a typically straight ball which kept a shade low.

Ten runs later, Favell's streaky innings came to an end. Tyson delivered a ball of venomous velocity that was homing in on the Australian's off stump. Almost involuntarily Favell stepped back out of the line, his crooked, stabbing shot offering a thin edge, which flew at blistering speed to Edrich, the deeply-placed first slip, who clung on bravely to a head-high catch. Elated by his success, Tyson was almost bull-like as he pawed the ground awaiting the appearance of new batsman Neil Harvey.

Tyson tore in, sending two express deliveries scudding past Harvey's tentative strokes, but, thereafter, the Victorian put his body in line, repelling the storm raging around him with growing confidence. Resolute, but unhurried, Harvey was content to nudge the ball around, collecting the occasional single while his partner, Jimmy Burke, dropped anchor. It was only when Appleyard and Wardle were introduced that more attacking shots were risked. Even a last fling from Tyson and Statham failed to trouble the pair's composure. Australia completed the fourth day on 72-2 – 151 more were needed for victory.

The final day dawned bright. The pitch had a dun pallor suggesting that it would continue to play as easily as it had for much of the previous evening. However, the new day began explosively. Tyson's headache had gone, but his anger had not. Off his shortened run, and visibly loose and lithe in movement, he quickly attained fearsome speed. Only five runs had been added to the overnight total before he slanted a lightning yorker beneath Burke's blade and up-rooted the off stump. Burke, who employed very little backlift, seemed bewildered by this breach in his defence.

Staring with disbelief at the carnage behind him, only the ecstatic English celebrations convinced him that his game was up. Hanging his head in disappointment, he shuffled towards the pavilion. Two balls later, Hole followed him, having lost both his off and middle stump to a similar delivery. Harvey was unfazed, though, quietly gathering runs, while Benaud played the pace bowlers cautiously, but with mounting confidence. Hutton changed tack, and brought on Appleyard to bowl into the freshening breeze.

Among Appleyard's many assets was his ability to vary his pace, flight and dip. Benaud became less sure of himself. Just after the Australian score had passed 100, Benaud misjudged a sweep off Appleyard, sending the ball skywards in the direction of square leg. Tyson had difficulty judging the catch because the soaring ball was slewing in the blustery breeze. With palpable relief he managed to take the chance, on one knee, with his hands stretched out well in front of him (102-5). At lunch, Australia was 118-5, still over a hundred runs short of their target, but Harvey was still in.

After lunch, Tyson returned to the fray refreshed and re-energised. Determined not to feed Archer's array of attacking shots, Tyson pitched shorter. Archer looked to cut which proved to be his undoing. With four runs added to the total, Tyson fired in another blazing delivery, slightly short of a length, and just outside Archer's off stump. Archer freed his arms to play a slashing shot backward of point. To his horror, the ball jagged back off the seam, and shattered his stumps (122-6).

Five runs later, Statham produced an equally malevolent leg-cutter to the left-handed Davidson. The ball ricocheted from Davidson's involuntary stroke in the direction of the slip cordon, but it seemed to be falling short until Evans intervened. Scurrying to his left he hurled himself in front of second slip, gloves outstretched, holding the ball aloft as he rolled over. It was a magnificent catch (127-7).

Enter Ray Lindwall, the man who had sown the wind. Now, Tyson was intent upon reaping the wild wind. Lindwall was expecting a retaliatory bumper. Edging onto the back foot, he was wickedly confounded, castled by a flashing half-volley. Aghast, Lindwall threw his head back in despair (136-8). When Statham bowled Gil Langley for a duck, nine runs later, it seemed all over for Australia. But as in the magnificent Ashes Test match at Edgbaston in 2005, the tip of the Australian tail wagged furiously.

While Johnston hid, Harvey cut, drove, smashed and scuttled, defying Hutton's attempts to isolate him by his speed of thought and movement. Thirty-five runs were added with Harvey raising his personal score to 92. Trudging wearily back to his mark, with his radar shot, and his arm lowering with fatigue, Tyson seemed blown out. Hutton persisted with him, though, knowing that one ball in the right area would probably be too good for Johnston.

Hutton at last managed to strand Harvey at the non-striker's end. Tyson had a full over to bowl at Johnston. Once again, Tyson strayed down the leg-side. Johnston flicked one wayward ball off his left boot for a boundary to fine leg. The next he tried to play off his hip without success. Statham then suggested to Tyson that he bowl a little shorter and nearer to Johnston's body. The ploy worked. Johnston made the finest of contacts, leaving Evans to gather the edged ball safely. England had won by 38 runs, and Tyson had taken six wickets for 85 runs, and ten for 130 in the match.

Len Hutton remarked in his autobiography *Fifty Years in Cricket*: "[Tyson's] pace at Sydney, on that decisive and extraordinary day, was nothing short of frightening. After one ball, Evans and the slips exchanged significant glances and moved back several paces. I never saw Evans so far back, and I'm told exactly the same retreat was made when Frank bowled his first over for Northamptonshire under Freddie Brown. Soon the English fielders were saying: 'If we can get Ray to nut Frank again there'll be no holding him.' I could hardly suppress my delight."

Trevor Bailey later recalled, during a BBC *Test Match Special* broadcast:

"After Brisbane [Tyson] shortened his run which made the crucial difference. He had been charging in from between 25 or 30 yards...It was spectacular, but, if everything didn't go exactly right, which it frequently didn't, he ended up all over the place...It's much more difficult getting your timing right from that distance with arms and legs going everywhere...So, he cut his run down to eight or nine paces, gaining a lot of control and not losing any pace...He was frighteningly quick. [Only] when watching Michael Holding have I seen bowling as fast as that."

For the Melbourne Test, Hutton restored the fit-again Bedser to the squad. Compton had also recovered from his broken finger, so he was chosen ahead of the disappointing Graveney. Hutton forsook his experimental use of Bailey as an opener and promoted Bill Edrich instead. For Australia, Ian Johnson was better, so led the side. Davidson made way for him. Miller was considered fit to bat, but probably not to bowl, having damaged his knee at Brisbane after colliding with the boundary wall. He replaced Jimmy Burke. The Victorian wicketkeeper Len Maddocks was also brought in to substitute for the injured Langley. Unlike Langley, Maddocks was considered to be an accomplished batsman.

The Test match began in bizarre circumstances. Alan Hill, author of *Bill Edrich: The Biography*, explained: "Hutton had to be persuaded to play at Melbourne...he was in a low state [he had scored only 75 runs in four innings]...Appleyard said Hutton was struggling to maintain his fitness. [Tour manager] Geoffrey Howard said Hutton was so overwrought that he asked for a doctor...It was thought to be a psychosomatic illness. [However, Hutton did have a heavy cold and a stiff neck caused by fibrositis]. 'Len was devastated; he wanted to be told he was unfit,' said Howard."

According to Hill: "The reason for Hutton's indisposition was that he had decided to leave Alec Bedser out of the team...Howard recalled: 'Len didn't want to hurt Alec; but he refused to delegate the task to Edrich [his adviser and fellow selector on this tour], who was prepared to convey the sad news.' To make matters worse, Hutton did not advise Bedser of his decision... 'Len had actually taken Alec out to inspect the wicket,' said Howard. 'With all the other problems pressing on his mind he still couldn't face communicating his decision to Bedser.'"

Hill continued: "Godfrey Evans recalled that it was largely at Edrich's instigation that Hutton was prevailed to play...Evans and Edrich shepherded the England captain into a cab and travelled with him to the ground, saying: 'We don't care a bugger what you do, Leonard, but you must go out on to that field.'"

Hutton was a fine tactician, but a hesitant manager of people. It wasn't as if he was insensitive to others' feelings, though, quite the contrary. For example, in his autobiography *Fifty Years of Cricket*, Hutton recalled hearing of the sudden death of Colin Cowdrey's father, shortly after MCC's party had arrived in Perth in October 1954. Hutton wrote: "At dinner I put my hand on his shoulder and told him I was sorry, which I felt to be a pitifully inadequate gesture, but from then on I made sure Colin was kept busy."

In his autobiography, *M.C.C.*, Colin Cowdrey remembered that Hutton had tears in his eyes as he made this small, but important consoling gesture. Perhaps it was because Hutton doubted his ability in handling others' distress that he tended to retreat from these situations, instead, wrestling in private over what he should do as seemed to be the case with Bedser.

Possibly, his relationship with Trueman, after their Caribbean tour, suffered for similar reasons. This is purely speculative, though. Cowdrey felt that Hutton's mental strain was exacerbated because he had no prior experience of leadership before accepting the England captaincy. If true, Hutton disguised this pressure better while he was on the field of play.

As hard as it was for him, Hutton probably made the right decision in excluding Bedser from the crucial Melbourne Test match. Alec Bedser had been badly debilitated by shingles, not helped by having to bowl in the extreme heat and humidity of Brisbane, with, as he put it, "a back full of sores". When asked by a member of the Australian press whether he regretted not selecting Bedser, Hutton replied: "We always miss Alec." Hutton was well aware of the massive debt he owed to Bedser. It was unfortunate that Hutton felt unable to communicate this to him.

Having won the toss, Hutton had a dilemma – whether to bat first, and risk a tricky morning session on a damp surface, or to field first, and risk a repetition of Brisbane. Hutton even donned spiked boots to test the degree of moisture in the pitch. It was small wonder that he wanted Bedser's expert advice. With Melbourne sweltering in a humid heatwave, Hutton decided that fielding first was too much of a risk. So, at high noon, he and Bill Edrich marched out to face Lindwall and, much to their surprise, Miller.

Seeing the dark, damp patches on the surface, Miller forsook his doctor's advice, and announced to Johnson that he was ready to bowl. It wasn't difficult to understand Miller's keenness because the wicket was a minefield – the ball swung and seamed all over the place, and spat off the glassy surface. After an hour's play, England was reeling at 41-4, with

Miller having taken three big wickets – those of Hutton, Edrich and Compton.

Hutton had been guilty of not placing his left foot far enough across to counter the away swing. It was a fault that had begun to creep into his game, and once again he paid the penalty, being caught at slip by Hole off Miller. Lindwall also dismissed May for nought – hardly the 25th birthday present that May had hoped for. Being the last of the recognised batsmen, Cowdrey and Bailey set about damage limitation. Cowdrey started sketchily against Lindwall's swing, squirting the ball to the third man and long-leg boundaries off thick edges, whereas Bailey blocked resolutely. At lunch, England was 59-4. Miller's analysis read: nine overs, eight maidens, five runs and three wickets – so much for his damaged knee!

After lunch, Cowdrey and Bailey batted in greater comfort. Johnson continued to employ an attacking field for his fast men, consisting of two slips, two gullies and three short legs, so there were plenty of gaps to plunder. Renouncing stagnant defence, Bailey began to knock the ball carefully into the unguarded areas, picking up a succession of singles.

Cowdrey was more adventurous, once hitting Lindwall for consecutive fours: a sumptuous off-drive that despatched the ball to the fence at a speed which belied the ease of his stroke, and an all-run effort from a crisp on-drive. Cowdrey was equally uninhibited against Benaud. Two exquisitely timed late cuts earned him eight runs and took him to his fifty, in 103 minutes, and England to 90-4. Inspired by Cowdrey's success, Bailey immediately swept Benaud for his first boundary.

Because Cowdrey and Bailey were playing with so much comfort, Johnson adopted a defensive strategy in the hope of inducing an indiscretion. With Johnston bowling floated half-volleys outside the off stump, to a packed cover field, Cowdrey's scoring was scotched, arousing the crowd's derisive impatience. Feeling safe from harm, Johnson brought himself on, serving up a succession of high, looping off breaks which Cowdrey patted back gently from the safety of his crease. In this period of stalemate, Cowdrey went 11 overs without adding to his score.

Ironically, it was his normally imperturbable partner who perished in trying to lift the blockade. Having also become becalmed, Bailey's eyes lit up when Johnston produced a rare long-hop on his legs. Unused to such gifts, Bailey mistimed his pull shot badly. The ball cannoned off a bottom edge onto his pads and looped up in a gentle arc before plopping into Maddocks' grateful gloves. Bailey had contributed 30 runs to a 74-run partnership with Cowdrey (115-5).

With Evans' arrival, Cowdrey realised he had to assert himself. He began by taking Johnson on, dancing down the track to him, and lifting the ball towards mid-on where Archer was stationed. For an agonising moment it appeared that he had holed out, but his shot had just enough power to elude Archer's leap, and find the pavilion railings. With the siege lifted, Cowdrey felt encouraged to produce a raking drive which sent the ball flashing through the covers to the boundary. He then hooked Johnston for four more. This spurt of scoring took England to 130-5 at tea, with Cowdrey on 68.

Lindwall returned after the interval to accompany Johnston, but Cowdrey remained unruffled. Cowdrey drove Johnston imperiously through the covers before sweeping his in-swinger for a further boundary, taking his score into the 80s. Miller returned to the attack, but it was clear that his morning burst had withered him. After bowling stiffly, in evident discomfort, he was replaced quickly by Archer, who dismissed Evans, but not before the wicketkeeper had contributed 20 valuable runs (169-6). With England's tail now exposed, Cowdrey went for his shots. He promptly produced a deft late cut off Johnson, and a crashing straight drive off Archer, both of which went for four.

After his early dismissal, Hutton had been inconsolable. Returning dejectedly to the dressing room, he had slumped in a corner, speaking to no one. He remained unmoved in that position until lunch, staring glumly at the floor and making no attempt to remove his pads.

He remained in a sombre, uncommunicative mood all afternoon, too. It was not until he heard the excited shouts from the balcony that his curiosity was aroused. Responding to his players' insistent invitation, he saw the climax of Cowdrey's brilliant innings. Infected by their exhilaration, he, too, urged Cowdrey on to his maiden Test century which was reached with three scampered runs. At last, Hutton's facial furrows relaxed as a broad, beaming, satisfied smile appeared.

Cowdrey was last man out for 102 when England reached 191. It was another disappointing team effort, salvaged in part by Cowdrey's "astonishingly mature" innings, as Hutton described it. Afterwards, Hutton gave a glowing testimony to his young batsman's skill in "fending off rising deliveries", complimenting him on a succession of "majestic drives", and "exquisitely-timed clips off his legs".

By the end of the second day, England's small total had assumed a more robust appearance with Australia rocking at 188-8. Tyson had made important inroads – trapping Morris lbw and clean bowling Hole with a full toss – without bowling particularly well. Statham had bowled steadily, and Appleyard splendidly, but Bailey seemed out of sorts. Wardle, too, struggled to find a length, despite bowling Archer with a shooter. Gratifyingly, the ball was beginning to turn. Appleyard had delivered a prodigious leg-cutter that clean bowled Harvey for 31.

After a rest day of furnace-like heat, with a fierce northerly wind whipping up clouds of dust, there was concern that the already fissured wicket might crumble completely. Its mosaic of cracks had already produced erratic bounce. Batting last on this surface threatened to be highly hazardous. So it was with some trepidation that Hutton and his men inspected the wicket before the start of the third day's play. However, they were astonished to find that the cracks had closed, and the surface was no longer glassy, but slightly soft.

The Age, a Melbourne newspaper, alleged that the pitch had been watered and rolled by the MCG ground staff in order to avert a controversial finale. Other theories included overnight sweating – Australian wickets were then covered – and rising moisture. A tributary of the Yarra ran beneath the MCG. It was thought that water might have been drawn to the surface by the extreme heat. No official explanation was given, though, apart from an emphatic denial of any wrongdoing.

The impact of this change was that the pitch played much more easily. Frustratingly for Hutton, Australia's tail wagged; their last two wickets added 80 runs, lifting the Australian total to 231, before Statham cleaned up, giving him an impressive return of five wickets for 60 runs. But the pitch's greater placidity also assisted the English batsmen overturn their 40-run deficit without loss. However, Edrich was bowled once that deficit was erased, and Hutton's scratchy innings of 42 came to a close when the England score had reached 96.

There were no heroics from Cowdrey this time as he was bowled by Benaud for seven runs, having made an indeterminate defensive stroke which failed to smother the spinning ball (128-3). May was in regal form, though, cracking the ball to the boundary on either side of the wicket with exceptional power. May hammered Lindwall with such force and regularity that the Australian was compelled to pitch shorter, and employ a deep mid-off and deep mid-on as protective cover. Despite being troubled by a bruised thumb, Compton kept May company as England closed the third day on 159-3 – 118 ahead.

The fourth-day wicket proved much more challenging, though. May departed quickly, bowled by Johnston's sharp legbreak, having added a boundary to his overnight score of 87. Compton did not last much longer, either, glancing Archer to Maddocks when he had scored 23 (185-5). The remaining five wickets then fell for 94 runs with Wardle contributing almost half of these with some typically lusty blows. He accumulated 32 runs in just two overs from Johnston and Johnson. Bailey held the remnants together in a three-hour knock which realised 24 runs.

The upshot was that just after tea, in a much cooler temperature, Australia began their quest of the 239 runs needed for victory. By the close, they were well on their way at 75-2. Once again they lost Morris for a single-figure score, brilliantly caught by Cowdrey, diving forward at short leg, off a short ball from Tyson. His opening partner, Favell, departed too, for 30 runs, having yorked himself by Appleyard's late in-dipper; it was Favell's penalty of playing too aggressively.

The scene was set for a pulsating final day's play. Some 50,000 spectators poured into the MCG to witness an astonishing feat, because in less than 90 minutes of play, the Australians were dismissed for 111 with Tyson taking seven wickets for 27. Hutton must take some credit for this as it was his idea to bowl Tyson from the southern end, hoping that Tyson might achieve the lift that Miller had gained at the start of the match.

The huge crowd had hardly settled into their seats before Harvey was sent on his way, dejectedly dismissed by Tyson's seventh ball. Harvey played an authentic leg-glance to a delivery fizzing past his right hip. He had every right to expect four runs. Instead, Evans launched himself to his right to pull off an astonishing catch (77-3). Only nine runs later Benaud followed Harvey. Hooking wildly at a short delivery outside his off stump, the ball flew off a bottom edge into his stumps (86-4). He rightly berated himself for his irresponsibility. Then, having found a bail lodged inside his pad, Benaud threw it behind him, disgustedly.

One run later Miller was despatched by probably the fastest delivery Tyson ever produced. The ball reared brutally, clipped the shoulder of Miller's bat and flew high in the direction of the slips. Hutton, at second slip, threw up a hopeful hand. Making agonised contact, crucially, he did just enough to divert the ball towards Edrich to his left. Ever alert, Edrich grasped the chance (87-5), and was immediately mobbed by his excited colleagues. Tyson had taken three wickets for three runs in two overs.

Hole and Archer resisted briefly, with Archer's savage cut smashing one ball to the point boundary. Then, Statham prised Hole out, softening him up with three yorkers before slipping in a shorter delivery that moved slightly off the wicket. Hole edged, and Evans gobbled up the opportunity (97-6). Tyson then produced a lightning yorker that caught Maddocks on the back foot. Being late on the stroke, the ball spun off the bottom edge and onto the stumps, dislodging a bail (98-7).

Lindwall was dismissed by his second ball from Tyson, an out-swinger that the Australian tried to force to leg. He missed and was plumb lbw (98-8). A deathly hush had descended on the huge crowd. Archer played two more expansive attacking shots before Statham yorked him (110-9). Tyson summoned up one last thunderbolt. Johnston poked at it and Evans pouched the edge diving to his right (111 all out).

Melbourne newspaper *The Age* carried a story entitled "They Said He Would Never Be Really Fast". It read: "London January 6 – just one year and six days ago – Frank Tyson the wrecker who captured six Australian wickets for 16 runs yesterday – was convinced his bowling action was all wrong. It was at a New Year's Eve dance that Tyson whipped an imaginary ball down the dance floor and said to his companion:- 'Look. You see? My body doesn't carry straight through. I dip to the left as if I am bowling to the slips. I feel comfortable. But they say I'll never be really fast if I do that.' Newspapers tell how Tyson, while still growing, hurt his back playing too much cricket. He got instructions for 100 exercises and practised at least 10 every night. Last winter he went on a tree-felling course in Surrey."

The article continued: "'Frank was always crazy about physical fitness,' his proud 61-year-old mother said today. 'Every day at home he gets out his Indian clubs and does his exercises with them.' In Frank's home town of Middleton today was Tyson's Day. Grey-haired Mrs Violet Tyson was knocked up at 6.30am by neighbours who went to shower her with congratulations. She recalled she used to play cricket with her son when he was a boy. 'When there was no one else he used to bowl to me,' Mrs Tyson said. According to the *Daily Sketch*, Mrs Tyson pleads that her son be called Typhoon – not Tiger. 'Frank's not really ferocious,' his mother says. But at least seven Australian batsmen are certain that in this matter mother does not know best."

Australia's all-rounder Alan Davidson said in his autobiography *Fifteen Paces*: "Frank Tyson plagued the Australian batting, turning the summer into the most miserable our country had experienced since the stormy days of 'Bodyline'. Speed, burning, scorching speed, was his weapon. There was no subtlety, no deceiving swing – he was too fast for that. Only when the ball was worn and he tired a little did he bend it back from the off...The wickets that summer responded to pace with the Sydney wickets the greenest and liveliest in memory...Tyson and Statham – Lancashire's tireless, penetrating speedster – reached the fastest pace of their careers and were able to maintain telling pressure at each end, just as Miller and Lindwall had done in 1948.

"If the initial blast had been repulsed, there was always Trevor Bailey who could bowl with infuriating accuracy... 'Typhoon Tyson' they called him, a stirring picture of an athlete as powerful as a rampaging bull, tall, loosely muscled and an awesome delivery in which he propelled himself airborne at the batsman. How his back did not break under the strain of that final whip I could never know...[In the second Test] Archer was caught at slip, the ball having hit the full face of the bat, but the force of the delivery had turned the bat in his hand."

Now the momentum was firmly with England. Not even three-figure temperatures or 90 per cent humidity could arrest the English charge at Adelaide. Although Australia posted a first innings total of 323 runs, with Colin McDonald contributing 48 runs, Miller 44, Maddocks 69, and Johnson 41, England trumped this with 341 runs of their own. Hutton made 80, his highest score of the series, and Cowdrey added to his burgeoning reputation with a composed knock of 79 runs.

Cowdrey recalled that at one point in his innings he became restive, as the Australians' defensive tactics held him in check. Seeing that Cowdrey might throw his wicket away, Hutton told Vic Wilson, his 'drinks waiter', to take out a couple of bananas for Cowdrey on the pretext that he might be hungry. The actual message was for him to get his head down.

Valuable supporting roles were also played by Compton, Bailey, Evans and Edrich. Once again, Australia collapsed in their second innings, emulating their abysmal display at Melbourne by scoring only 111 runs. This time, Appleyard made the breakthrough after only two overs from Statham. Appleyard promptly dismissed Morris, Burke and Harvey for just 13 runs, leaving the Australian innings in a parlous state overnight. Then, with the press identifying Appleyard as the man most likely to bring the Australians down, Hutton confounded all expectations, and turned once again to Statham and Tyson to finish the job.

Despite being set a victory target of less than 100 runs, Miller made England fight all the way. At one point England was tottering on 18-3. Compton strode to the wicket with Hutton's despairing words ringing in his ears: "The buggers have done us." *Nil desperandum* thought Compton as he and Evans took England to a five-wicket victory, sealing a series win and retaining the Ashes.

Immediately after Godfrey Evans had hit Miller for four, to win the game, an exhausted Hutton spoke on Australian radio: "It is a great moment here for me today...Of course, we are feeling pretty tired, and really I don't know what to say, except this morning we saw some magnificent fast bowling by Tyson and Brian Statham, and then this afternoon we saw a magnificent spell of bowling from Keith Miller who, I think, is the finest bowler with a new ball that I know. He bowled magnificently, and gave us all quite a lot of worries for some time this afternoon."

Hutton became the first England skipper to win and retain the Ashes. How he suffered, though! Ever since Wally Hammond's 1938/39 tour to South Africa, he had lived with a recurring pain in the small of his back. Throughout the 1954/55 tour, he was so troubled by the ailment that he took painkillers almost constantly. At Adelaide, the pain was particularly acute, bad enough for him to worry that he would not be able to complete the match. This was a measure of the man's courage.

The final Test at Sydney was almost washed out by incessant heavy rain. It was the worst deluge that New South Wales had experienced in 50 years, causing the first three days of play to be abandoned. Having been put in by Johnson on the fourth day, there was still enough time for new opener, Tom Graveney, to stroke a glorious century (111), and for May (79), Compton (84) and Bailey (72) to make substantial additions, as England racked up 371-7 declared, their highest total of the series. After Hutton declared, Wardle created havoc. Australia was dismissed for 221. Following on, they were struggling again, at 118-6, before time was called.

Alan Ross, author of *Australia 55,* observed: "Tyson was initially a selector's gamble: they owe it to Hutton's dogged faith that it succeeded beyond anybody's dreams...May at Sydney and Melbourne destroyed the legend of Lindwall...May dominated him to such an extent that he no longer dared to bowl his most deadly ball – the fast swinging half-volley... May put his left leg down the wicket and thrashed them to the sight-screen. Under this treatment, Lindwall aged noticeably...[Cowdrey's] defensive technique was of unassailable soundness, he got firmly behind the pace bowlers and he placed and drove the ball to the on with a distribution of balance that would have delighted Michelangelo.

"Statham was the unluckier bowler of the two, and without his sustained pace and onslaught on the stumps, which allowed the batsmen no rest, Tyson's success would have been greatly reduced...Bailey, whose all-round tenacity was little less invaluable than in 1953, as a bowler he largely ignored the stumps, but he moved the ball in the air more than any bowler on either side, and his skill at floating his slower ball across the wicket in both directions got him important wickets, particularly Harvey's...Appleyard's ability to make the ball hang and then quickly dip, found the Australians pushing out too soon, and the shade he was able to move the ball off the seam from the left-hander's leg to off twice accounted for Harvey at vital stages.

"Hutton was mostly a struggling batsman...Tactically, he seemed occasionally cautious, sometimes surprised one, but was thoroughly effective... He handled his bowlers with a conviction and understanding of their powers that made victory possible. He calculated exactly when to attack and when to slow down the Australian rate of scoring...If the genius of captaincy lies in the precise husbanding of resources, then Hutton frequently demonstrated it... He proved that the important thing about a captain is not whether he is amateur or professional, but what kind of man he is."

In his autobiography, *Fifteen Paces*, Alan Davidson added: "Hutton earned a place for himself among the great Test commanders...It is no coincidence that his name should be linked with Douglas Jardine...Though different in background...both men dedicated themselves to humbling Australia...Each jettisoned a famous bowler [Tate and Bedser] and each was prepared to stretch the rules to the limit to justify the results.

"Where Jardine exploited the bouncer and massed body-line fields, Hutton blue-printed slow-motion cricket, a frustrating pattern of play in which the number of overs was deliberately restricted to conserve the energy of the English speed bowlers. The fewer overs bowled, the fewer runs the opponents could score in a day. England was to apply sustained speed pressure bowling to play on the fickle concentration of the Australian batsmen. Finicky field placements, sometimes as many as three or four in an over, gave the English express bowlers breathing space before the next furious delivery.

"Hutton was an astute leader...He played the game hard and he was a stern and demanding disciplinarian. He did not encourage fraternisation with the 'enemy'. [When I] shook Alec Bedser's hand warmly [at the Oval in 1953 after Bedser had taken a Test series record 39th wicket] a voice over my shoulder said: ''Ere Alec, how do you expect to get batsmen oot if you're always talking to 'em.' [Like Bradman] Hutton was a distant figure. He stayed in his hotel room as a general might remain in his tent before the battle."

The pressure placed upon Hutton was enormous. Fretting about his form, troubled continually by pain, contorted with guilt and embarrassment at his treatment of Bedser, he also had to contend with the never-ending round of speeches and social functions. For an intensely shy man this must have been torture. Once on the field of play, though, he was as tough as they come.

Davidson remarked: "[Hutton] could 'needle' an opponent. When Richie Benaud came out to bat he said more than once: 'Come on Richie, let's get you over with', as though it was a tedious formality...Things had gone badly in the Tests and our confidence was badly dented. [Before the fifth Test when the Ashes had already been retained] Hutton suggested that if we liked to come to the nets he would give us each an hour's free coaching..." After the many Australian batting calamities, Davidson said he was prepared to take him up on the offer!

Alan Hill wrote in his biography of Peter May: "Colin Cowdrey said that he was conscious throughout the crucial Test at Sydney that Hutton was manipulating a campaign as though playing a tight and ruthless game of chess. One adroit ploy involved Richie Benaud. Johnny Wardle was just about to bowl to Benaud. The over was halted as Hutton moved within conversational distance of the batsman.

"Seconds passed while he apparently deliberated on some devious scheme. 'What's going on?' asked the perplexed Johnny. 'Put your sweater on,' said Hutton. He then briskly clapped his hands, looking over towards Tyson fielding in the deep. 'Come on, Frank, have a bowl. Richie's in.'..."

Having summoned Tyson, Hutton would then engage him in a long whispered conversation before handing him the ball. "Len did not believe in sparing the opposition once he got them on the floor," said former England bowler John Warr.

Speaking on BBC *Test Match Special* during the 1980s, Trevor Bailey commented: "Len Hutton was dour, but a very shrewd tactician, the type I always wanted to play under. He wasn't a leader from the front...He let you get on with your job. He was far more impressed by fast bowling than slow bowling, because he played slow bowling better, if anything, than he played fast bowling.

"So he did have a tendency to put great emphasis on the quicks and, of course, if you look at the modern game you realise they are pretty important...Hutton was a master batsman and beautiful to watch...He could make the forward defensive look attractive. His off-drive was very graceful...He was marvellous on bad wickets...Len needed to score a hundred because there was a tendency to regard anything less than a hundred as a failure."

Although unaware of the significance of this match at the time, Len Hutton bowed out of Test cricket with a half-century at Eden Park, Auckland where the host side subsided to 26 all out in their second innings to lose by an innings and 20 runs. Ironically, "Gubby" Allen was about to give Hutton an unprecedented vote of confidence by appointing him as captain for all five home Tests against South Africa.

Hutton would soon discover that he was no longer fit enough to play first-class cricket, let alone Test matches. Arthritis took hold due to the abnormal strain placed on his back. It seemed symbolic given the extent to which he had carried England's hopes during the post-war years. As Hutton said: "They expect me to stay in."

Tom Graveney remembered the Australia tour of 1954/55 as a wonderful experience, describing the country as "almost British" in character with so many people emigrating from the UK, having become disillusioned with their grey homeland. As part of the 'White Australia policy', white immigrants were encouraged to settle there with the inducement of "a £10 passage". Initially, immigration was encouraged primarily from Britain, but was subsequently widened to attract white Europeans from Holland, Italy, Greece, and Yugoslavia. In 1955, Australia celebrated the arrival of one million white immigrants since the policy was put in place.

The 'White Australia policy' originated in the 19th century when competition in the gold fields, labour disputes and growing nationalism created racial antagonisms. It was then accentuated during the 1930s and 1940s in response to Japan's aggressive expansion in the Pacific region. The Australian government sought to grow its white population in order to avoid the country being overrun by people of Asian ethnicity. It was in this climate that the slogan, 'populate or perish', was first coined.

During the war, many non-white refugees, including Malays, Indonesians, and Filipinos, arrived in Australia, but once the hostilities ceased, the Australian Government sought their deportation. The policy was gradually relaxed during the 1950s, partly because of Australia's growing labour needs in servicing major projects such as the huge Snowy Mountains Scheme.

Nevertheless, as writer Alan Ross indicated in his journal of the 1954/55 tour, the strong pro-white attitude of Australian people was evident in their treatment of the aborigines. Ross wrote in *Australia 55*: "The white races have not done well by [the aborigines], although under an exceptionally intelligent Minister the aborigines are now being [accommodated] in their remote Reserves that will once more make them part of the community. Unfortunately, it has been done too late.

"It was not so long ago that the police was allowed to hunt and kill them like dogs. Their number is so small that they cannot hope to survive as a race much longer. Missionaries in part clothe, feed and educate them: but by breaking down their tribal secrecies, they are removing the mysteries and pride that were the cause of their art, and the justification and meaning of their separateness."

Despite suffering long-standing discrimination, in 1868 an aboriginal team became the first Australian cricket side to play in England. And yet Jason Gillespie was the first indigenous player to represent Australia when he was selected to play, against the West Indies, in 1996. Remarkably, this came about only 16 months before Makhaya Ntini became the first black cricketer to represent South Africa.

Eddie Gilbert, Queensland's aboriginal fast bowler, might have been chosen during the 1930s, though, had there not been doubts about the legality of his action. Bradman considered him faster than Larwood. Not that England's record in recognising black talent had been much better. Roland Butcher became the first black British player to be capped by England in 1981, 33 years after the *Empire Windrush* had docked at Tilbury. By then, only two black players, Viv Anderson and Laurie Cunningham, had been chosen to play for the England football team.

'WAITING FOR GODOT'

'Stranger in Paradise'

During March 1955, Pathe News provided national cinematic coverage of the forcible eviction of 60,000 black South African people living in Sophiatown, on the western edge of Johannesburg, in order that their white South African neighbours could "live alone".

The Pathe News commentator explained that the South African Nationalist government was continuing to add "legal bite" to its policy of apartheid, while the newsreel featured a group of distressed and bewildered black people staring desolately at the camera. They were well-dressed as if preparing for church. What the Pathe camera did not show were scenes of 3,000 South African police, armed with sten guns, sweeping into Sophiatown, removing the black occupants and razing their homes.

The black occupants were taken to Meadowlands, a new township, 11 miles away. While they were freeholders in Sophiatown, in Meadowlands they were tenants only. This was an exercise in dispossession as well as displacement. The African National Congress was forbidden to hold public meetings or call strikes, but announced that it would protest by calling "Days of Prayer" to keep people from work. The ANC's Defiance campaign against apartheid escalated, with strikes, boycotts and organised civil disobedience.

By then, UK cinema audiences were shrinking rapidly, but few British people could feign ignorance of what was going on in South Africa. In October of that year, the United Nations debated "the racial conflict in South Africa, resulting from the policies of apartheid", which prompted the white South African delegate, WC du Plessis, to walk out in protest. He complained that the UN had infringed its own charter by intervening in his country's internal affairs. South Africa had repeatedly ignored the UN's human rights committee, which called apartheid a "seriously disturbing factor in international relations".

Despite their blatant disregard of human rights, Westminster submitted no official protest to the South African government. No disquiet was voiced about the South African cricket team's impending tour of England, either. By this time the horror of apartheid was known within MCC, and not only second-hand, as Billy Griffith, a senior MCC official, had direct experience of this during the 1948/49 tour.

Despite Pathe's selective coverage, and the constrained neutrality of its commentary, the suggestion was clear that these dispossessed black people warranted the viewers' sympathy. This was a bold political departure for a media company renowned for its faithful endorsement of the British establishment.

It can only be speculated whether any discussion took place within Westminster or Lord's about the morality of maintaining sporting links with a regime that institutionalised such gross inhumanity. There again, India and Pakistan had managed to establish sporting links with one another after thousands of Muslims, Hindus and Sikhs had been killed in the frenzied ethnic and religious conflict that accompanied Partition.

Until Macmillan delivered his "Winds of Change" speech to the South African parliament in 1960, the British government had not publicly criticised apartheid, although Macmillan's stand was probably prompted less by moral indignation as by a fear of a communism spreading among brutalised indigenous people. His speech was delivered one month before the Sharpeville massacre.

As former British diplomat David Summerhayes suggested in a 2003 interview, there were two principal reasons why the British government was so cautious about openly condemning apartheid. Firstly, with so many white British passport holders living in South Africa, there was no appetite for jeopardising relationships with its government through adversarial politics. Secondly, a large number of British businesses were situated there. An expression of outright condemnation was considered to carry risks for their economic interests, also.

Although Summerhayes did not mention this, during the 1950s there were some right-wing elements of the British Conservative party who strongly supported the South African regime. He maintained that, up until the seventies, a policy of persuasion and mediation was employed for the most part, although the D'Oliveira affair of 1968 and growing British anti-apartheid protests eventually brought about a suspension of sporting links.

With the British government equivocating about its relationship with South Africa, no decisive moral leadership was provided. Even at the height of the D'Oliveira affair, the attitudes of leading British politicians seemed pusillanimous. This is illustrated in Colin Cowdrey's autobiography *M.C.C.* Here, he recalled a conversation he held with Sir Alec Douglas-Home, a former Conservative Prime Minister, when seeking political advice on the potential selection of D'Oliveira. Although no longer in power, Douglas-Home had spoken privately with Dr Vorster, the South African premier, regarding South African reaction to this possibility.

Vorster was apparently dismayed at the prospect, but Douglas-Home counselled Cowdrey that it was politically expedient to maintain 'warm relations' with South Africa. While insisting that the team should be selected on playing ability alone, Douglas-Home advised against cancellation of the tour, suggesting it was not Britain's place to take a moral stand about apartheid. According to Cowdrey, he expressed the belief that the suspension of sporting relations would not affect South Africa's adherence to this policy. It was small wonder that Lord Cobham had been inclined towards adopting a policy of appeasement.

The problem with Otto von Bismarck's observation, "politics is the art of the possible", is that it can be used to vindicate all manner of shoddy compromises and grubby accommodations. Lest it be forgotten, though, the rapprochement that India and Pakistan achieved, during the early 1950s, was also an expression of this principle. Nevertheless, there were no angry voices or protesting placards to greet the South African tourists as they arrived in a wet, cold Britain in April 1955.

By the end of May, the Test series threatened to be another kind of washout. Shrivelled by the intense cold and damp, the South African tourists performed badly in their opening county games. Any notion that these were 'warm-up' contests was lost on them as they shivered under multiple layers of sweaters. To make matters worse, they had to contend with a national railway strike, forcing them to spend many tiring hours on the coach.

With the sun finally emerging in June, though, their mood and form lifted. Opening batsman Jackie McGlew and free-scoring Roy McLean put Trevor Bailey's Essex to the sword at Colchester, as South Africa scored over 500 runs for the loss of four wickets. With the drying wickets allowing pace bowlers Adcock and Heine firmer footholds, Jack Cheetham's side began to display an opening attack of real menace.

Hutton was unable to complete MCC's game against the tourists at Lord's, on account of an attack of lumbago. It was clear then that England would need to find another captain. Because Sheppard was embarking upon his church ministry training, May was spared a tussle for the vacant captaincy. Having appointed May, in Hutton's place, MCC had reverted to their cherished policy of choosing an amateur leader. But, May was no Freddie Brown. According to the journalist and broadcaster Alan Gibson: "[May] crammed himself into the mould of Hutton."

As quoted by his biographer, Alan Hill, May commented: "I was well aware that although I was an amateur – and a genuine one unsupported by sponsors or advertisers – I did not always play in the obviously light-hearted way which had been associated with some amateurs in the past." He certainly didn't.

May was equally ruthless in the pursuit of victory, and in resisting defeat, as Hutton. He demanded committed, wholehearted efforts from each member of his team, and was intolerant of reckless batting when the chips were down, but preferred to convey his disapproval with a judicious frown. While he was a team man who entertained no cliques, being appreciative and fond of the professionals who played under him, he was no more cordial with his opponents than his predecessor.

Like Hutton, he was disinclined to fraternise with the opposition. May considered he was there to win Test matches, not friends. And, according to Sheppard, who played under May during the 1956 Ashes series, the award of the England captaincy did not diminish his appetite for runs – quite the contrary, for he became even more voracious in his pursuit of big scores, as underlined in 1957, when he scored a demoralising 285 not out, at Edgbaston, to tear the initiative away from the visiting West Indians.

Although the warm sunshine of June had helped revive South African fortunes, they were comprehensively outplayed in the opening Test at Nottingham. They started poorly, when the normally reliable Tayfield dropped Kenyon, at short leg, in Adcock's opening over. Kenyon profited by making 87 runs, helping Graveney (42) add 91 for the first wicket despite numerous close calls. May (83) and Bailey (49) then helped England to put 334 runs on the board, at a customary snail's pace, before exposing the South African openers, McGlew and Goddard, to Statham and Tyson in poor light.

South Africa collapsed. Goddard was lbw to Statham's leg-cutter for 12 while Endean was trapped lbw by Tyson for a duck. After Waite was calamitously run out, also for nought, South Africa was rocking at 19-3. There was no let-up. Bowling as fast as ever, Tyson bowled McLean for 13, while Appleyard dismissed Winslow for two, leaving South Africa at 55-5. Although captain Cheetham and McGlew forged a partial recovery, Wardle wrapped up the South African innings for 181 by taking four for 24 runs off 32 overs.

Wardle's command over the tourists' batting was so great that he created a new Test record by bowling 13 consecutive maiden overs. After being asked to follow on, once again South Africa had to contend with difficult batting conditions. On a rain-affected wicket, Tyson routed them with his searing pace and sharp lift, taking six wickets for 28 runs in 21.3 overs. Remarkably, Tyson had taken 52 wickets in just nine Test matches.

Sadly for Tyson, his intense labours on the concrete-like Australian surfaces had taken a heavy toll on his feet and ankles. Henceforth, he would be troubled by a succession of injuries which would rob him of his health, fitness and, crucially, his blistering pace. The Nottingham Test would also witness the decline of Bob Appleyard as a Test bowler. Troubled increasingly by muscle wastage in his shoulders, he began to lose his mesmerising control and guile. His bowling at Nottingham contained an erratic mixture of wild full tosses and long-hops that forced wicketkeeper Evans into making a flurry of desperate, bruising saves.

At Lord's, Peter Heine made his debut for South Africa. Until then South African cricket was largely untouched by past Boer grudges. This was simply because few Afrikaners played the game. For much of the 20th century, South African cricket was played and watched predominantly by its English-speaking populace. Before the days of Hansie Cronje and

Allan Donald only two players with a Boer heritage represented South Africa. The first was Johannes Kotze, a Boer farmer who preferred cricket to war. He toured England in 1901 while the Second Boer War was being fought. The second was Peter Heine.

Heine was a scowling, powerfully-built 6ft 4in fast bowler. While reputedly mild-mannered when off the pitch, upon receiving the ball he hissed with Afrikaner fire and brimstone. During the 1956/57 series in South Africa, he sneered maliciously at Trevor Bailey, England's obdurate all-rounder: "I want to hit you, Bailey – I want to hit you over the heart." He also snarled at Peter Richardson, whom he had felled with a bouncer: "Get up! I want to hit you again!" Cricket seemed to be not so much as an escape from the Boer War as a chance to re-wage it. In his book, *Over to Me*, Jim Laker referred to Heine as "the bloody Dutchman".

At Lord's, Heine and Adcock teamed up as a Test opening attack for the first time. Jackie McGlew reckoned that, at their peak, the Adcock–Heine partnership was as good as those of Lindwall and Miller, Statham and Tyson, or Statham and Trueman. In his book, *Cricket for South Africa*, McGlew stated that the Australian openers, Colin McDonald and Jimmy Burke, agreed. Both Heine and Adcock bowled with considerable fire, banging the ball into the pitch just short of a length at a furious pace, discomforting opposing batsmen with their bruising bounce.

Colin Cowdrey had cause to reflect upon his favoured front-foot technique after being battered black and blue by the pair at Manchester. It was a torrid summer for Cowdrey. Having been censured in public by Sir Gerald Nabarro MP for supposedly dodging National Service – actually, Cowdrey had been pronounced medically unfit on account of a hereditary toe problem – he then had the 'temerity' to be selected for the Old Trafford Test only to suffer so much, from Adcock and Heine, that he was not fit again until the following winter.

Heine and Adcock had more in their lockers than brutal pace, though. Heine improved the potency of his out-swinger, in taking ten wickets at Taunton, also adding a jagged off-cutter to his armoury to complement Adcock's mix of out-and in-swing. Both South African bowlers possessed amazing stamina to add to their fierce determination. Had both played in all five Test matches the result of the series might have been different.

At Lord's, May once again won the toss, and decided to bat on a fiery pitch. Heine and Adcock steamed into the action. Kenyon was bowled by Adcock for one while Heine had May caught by Tayfield off a lifter for a duck. England was then 8-2. Graveney remained briefly before Heine had him caught at the wicket for 15 (30-3). Compton did little better, dismissed by Heine for 20 (45-4). Although Ken Barrington, a debutant at Nottingham, batted adhesively for 34, he, too, was castled by Heine's pace. Despite Wardle striking some useful late blows, England subsided to 133 all out.

Heine had bowled almost continuously, taking five wickets for 60 runs off 25 ferocious overs. Surprisingly, his co-assassin was not Adcock, but all-rounder Trevor Goddard, also playing in his first Test series. His nagging, accurate medium-paced seamers accounted for salvage expert Bailey, new-cap Fred Titmus, Wardle and Statham for 59 runs off 21.2 overs. Like Tayfield, Goddard had the knack of strangling batsmen's shots, tucking them up with an irksomely accurate leg stump line of attack, supported by a ring of on-side fielders.

Fred Trueman was recalled to the England attack, following Tyson's withdrawal with a damaged heel. He started well, helping Wardle add 22 runs for the last wicket. And when it was his turn to bowl, he removed Goddard in his first over for a duck as Evans took a magnificent diving catch. This left South Africa tottering at 7-2, since Statham had McGlew caught at the wicket for nought. South Africa's plight might have been worse had Evans not unaccountably missed Cheetham off Trueman's third delivery. Thereafter, South Africa prospered. McLean had reason to count his blessings as he was dropped five times in blasting 142 runs. Admirably supported by Keith (57) and Endean (48), South Africa established a 171-run first innings lead in the improving batting conditions.

Trueman also took the wicket of wicketkeeper-batsman Waite for eight, but in his desperation to prove his worth he bowled far too many loose deliveries which were punished ruthlessly, notably by McLean. Trueman's humiliation was complete when he was forced to bowl with a single slip, and a ring of fielders protecting the boundary.

Although Kenyon failed once again, May struck a crucial century (112), assisted by Graveney (60) and Compton (69), to take England patiently to a lead of 182 runs. Tayfield took five wickets for 80 runs in 38.5 demanding overs, while Goddard closed up the other end.

Chasing a modest victory target, the South Africans were immediately in difficulties in the closing overs of the third day. Statham dismissed both McGlew and Goddard while Trueman hit Cheetham on the elbow forcing him to retire hurt, and leaving the tourists effectively at 17-3, as it was unlikely that Cheetham would be fit to resume his innings. With poor light on Monday providing regular interruptions, Statham was able to bowl unchanged. He almost single-handedly destroyed the South Africans, taking seven wickets for 39 runs in 29 overs. England won by 71 runs.

At last, Manchester flouted its reputation for dull, wet weather, as the tourists were treated to five days of uninterrupted sunshine. And how they prospered! Helped by a rash of missed chances, McGlew, Waite and Winslow struck centuries as South Africa made 521-8 declared, in response to England's inadequate first innings total of 284 in which only Compton had excelled. His glittering knock of 158 had seemingly turned back the clock eight years.

For South Africa, the lean, lanky and bespectacled Paul Winslow defied all expectations. Looking like an unobtrusive civil servant compelled to exchange his pinstripes for whites, he blazed his way to a century in a fraction over three hours. Having decided that his bludgeoning blade required no defensive application, he clouted the England attack to all quarters, completing his century with a massive blow that cleared the sight-screen and found the BBC television gantry. Bedser, playing in his last Test match in place of the injured Statham, was treated with disdain by the rampant Winslow.

In attempting to clear a deficit of 237 runs, England started disastrously as Heine and Adcock swept away the openers, Kenyon and Graveney, with only two runs on the board. A 124-run third-wicket partnership between May (117) and Compton (71) restored a steadier platform, helping England clear the arrears and eventually establish a 144-run lead. Helpful contributions were also made by an ill-at-ease Cowdrey (50), a doughty Bailey (38 not out) and a brave Evans (36), who had broken his little finger. Together they faced sustained hostility from Heine who took a further five wickets and Adcock who took three.

May probably thought that England's slowly-compiled score of 381 had insulated them from defeat. When Evans was England's last man out, the South Africans were left with 132 minutes, or around 30 overs, to reach the 145-run victory target. The required run-rate was twice as fast as that achieved in most 1950s Test matches. McGlew had no qualms about chasing down the target, though. He and McLean played starring roles as the Springboks sprinted home with three wickets and three minutes to spare.

As the game approached its nail-biting finish, McGlew instructed Heine, his next batsman, to wait on the boundary edge to conserve precious time. Heine was so desperate to comply that he tripped on the Old Trafford steps, falling to his knees. As he did so, a roar went up from the crowd. An elderly Lancastrian leant across him, kindly suggesting: "You can stop praying now, lad, your team has just won."

Tyson's ankle suffered badly, having bowled 50 overs on the hard, worn Old Trafford track. Much to his dismay, "Gubby" Allen ruled that he was unfit for the next Test at Leeds. After his undignified treatment by the South Africans at Manchester, Bedser was also omitted from the fourth Test squad. At the age of 37, his superb international career had been brought to a close. His Surrey new-ball partner Peter Loader was selected in his place, while Statham returned for the injured Tyson. Fit-again Wardle replaced the tidy, but ineffective young Middlesex off-spinner Titmus, while Essex batsman Doug Insole was brought in instead of Kenyon.

With England's opening partnership failing once again, Yorkshire's Frank Lowson was recalled to the side, where he was accompanied by Trevor Bailey, promoted once more from the middle order. To accommodate this move, Graveney was pushed down the order to bat at number six. Evans who was nursing a broken finger was replaced by Surrey's Arthur McIntyre.

Stung by their defeat at Old Trafford, England seized an early advantage at Leeds, reducing South Africa to 38-5 on a perfect wicket. Loader fully justified his selection by taking four of the seven South African wickets that fell before the hundred was up. A rearguard action involving Endean (41), Tayfield (25) and Heine (14) achieved a small recovery, but South Africa's first innings of 171 seemed far too small to be defensible. Not so, for England's all-too-frequent batting frailties were once again exposed by Heine's aggression and Tayfield's wiles.

Both openers were shot out for single figures, and only May (47) and Compton (61) batted with distinction, as England managed a dismal total of 191 in reply. The South African effort had been all the more commendable since Adcock had twisted his ankle, also chipping a small bone in his foot, leaving them with only three front-line bowlers.

As if to rub in the inadequacy of the English efforts, South Africa then scored 500 runs at their second attempt in temperatures hovering in the 90s. Both McGlew (133) and Endean (116) reached three figures, while Goddard and Keith chipped in with scores in the 70s. The left-handed Keith's batting technique was particularly impressive, in proficiently blunting the threat posed by Wardle who bowled persistently into the rough outside his off stump.

Even against South Africa's depleted attack, England fared little better the second time around. May fell three runs short of a century, and Insole made 47, but no one mastered Tayfield or Goddard who bowled with suffocating accuracy and skill. Goddard's analysis read 62 overs, 37 maidens, 69 runs and five wickets while Tayfield's was 47.1 overs, 15 maidens, 94 runs and five wickets. Goddard bowled unchanged for four hours. The English batting eventually succumbed to the pressure the pair created, disintegrating from 204-3 to 256 all out.

At Nottingham and Lord's, the victorious England side had the better of generally poor batting conditions, whereas its defeats had taken place on the truer surfaces at Manchester and Leeds. Therefore, May must have been reassured at the prospect of playing the deciding Test at the Oval, his home ground, which was likely to favour his spinners, particularly if he could win the toss and bat first.

With England's status as unofficial world champions in some peril, MCC's selectors made five changes for the final Test. Their priorities were to strengthen the middle order, improve the quality of the English out-cricket, notably the close catching, and to exploit the degree of turn that the Oval wicket frequently allowed. Consequently, Jack Ikin and Brian Close, both excellent close catchers, were chosen to open the innings. This was England's fourth opening combination of the summer. Len Hutton had been sorely missed!

With Ikin and Close deputed to face the new ball, Bailey was asked to bolster the middle order, as was the returning Willie Watson, a good outfielder. Warwickshire wicketkeeper Dick Spooner was considered to be a better batsman than McIntyre, so he replaced the Surrey stumper. Jim Laker was brought back, too, on his favoured home turf, to accompany Lock, his spin partner, who had yet to make much impact in this series. Given that Wardle, Lock's left-arm Test rival, had taken three times as many wickets in this series, at almost a third of the cost, Lock seemed fortunate to be playing at the Oval.

And yet Lock was not only a brilliant close-to-the-wicket fielder, he had taken a stack of wickets on his home strip. And hadn't he and Laker sunk the Australians there, two years before? It seemed to be a case of horses for courses.

As for the South Africans, fit-again Jack Cheetham relieved McGlew of the captaincy, and replaced Winslow who had not batted well at Leeds. Adcock had also recovered, but he was passed over in favour of the fast-medium Eddie Fuller, who had bowled well in the previous county games.

The result of the toss was expected to be crucial, and so it proved. May won it and decided to bat. In the two-and-a-half hours of play that was possible on the opening day, England progressed at funereal speed, to 70-3, having made 51 for the first wicket, their best opening partnership since Nottingham.

Weekend rain then rendered the pitch particularly spiteful, so by the end of play on the second day, both England and South Africa had completed their first innings. Seventeen wickets had fallen for the addition of 182 runs. While England had groped and ground their way to 151 all out, in a shade under 90 overs, with only Close (32), Compton (30) and Watson (25) making even passable contributions, the South Africans were sent packing for 112 runs in just 65 overs.

The principal South African wicket-takers were Goddard and Tayfield. They shared eight wickets at miserly cost, before the Surrey spinners, Laker and Lock, set to work, taking two and four wickets respectively. In easier conditions on the third day, May and Graveney enabled England to exert a strong grip on the game. Nevertheless, once Graveney was dismissed for 42, there was another unseemly slide.

From a position of dominance at 157-3, England closed the third day on 195-8 with May 81 not out. McGlew was particularly vexed, though. He was convinced that May had been lbw to Tayfield, when he had scored only four runs, but the umpire, Bartley, shook his head. Had that perilously close decision gone against May, the result of this game and series might well have been different.

As it happened, May went on to register a match-winning score of 89, lifting his average for the series to almost 73 runs per innings. Apart from Compton, who achieved a series average of 55 in spite of his troublesome knee, no other English batsman had performed well. Third-placed

Graveney averaged just 24 runs per innings. May's place, in this all-too-fallible England batting order, had already assumed Hutton-like status.

England was dismissed quickly on the fourth morning for 204, giving Tayfield the incredible figures of 53.4 overs, 29 maidens, 60 runs and five wickets. Consequently, the South Africans were set a victory target of 244 runs, but once Laker and Lock were called upon the outcome was a foregone conclusion. Keith, Endean and McLean were all dismissed for ducks, leaving South Africa on 33-4.

Only Waite (60) offered stern resistance, showing admirable footwork, and driving and cutting with impeccable discretion and timing. South Africa was ultimately beaten by 92 runs, Laker taking five wickets for 56 runs and Lock four wickets for 62 runs. Between them, they had taken 75 per cent of the Springboks' wickets in this decisive Test. But the South Africans' admirable performances during this series suggested that on true surfaces they were at least England's equals.

'LOOK BACK IN ANGER'

'Whatever Will Be Will Be (Que Sera Sera)'

In 1956, a new term of rebellion entered the British vocabulary – "angry young man". It was applied loosely to a disparate group of almost wholly male, middle- and working-class playwrights, novelists and thinkers whose only shared feature seemed to be a love of iconoclasm. Among the so-called 'angry' brigade were playwrights John Osborne, Arnold Wesker, Harold Pinter and Shelagh Delaney; novelists Kingsley Amis, John Wain, Alan Sillitoe and John Braine and self-styled intellectuals such as *The Outsider* author, Colin Wilson.

Few members of this group seemed to be particularly angry, although most of them managed to be a bit sardonic. The term "angry young man" derives from Osborne's play *Look Back in Anger* which was staged at the Royal Court Theatre, London, in May 1956. The play is considerably less remarkable than the brouhaha it aroused among its reviewers.

Excited drama critic Kenneth Tynan wrote in the *Observer* on 13th May 1956: "[The play] presents post-war youth as it really is, with special emphasis on the non-U intelligentsia who live in bed sitters...all the qualities are there...the drift towards anarchy, the instinctive leftishness, the automatic rejection of 'official' attitudes...the lack of a crusade worth fighting for..."

However, not all critics were as enthusiastic about the play as Tynan. In fact, opinions were sharply divided. While some, like Tynan, saw the play as providing welcome relief from the stifling stagnancy of genteel privilege and understated emotions, as found, perhaps, in a Terence Rattigan play, others saw it as gratuitous cultural contamination. Not that this jousting raised much interest beyond the review pages.

That said, the output of these 'slightly aggrieved' writers helped shift British cultural focus, albeit haphazardly. Novelists as varied as John Wain (*Hurry on Down*), Kingsley Amis (*Lucky Jim*) and Keith Waterhouse (*Billy Liar*) introduced their readers to the middle-class 'outsider', typically, a bright, young, well-educated *man* who finds himself at odds with or distanced from the standards of conventional society.

But it was the grittier offerings of Alan Sillitoe, Arnold Wesker and Shelagh Delaney that helped re-awaken public interest to the harsh realities of working-class life, fostering the growth of 'kitchen sink' dramas, and the British 'new wave' cinema of the late 1950s and early 1960s.

Coincidentally, 'pop' music, grasped by predominantly working-class teenagers, at least during its earliest manifestations, emerged as an abrasive rival to the 'popular music' much loved by the easy-listening, middle-class public. Bill Haley lit the tinder, in late 1954, but Elvis fanned the blaze with his mega hit of 1956, 'Heartbreak Hotel'. Jeff Nuttall, author of *Bomb Culture,* observed that while 'pop' largely represented the voice of working-class rebellion, Beatnik folk music and 'trad jazz' were predominantly expressions of middle-class protest. Certainly, there were jazz lovers aplenty within the duffle-coated Campaign for Nuclear Disarmament of the late 1950s, a protest group which had strong academic, affluent trappings, hence the historian AJP Taylor's jibe that it was primarily "a movement of eggheads for eggheads".

By the latter half of the 1950s, the social profile of the British working classes was strengthening. This was partly a reflection of the increased educational opportunities granted by the 1944 Butler Education Act, augmented, perhaps, by the vibrancy or disturbance aroused by the new 'pop' culture. But, above all, the enhanced status of the lower classes owed much to the growing potency of the British economy.

In print, on film and on the stage, the daily struggles of British working people began to receive candid, sympathetic treatment, but there were more alarmist reactions, also. Two major British films of the late 1950s illustrated a growing disquiet at the increasing power being exerted by the working classes: *The Angry Silence* and the satirical *I'm Alright Jack.*

These films signalled, and played upon, middle-class anxieties about the rebellious actions of the British trade unions. The national rail strike, in 1955, stirred middle class unease compounded by the British government's decision to announce a state of emergency.

A spate of 'wildcat' stoppages, notably in car manufacturing plants, did little to allay their misgivings. According to the best traditions of 'folk devilry', *The Angry Silence* and *I'm Alright Jack* portrayed shop stewards as petty, militant, shop floor 'Napoleons'. Although the middle-class fears of worker insurrection were well off beam, there was little doubt that, with consumer demand increasing, and employment levels remaining high, trade union militants had better opportunities to flex their muscles. After the mid 1950s, class deference began to beat a retreat as the working classes became aware of their greater might.

Not that MCC seemed aware of the accelerating pace of social and economic change. Insulated within its citadel at Lord's, MCC was so preoccupied with its Edwardian heritage that, even by the mid 1950s, it still sought to restore the prominent position of the (gentleman) 'amateur' within the first-class game. Diana Rait-Kerr, MCC's first curator, insisted that this preoccupation was not motivated by "old school tie" considerations. It was said to represent a fervent desire to recover an "unfettered spirit of high adventure" which the gentleman amateur had supposedly provided during the Edwardian "golden age". If the Church was "the Conservative party at prayer", MCC seemed to be English conservatism at play.

In his autobiography, *M.C.C.*, Colin Cowdrey recalled that when he became the captain of Kent in 1955, he was given a book in which he was required to document the availability of various amateur players for county games played during July and August. Irrespective of their form and ability, Cowdrey was expected to give precedence to these players, once they had confirmed their availability. Not only were Kent's professional players, who relied upon the game for a living, expected to stand aside, no consideration was given to tactics, playing conditions or the strength of the opposition in the amateurs' selection.

Of course, there were few genuine amateurs then playing first-class cricket. Most of them earned a living either through extramural activities at their county club or via sympathetic commercial employers – hence the charge of 'shamateurism'.

MCC had been in charge of English cricket since the Victorian period.

By the Edwardian age, MCC had established complete authority over the domestic game through its Advisory County Cricket Committee. It ran the England team via its Board of Control for Test Matches, and held a commanding position within the Imperial Cricket Conference, which was initially only open to white members of the British Empire.

With its president and secretary occupying equivalent roles within the Imperial Cricket Conference, MCC was assured of a leading stake in the administration of all international cricket. Having become accustomed to this position of unrivalled authority, MCC of the 1950s was reluctant to make the necessary accommodations to the changing world outside, other than to commission a series of largely ineffective investigative and fact-finding committees.

Only the worsening financial climate of the latter 1960s caused MCC to reconsider its position. In 1968, MCC finally conceded its role as cricket's governing body to a separate Cricket Council. An independent Test and County Cricket Board (TCCB) was also set up to administer the professional game and a National Cricket Association (NCA) replaced MCC Cricket Association in looking after recreational cricket.

This was done, under duress, in order that the cash-strapped game might avail itself of public or government funding, which was not possible while MCC, a private club, remained in charge. As Derek Birley observed in his extensively-researched and wonderfully iconoclastic book, *A Social History of English Cricket*, even then MCC's senior officials clung to power, filling most of the influential positions within these new institutions.

Back in 1956, such heresies were not even contemplated, at least as far as can be ascertained. Although MCC was then rightfully concerned at the persistent decline in county cricket attendances, they seemed heartened that Test match revenue might offset the losses. The 1953 Ashes series netted £200,000, worth around £10m in modern currency. Television receipts were swelling the coffers, too, but this was a double-edged sword in that TV Test match coverage was thought to discourage attendances at county cricket games.

However, if Test match revenue was to indemnify county losses, the England team needed to perform successfully. It was unsurprising that Hutton and May sought their Test victories with such caution. As if to lessen their burdens, RAB Butler, the Conservative Chancellor of the Exchequer, exempted first-class cricket of liability for entertainment tax. How droll.

Although the MCC of 1956 remained wedded to its 'amateur first' catechism, this principle was no longer upheld by all county cricket clubs. As Cowdrey pointed out in his autobiography, during the post-war period there was a rise in professional standards leading to a levelling in players' abilities. Amateurs were not necessarily star cricketers any more. Even amateurs like May and Cowdrey, who captained their county sides, felt they could not ask their professional players to relinquish their places out of social deference rather than reasons of form or tactics.

Cowdrey wrote in his autobiography *M.C.C.*: "[By the mid 1950s] at Test level, Peter May and I were the last genuine amateurs, in that neither of us received any money for playing and our expense allowance did not cover our costs. Moreover, we were not really accorded any privilege, and quite right too. We appeared on the first day of pre-season training, played in the county or Test sides, right through to September, and played in the fund-raising benefit matches on Sundays.

"It was this change in outlook which altered the traditional character of county cricket. With it went, too, much of the glamour of the individuals, the real personalities...there has been such a levelling up of talent and such all-round improvement in standards that the stars no longer stand out so prominently."

The winter of 1955/56 had been deeply unpleasant. A heavy snowfall in January had brought down electricity and phone lines while there were record levels of smog, giving additional impetus to the passing of the Clean Air Act of 1956. More British troops were despatched to Cyprus as the Greek- and Turkish-Cypriot crisis intensified. Like a latter-day Napoleon, the British deported Archbishop Makarios, the leader of the Greek-Cypriot community, for fostering EOKA terrorism. Makarios would spend a period of exile in the Seychelles – not too punitive, then. But soon, Britain would be embroiled in a bigger, much more controversial action – Suez.

Since their decimation by Tyson and Statham Down Under, Australian fortunes revived spectacularly as they thrashed the West Indies in the Caribbean, during the spring of 1955. In the five-match series, four Australian batsmen averaged over 60 runs per innings. Incredibly, Harvey recorded a Test average of 108 after scoring three centuries, including one innings of 204, while his team-mates managed to score another nine Test tons between them.

Colin McDonald nailed one of the troublesome opening slots, having scored 449 Test runs with two centuries, to attain a series average of 64, while Ron Archer's batting average of 61 suggested that he might prove as useful with the blade as with the ball in England. Although leg-spinner Benaud and off-spinner Johnson headed the Australian Test bowling averages sharing 32 wickets at averages of less than 30 runs each, the series featured an outstanding all-round performance by Keith Miller.

Not only did he manage to take 20 West Indian Test wickets on the unforgiving Caribbean tracks, for a shade over 30 runs each, he cracked three Test centuries for a batting average of 73 runs. Not to be outdone, Lindwall bludgeoned a Test century of his own, at Bridgetown, to accompany a series bowling return that almost matched Miller's.

As for the West Indies, Clyde Walcott enjoyed a phenomenal series, scoring over 800 runs, five centuries and two fifties to earn an average of almost 83 per innings. Captain Denis Atkinson played an outstanding innings of 219 at Bridgetown, as did wicketkeeper Depeiza (122). Together, they amassed a 348-run seventh-wicket partnership – then, a new world first-class record – to help their side scrape a draw in the fourth Test.

Everton Weekes also played two outstanding innings at Port-of-Spain of 139 and 87 not out to help achieve another draw while Sobers gave further notice of his considerable talents. However, there were few other West Indian performances of note. Ramadhin and Valentine took only ten wickets between them at a combined average of over 70 runs per wicket. Achieving hard-won parity seemed to be the summit of West Indian hopes in this largely one-sided series. England had good reason to expect a tough Ashes challenge in 1956.

The Australian team chosen to contest the Ashes included Keith Miller and Ray Lindwall, for their third and final tours of England. Miller was then aged 36 years old while Lindwall was 34. As the ocean liner *Himalaya* left Fremantle, Miller turned to his pace bowling partner and remarked, "Take a good look, Ray. This is the last time we shall have this view."

Lindwall responded morosely, reluctantly acknowledging that their time was passing. Miller was rueful, too, having never had the opportunity to captain his country. After Ian Johnson was awarded the Australian captaincy once again in 1956, Miller knew that his chance had passed. He later told his biographer Mihir Bose, in *Keith Miller: A Cricketing Biography*: "I never seriously thought I would be captain. I'm impulsive; what's more, I've never been Bradman's pin-up and The Don rates high when it comes to policy matters in Australian cricket."

Miller's relationship with Bradman had often been prickly. When playing under him, Miller was irritated by Bradman's habit of claiming credit for each dismissal, attributing this to his encyclopaedic tactical knowledge. The cavalier, fun-loving Miller also disliked Bradman's win-at-all-costs mentality, particularly in 'bun fights'. And because Bradman had not gone to war, Miller thought this disqualified him from playing the reproving headmaster.

It was no surprise, then, that Miller should play the party pooper in Bradman's valedictory match, in Sydney, in 1949. Miller recalled Bradman's ruthless employment of bouncers, even in festival or benefit games, as a means of flaunting his power. As Miller prepared to bowl to Bradman in his final first-class innings, he mused: "I wonder how much he likes bouncers."

With a characteristic toss of his mane – a sure sign of trouble ahead – Miller gave "The Don" the works. Having easily hooked Miller's first, deliberately mild, effort for four, Bradman skied a catch off the next much quicker delivery, prompting hoots of derision from the disappointed Sydney crowd. The ostentatiously triumphant Miller was dropped promptly from the Australian tour party to South Africa, although he was reinstated later after the accident-prone Bill Johnston incurred an injury. Miller knew he would never be Australia's captain, though, while Bradman ran Australian cricket, despite leading New South Wales to a Sheffield Shield triumph.

Although 37-year-old Ian Johnson was a less compelling Test performer – he wasn't thought worthy of selection for the 1953 Ashes tour – and an unremarkable captain of Victoria, he had 'blue blood' in his veins. He had attended a prestigious school, and was related, through birth and marriage, to two Australian selectors. Even the more egalitarian-minded Aussies were not averse to nepotism, it seems. Besides, Johnson was an arch diplomat. In Miller's disappointed view, the choice was simple, and yet he bore Johnson no grudge. War had left Miller with a determination to enjoy life to the full. He did not succumb to petty jealousies. As at The Don's farewell, a moment of malicious fun was as much as he would allow himself.

The Australians' Ashes touring party comprised a glut of all-rounders. Apart from Miller, there were: Benaud, Davidson, Archer and the oxymoronically-named "Slasher" Mackay, while Lindwall boasted two Test centuries as well. Jimmy Burke and Colin McDonald offered solidity and reliability at the top of the order while Harvey had emerged as the best Australian batsman since Bradman. But the middle order had proved frail against the pace of Statham and Tyson. It was also unclear whether newcomer Peter Burge and 1953 tourist Ian Craig were good enough as specialist batsmen to buttress the long cast of all-rounders, who had contributed only cameo performances with the bat on the previous tour.

The *Himalaya* made for Tilbury via the Suez Canal providing the Australian party with a preview of the conflict about to unfold. Former Australian opener Arthur Morris sailed with them, this time as a journalist. He remarked in his journal, *Operation Ashes*, that the Egyptians he met, in Port Said, did not hold anti-British views, deploring, rather than greeting, the depletion in British troop numbers which were then said to be fewer than 200.

Morris was not to know that the Suez crisis would deepen soon after, in the wake of US and British refusal to help finance Colonel Nasser's Aswan Dam project, a scheme, considered essential, for reviving the Egyptian economy. When Nasser reacted, by seizing the Anglo-French Suez Canal Company, threatening the movement of Gulf oil supplies, Jim Laker's monumental bowling feat at Manchester was pushed from the headlines.

The Australian team disembarked at Tilbury on 24th April. A welcoming committee of pressmen awaited them, but so did dreary skies and insistent rain. Having charmed them with his winning smile and courteous manner, Johnson dampened expectations by announcing that the county games, while of "some importance", were secondary to his aim of recovering the Ashes. In those days, the county games were expected to be competitive, not just extended net practices.

Johnson was a good as his word as his team treated the initial warm-up games with cursory interest. Because they were mostly played in damp, chilly, gloomy conditions, there was little appeal for the scattered, spartan spectators, clad in heavy woollens and plastic macs. Not that the county sides put up much resistance in the early contests. Worcestershire was shot out for a pathetic total of 90 runs without any of the Australian bowlers having to extend themselves.

Australia then posted 438 carefree runs in reply with Benaud smashing 160 incandescent runs. The Australian reporters welcomed the fireworks as they endured press box facilities so primitive and austere as to be almost 'Stalinist'. The only interest for MCC's selectors was the form of Worcestershire's left-handed opener Peter Richardson, a farmer, who scored a defiant innings of 130 not out as Worcestershire escaped with a draw. But as admirably as Richardson had played, he seemed all at sea against the new ball at the start of his knock.

Johnson's decision to bat for ten hours at Leicester won him few friends. It allowed Keith Miller to strike his best first-class score of 281 not out and Burke to make a century, as Australia accumulated 694 runs for the loss of six wickets on a benign Grace Road strip. However, a much more challenging surface at Bradford had the tourists reeling, as Appleyard and Wardle shared nine wickets, in dismissing Johnson's men for just 94 runs in less than 42 overs. While rain had made the Park Avenue track problematic, the degree of turn was not as savage as to account for Australia's hapless performance. The 'phoney' war was over.

Johnson's side had been selected with Tyson and Statham in mind. However, the English wickets were prepared to favour spin not speed. And after Bradford, it was clear that the Australians' mastery of top class slow bowling was highly suspect. More flat-track bullying took place at Trent Bridge, with McDonald scoring 195 and Burge 131, but Australia was then humiliated at the Oval, losing heavily to the county champions. Jim Laker and Tony Lock took 19 Australian wickets between them, with Laker bagging all ten in their first innings. It was the first time, since 1912, that an Australian touring side had been beaten by an English county team.

The Australian pressmen became incensed at Johnson's captaincy. They were dumbfounded at his insistence at bowling himself for 60 overs, while Lindwall, and his new-ball partner, Crawford, were allowed to graze for hours on end in the outfield. While Surridge armed Laker and Lock with a clutch of close catchers placed at whispering distance from the batsman, Johnson packed the covers and picketed the boundary ropes. Certainly, Peter May benefited more from this dress rehearsal than his opposite number.

The state of health and fitness of the Australian squad was an even greater worry. Ian Craig was admitted to hospital with abdominal pain, Burke aggravated an old leg injury, Maddocks damaged a thumb, Lindwall sustained a groin strain, Archer tore his back muscles and McDonald strained his thigh. On the plus side, Harvey found form, smiting a brilliant double century against a strong MCC XI at Lord's. Rutherford also did well, notching his best score of the tour before being dismissed, two runs short of a ton, by England hopeful Alan Moss. MCC's selectors looked once again at Worcestershire opener Peter Richardson. They learnt little, though, as a viciously lifting ball, from Archer, hit Richardson on the temple, forcing his dazed retirement.

The two county games which followed gave Johnson less joy, though. Davidson, in his faster guise, Lindwall, Archer and Crawford collectively demolished Lancashire for 108 on a quick strip at Old Trafford. But Statham returned the compliment. Had he been supported by a partner of similar pace, Australia might have struggled to achieve parity. As it was, they managed to establish a lead of just over 50 runs, but with the pitch easing and the light fading, Wharton's second innings century ensured that Lancashire earned a deserved draw.

At Hove, Sussex became the third county side to achieve a first innings lead over the tourists. Despite his limited match practice, the Rev. David Sheppard made 97 runs in one of his rare outings for the county. Almost inevitably, wistful thoughts turned to his inclusion in the Test side. With rain wiping out any chance of a result, Australia was left to reflect upon their unprepossessing start. In ten warm-up games they had managed only two victories, both against varsity teams, and had demonstrated their vulnerability against spin bowling.

The first Test match at Nottingham was also disturbed by bad weather. An equivalent of two days' play was lost to rain. Not only was the weather disappointing, so were the number of injuries sustained by either side. Before the match started, England had to dispense with three main strike bowlers – Tyson, Trueman and Statham.

Australia fared worse, though, after Lindwall and Davidson sustained injuries during the first day's play. Lindwall was incapacitated by a recurrence of his groin problem while Davidson's ankle folded beneath him as he came in to bowl, chipping a bone and sustaining ligament damage. The England team was deprived of their replacement fast bowler Alan Moss, too, after he had slipped badly on the wet Trent Bridge outfield.

Without Lindwall and Davidson at his disposal, Johnson was forced onto the defensive and, while May was in a stronger position to achieve victory, there was insufficient time and devilry in the pitch for Laker and Lock to break through twice. Although Australia was briefly in peril of losing on the final day, when Laker and Lock dismissed McDonald, Harvey and Miller with only 41 on the board, birthday boy Jimmy Burke and Peter Burge applied themselves splendidly to bat out time.

The match was a personal triumph for debutant opener Peter Richardson who made two impressive scores of 81 and 73, suggesting that he had solved one of the vexed opening conundrums. He had curbed his tendency to 'fish' outside the off stump, scoring well off his legs and square, through point. However, he should have been run out for four in the first innings, after a calamitous mix-up with Cowdrey, and caught for nought in his second innings when Burge put him down at short leg off an involuntary leg-glance.

His opening partner Cowdrey had played imposingly also, in his unaccustomed position, scoring 25 and 81 with a profusion of stately off-drives. In England's second innings, Cowdrey put on 151 runs with Richardson for the first wicket. It had been England's best opening partnership against Australia since Hutton and Washbrook had scored 168 runs together at Leeds in 1948.

Apart from May, the remaining England batsmen exhibited all-too-familiar weaknesses. In their first innings, England subsided from 180-2 to 214-8 before May declared three runs later. However, had it not been for Harvey, who scored 64, and Archer (33), the Australians might have followed on. Hampered by a rain-affected surface, Johnson's side totalled only 148 runs in reply. In 76 exacting overs of spin and cut, Laker, Lock and Appleyard took nine of the Australian first innings wickets, between them, for 136 runs. England no longer needed the 'Sultans of Swing' to leave their opponents in dire straits.

From Nottingham, Johnson's team moved south to Northampton, and promptly found themselves in a pickle. On an easy-paced County Ground pitch, Dennis Brookes hammered an Australian attack, comprising Archer, Crawford, Benaud and Wilson, in scoring a sublime century (144). Aided and abetted by Livingston (85) and Barrick (37), Brookes took Northants to 339-3, before declaring. Harry Kelleher then tore a hole in the tourists' top order, removing McDonald, Rutherford and Craig to leave the Australians stumbling at 17-3.

Their first innings recovery, begun by Mackay and Burke, was eventually completed by Miller and Archer. However, there was still time for a few palpitations, on the final day, with Australia closing on 98-6 in chasing 197 runs for victory. Arthur Morris was so affronted by this feeble performance that he declared Johnson's men to be no better than those of Kent who were currently at the bottom of the County Championship. As if to put Morris's claim to the test, the Australian party moved on to Canterbury. Here, Craig and Rutherford failed once more, but the Australians had the better of the game until rain and a determined Kent rearguard frustrated Johnson's hopes of victory.

With the tourists performing so ineffectually, it was unsurprising that England was backed heavily to win the second Test at Lord's. The injured pair Lindwall and Davidson were replaced by Crawford and Mackay. Mackay deserved his first cap for he had batted with surprising fluency at Canterbury, demonstrating a confident, nudging acquisitiveness instead of his characteristic crab-like stolidity.

As for England, Statham and Trueman were recalled, in place of Moss and Appleyard, while Wardle replaced Lock, which seemed surprising since the Surrey bowler had performed well at Nottingham. It was academic, anyway, as just before the game Lock was rushed into hospital with suspected appendicitis. As expected, May was confirmed as England's captain for the remainder of the series.

Ian Johnson's luck improved when he won the toss, and chose to bat on a wicket rendered placid by the heavy volume of recent rain. Also, due to their limited match practice, neither Statham nor Trueman hit top form during the Australian first innings. Statham had not been in the best of health either. He had been suffering with an infected tooth until "Gubby" Allen arranged for him to have the tooth extracted on the eve of the match.

Batting with estimable resolution and concentration, McDonald and Burke took advantage of the conditions, below par bowling, and poor catching, raising 137 runs for the first wicket. Although Bailey eventually removed McDonald for 78, and Harvey for nought, while Laker had Burke brilliantly stumped by Evans for 65, Australia had the better of a turgid first day's play. When bad light brought about a premature close, Australia was well-placed at 180-3.

On the following day, Statham and Trueman proved much more menacing. The wicket had quickened, thanks to overnight rain, and with a relatively new ball at their disposal, they were able to achieve greater lift and movement. Burge was given a torrid time, particularly by Statham who soon removed the burly Queenslander's middle stump via a faint inside edge (184-4). Not to be outdone, Trueman took out Miller's off stump with a very fast delivery that Miller played inside of (196-5).

With the Australian innings faltering, Mackay (38) and Archer (28) took root, refusing to touch anything outside the line of their stumps, and playing the straight balls very watchfully. By so doing, they managed to add 53 invaluable runs for the sixth wicket. Nevertheless, Johnson was disappointed not to score more than 285 runs, after his openers had made half of that total.

His mood was not improved when his opening bowler Pat Crawford pulled a thigh muscle after only five overs. If he was downhearted, though, Miller was not. Fired up through adversity, he exposed Richardson's residual vulnerability outside his off stump, having him caught by wicketkeeper Langley for nine. As proof of his serial frailty, Richardson exited in a similar way in each of his innings during this series. Then, Miller bowled Graveney with a ball that moved back up the hill, kept low and seemed to clip an inside edge (32-2). He nearly dismissed May first ball, too.

Setting aside the pain from his bothersome back, Miller bowled unchanged for two hours, serving up everything in his extensive repertoire, with no discernible change of action. Meanwhile, Cowdrey contently stroked the ball around with almost nonchalant ease. But he, too, departed before stumps, as a result of a stupendous catch by Benaud, at gully, from a flashing thick edge off Mackay's restraining medium pace (60-3). Watson arrived to help May take England to 74-3 at the close of play.

May began the third day confidently, taking ten runs off Miller's first two overs, with a straight drive for four the outstanding shot. Watson did not tarry long, though. Miller brought a ball down the hill which he edged onto his pads whereupon the ball flew in a gentle arc to Benaud in the gully (87-4). Bailey proved to be a more robust partner for May, though, seemingly oblivious of the gaggle of close catchers hemming him in. While May swung the bat with finesse and power, Bailey blocked. The strategy seemed to be working until May, on 63 runs, misread Benaud's top-spinner as a leg break, and was bowled (128-5).

Thereafter, the England batting collapsed as if hit by a wrecking ball. Miller, as head hunter, added a couple more scalps to his impressive haul – the obdurate Bailey (32) and Trueman (7). These spoils enabled him to wrap up the England innings for 171 runs, earning him the immaculate figures of 34.1 overs, nine maidens, 72 runs and five wickets.

England then fought back furiously after Burke and McDonald had put together a relatively untroubled partnership of 36. Performing a fair impersonation of Benaud, Cowdrey clung onto a scorching catch in the gully to dismiss McDonald off Bailey, while Bailey produced an equally spectacular diving catch at leg slip to dismiss Harvey, from a leg-glance-off Trueman (47-2). Suitably inspired, Trueman produced a magnificent spell of fast bowling to send back Burke (16), Burge (14) and Archer (1), leaving the Australians in a sorry state at 79-5.

Miller and Mackay partially repaired the damage, with a stand of 33 runs, before Trueman returned shortly before the close to induce Miller into playing at an out-swinger which found an edge, and was brilliantly caught by Evans diving in front of first slip (112-6). There was still time for Benaud to survive a ferocious appeal for a catch at the wicket, also off Trueman, before play closed with Australia 115-6 – 229 runs ahead.

When play started on day four, it was imperative that English bowlers wrapped up the Australian innings quickly if their side was to have any chance of victory. Benaud obliterated those hopes, though, with a combustible innings of incredible power and verve, smashing both Trueman and Statham to all points of the compass. Fifty runs were added in the first 40 minutes of play in a blizzard of boundaries. May seemed bewildered by the punishment, persevering rashly with his quicker bowlers rather than risk his spinners.

By lunch, the Australians had progressed to 221-6 with Benaud on 90 and Mackay on 26. Already the game seemed well out of England's reach. However, if anyone thought that Benaud would play carefully for his century, they were wrong as he continued to smite mightily. It was a rash policy, for on 97 he skied a catch to Evans, having vainly tried to hook Trueman to the square leg boundary. Benaud left the field to rapturous applause. He had provided uncommon entertainment.

The Australians were dismissed shortly afterwards for 257, with Trueman easily the pick of the England bowlers, having taken five wickets for 90. This left England 372 runs to chase for victory. There was little chance that a fallible England batting order, with its long tail, would achieve this target even with the Australians having a bowler short.

Richardson began edgily, playing and missing outside his off stump. Although Craig dropped him off Miller, Richardson's reprieve was brief. Archer induced another snick and Langley grasped the chance (35-1). Graveney began his innings looking ill-at-ease, but managed to keep Cowdrey company for 35 largely unproductive overs – 18 of which were maidens. Then Miller returned to bowl around the wicket. Unable to counter the shift in direction, Graveney edged a ball moving across him to Langley (59-2). By stumps England was 72-2.

On the final day, Cowdrey and Watson began as if only intent upon survival. It seemed like a reprise of 1953. Cowdrey employed pad play to try to blunt the threat from Johnson and Benaud who were producing sharp turn at times. Johnson reacted by placing his close catchers suicidally close to him, hoping to snaffle a bat-pad chance. As hard as he tried, Watson could not repeat his heroic performance of three years before. With the siege-like pressure mounting, he unaccountably hit across a Miller yorker, and was bowled for 21 (89-3).

Worse was to follow. Cowdrey was made restive by Johnson's crowding tactics. Burge, perched right under his nose, was clearly a distraction. However, the umpires saw no reason to intervene. It was a question of who would crack first. Having become completely becalmed by Benaud's persistent leg-stump line of attack, Cowdrey was fooled by a top-spinner that hurried through, trapping him lbw (91-4). Thereafter, May and Bailey added 51 carefully-gathered runs before Archer had Bailey caught at backward short leg (142-5).

Miller then produced two vicious, leaping deliveries which Evans and

May could only edge to Langley, while Wardle was utterly confounded by Miller's off-cutter that jagged back, and hit his middle and leg stumps. Fifty minutes after lunch it was all over. England had been beaten by 185 runs. Miller had taken a further five wickets, giving him match figures of ten for 152 off 70.1 overs. As far as swansongs go, this one was Zeus-like. Strolling casually towards the Lord's pavilion, Miller suddenly reached into umpire Lee's coat pocket, extracted the bails, and tossed them breezily into the crowd. The man had so much style.

Speaking about Miller's performance on BBC *Test Match Special*, 30 years later, Freddie Trueman said: "Keith Miller was a magnificent cricketer. As a bowler he was an enigma. You never knew what the bloke would do. He'd run up and bowl quick – and I mean quick – then he'd bowl a googly, then an off-cutter, then a slower ball, then a bouncer...and they were all difficult to spot. During a game against MCC, I once saw him bowl David Sheppard with a googly using the new ball! His attitude was that he played to win, but if they lost, they lost. He would never moan or whinge about it. He'd try to knock your block off on the field, but, afterwards, in the bar, he'd be the first to buy you a drink."

Lifted by this comprehensive victory, Australia upped their game in the ensuing county fixtures. At Bristol, Gloucestershire was thrashed by an innings, inside two days, with the 'forgotten' Australian left-arm spinner Jack Wilson picking up career-best figures of 12 for 61. The Australians also showed much greater resilience in their second fixture with Yorkshire, and were clearly the moral victors in their other drawn games at Taunton and Southampton.

Consequently, Johnson's men approached the Leeds Test with confidence. The Australian press was won over, switching their line of attack to the stumbling Englishmen. The Australian team might have been the weakest seen in Britain since Edwardian times, but they were beating England. Besides, Lindwall, the nemesis of English batsmen, was back in the fold having recovered from a groin strain. He replaced Pat Crawford.

Maddocks also took over from Langley whose thumb was still painful. The only bad news for Australia was that Miller was not fit to bowl on account of a painful knee. He had first experienced a problem during the Sussex game, and his marathon shift at Lord's hadn't helped.

The Australians were confident about playing on firm, true surfaces. These were the conditions with which they were familiar. They had shown in the West Indies how formidable their batting could be on such tracks, particularly where there was little deviation. However, they were unused to, and distrustful of, playing on the tricky uncovered pitches in England.

Their hapless performances against spin on the turning, rain-affected wickets at Bradford and the Oval had exposed their almost pathological nervousness.

As yet, England had not produced a Test wicket on which May's spinners could really exploit the Australians' weakness. At Nottingham, it was only in the first innings that Laker and Lock had the conditions to their liking. And, as well as Laker bowled at Lord's, it was not until the final day that the ball turned with any great menace. By that time, of course, Australia had enough runs on the board to call the shots, and it was the English batsmen who had their backs to the wall, prodding tentatively at Johnson and Benaud.

However, if the England players were to exploit Australian vulnerability on tricky surfaces they had to bat better. Hutton's departure had left a yawning gap. His assured ability to score prolifically on poor surfaces often held a suspect batting order together. May and Cowdrey seemed capable of stepping into that breach, but they were still developing their craft. They had yet to occupy the crease for the long hours that Hutton managed, or compile the big hundreds that he produced. Bailey had something of Hutton's resilience, but not his weight of runs.

The chairman of the selectors, "Gubby" Allen, then had a brainwave – if England could no longer call upon Hutton, what about turning to Cyril Washbrook, his preferred opening partner? Although Washbrook was then 41 years old, Allen's notion was not as hare-brained as it might have seemed. Admittedly, Washbrook had not played Test cricket for five years – another unaccountable omission given his Test average score of more than 40 – but, he had kept his eye in, continuing to rack up the runs for Lancashire, his county side. Besides, Allen might have recalled that Hutton had pressed strongly for Washbrook's recall three years before. Belatedly, MCC's selectors realised that Hutton was probably right. After all, he had seen at the closest quarters how well Washbrook could play.

Whatever inspired his recall, Washbrook was back. At Headingley, he replaced the gifted, elegant, but frustratingly inconsistent Tom Graveney. Peter May was less convinced of the wisdom of the move, remarking to Allen: "Surely the position is not as bad as all that." Behind May there was a chorus of 'gob-smacked' pressmen. Frank Rostron of the *Daily Express* wrote: "Dear Cyril. No, you're kidding. I don't believe it. Are you doing a leg pull?"

Rostron pointed out that, as a Test selector, his presence in the side might undermine May's captaincy. He had expressed the same concern when Freddie Brown was recalled at Lord's in 1953. Brian Chapman of the *Daily Mirror* exclaimed: "What a crazy fashion to encourage all the splendid young talent there is in our cricket!" However, Jim Swanton of the *Daily Telegraph* and Crawford White of the *News Chronicle* kept their own counsel, wisely awaiting the outcome of this Lazarus-like selection.

Watson was axed, too. His place was taken by Essex batsman Doug Insole, who had played twice before for England, against the West Indies in 1950 and against the South Africans in 1955, without startling success. However, Insole had enjoyed a very productive summer, attaining an average of almost 45 runs per innings for his county side. Johnny Wardle, who had an undistinguished game at Lord's, was replaced by Sussex's all-rounder Alan Oakman.

Oakman had scored 80 runs for MCC against Johnson's Australians at Lord's in May. He had also performed well for his county, scoring four centuries, and taking vital wickets with his off-breaks. Besides, Oakman was an expert close catcher. Finally, Lock was recalled in place of Statham whose Lord's form had been below par. There was less need of three seamers because the Headingley wicket was expected to turn.

The revised England team comprised seven recognised batsmen plus a Test centurion, Evans, batting at eight. On paper, at least, this was the strongest batting side chosen since the decisive final Test against South Africa in the previous year. The strategy relied heavily upon May winning the toss and batting first. This would probably consign the Australians to batting on a crumbling wicket in the final innings.

The pressure placed upon Peter May must have been enormous. The pressure on "Gubby" Allen must have been no less, though. England had played poorly at Lord's, and was in imminent danger of losing the Ashes. And now he had a controversial selection to defend. Perhaps that is why he singled out Freddie Trueman for some impromptu coaching.

Allen seemed so concerned that England should not haemorrhage runs, as they had done at Lord's, that he made Trueman practice pitching the ball on a good length, laying down his own handkerchief on the ground to guide his aim! Needless to say Trueman was not amused. After all, he had been England's best bowler at Lord's. He found this public examination utterly humiliating. But rather than sound off at the chairman of selectors, in front of the large crowd that had gathered at the Headingley nets, he diplomatically left it to his mentor, Bill Bowes, to condemn Allen's actions in newsprint. Trueman remarked in a later radio interview that he felt that members of the "cricket establishment" had been keen to put him down, citing several professional colleagues who had felt similarly.

Although May won this important toss, his sense of relief had almost evaporated after only 70 minutes of play. During this period, Ron Archer had dismissed Cowdrey, Richardson and debutant Oakman for only 17 runs. With his smooth, high, relaxed action Archer was able to move the ball disconcertingly late in the air and off the pitch. Cowdrey and Richardson were both caught by Maddocks off deliveries which they had to play, undone more by the quality of the bowling rather than any technical error. Oakman, on the other hand, looked out of his depth, vainly thrusting out against Lindwall and Archer, and exhibiting little conviction in his footwork or shot selection. Archer ended his torrid 20-minute stay with a ball that swung into him, beating his back foot stroke, and bowling him.

Washbrook strode commandingly to the wicket, and proceeded to play with reassuring confidence. His late cut for four off Archer oozed class, but he was fortunate to survive an lbw shout by the same bowler as he shuffled across his stumps. The crowd held their breath, but umpire Buller shook his head and Washbrook proceeded with his composed restorative work. Lindwall posted Burge at long leg for him.

Perhaps he recalled Washbrook's fatal predilection for the hook in former days, but having laid the trap, Lindwall surprisingly failed to provide the bait, preferring to bowl to a fuller length. Johnson introduced Benaud into the attack, but apart from one delivery, which fizzed past the edge of Washbrook's bat, there were no further alarms. With lunch approaching, May began to demonstrate greater fluency, cutting and driving Benaud with glorious timing and power. England lunched in a little more comfort at 54-3.

With Miller indisposed, Johnson felt compelled to retain Archer in the attack for longer than he would have wished. Lindwall had been only briefly threatening, Mackay had been easily collared, and Benaud was largely innocuous. Consequently, Archer was asked to bowl 13 overs on the stretch, in which he took three wickets for 13 runs. It had been a magnificent effort, but the lad had almost shot his bolt in that very first session.

Not that this deterred Johnson as he turned once again to Archer at the resumption of play after lunch, but to no avail. With May and Washbrook playing with increasing certainty, the Headingley crowd was treated to a torrent of forceful shots that took the England total to 140-3 at tea. May and Washbrook had 65 runs each. Lindwall had never been treated so disdainfully in a home Ashes series.

The new ball came and went, but still the two English batsmen remained in command. May stormed to his hundred with a sequence of immaculate shots, the most powerful of which resounded like the crack of a gun. There was little doubt that this was his finest innings for England, thus far. However, just before the close Johnson fed May a lollipop, a high full toss outside his leg stump. The ball should have been smashed out of sight, but May only succeeded in swatting it to Lindwall at fine leg, who took an excellent catch. May and Washbrook had added 187 runs for the fourth wicket, turning the game around. But as brilliant and essential as his knock had been, May had yet to match Hutton's knack of turning hundreds into huge ones. At stumps, the England score stood at 204-4.

The next day started disappointingly. Washbrook missed his richly-deserved century by two runs, and, following his departure, England collapsed abjectly, despite bright knocks from Evans (40) and Lock (21), and a typically resolute one from Bailey (33 not out). England closed their innings on 325 – considerably more than May might have expected, after that traumatic start, but much less than he hoped for, just before holing out to Johnson.

During the latter stages of England's innings, *The Times* cricket correspondent had his binoculars trained on the wicket. The Australians were watching with growing consternation, too, as puffs of dust were flying up each time the ball pitched. More in hope than expectation, Johnson looked to the roller to ease their worries.

At 3.30pm on the second day, McDonald and Burke began the Australian reply. Pumped up by his home crowd, and incensed by Allen's treatment, Trueman worked up a ferocious pace. In his first over McDonald could not extract his bat from an express delivery that left him and Evans threw up the ball in exultation (2-1). Although he knew that his spinners would cause the greater problems, May allowed Trueman and Bailey half an hour with the new ball. But just before tea, Laker was asked to accompany Trueman, and soon after, Laker and Lock were operating in tandem. The Australians were soon in deep trouble.

In one hour after tea, the Aussies had crumpled from 38-1 to 69-6. A cold wind blew across Headingley – 'Ashes to Ashes, dust to dust...' it seemed to whisper. The Australians played Laker and Lock with acute apprehension as if each ball would bring about their execution. Harvey was caught, at leg-slip, as he so often was, by Trueman (40-2). Burge played imprudently back to Laker and was caught in front of his stumps by the abruptness of the turn (59-3). Burke was despatched in an identical fashion except the bowler was Lock (59-4).

After a wretched stay, Mackay was finally seen off by Laker, snaffled off bat and pad by Bailey (63-5). Lastly, Laker breached Archer's hesitant defence to bowl him (69-6). Miller and Benaud then took Australia through the encircling gloom to stumps, at 81-6. As Keith Miller left the field a young female admirer told him she'd be coming to watch him bat on the following day. Miller warned her: "You better come early."

Much to May's horror, heavy rain began to fall at 7pm on that Friday evening, not relenting until the Sunday night. Undaunted, the Leeds ground staff worked industriously to mop up, but play could not resume until 12.45pm on Monday, the fourth day. It also became quickly apparent to Jim Laker that, because of the weight of rain, the wicket had lost its bite, and was sluggish and unresponsive to his spin.

However, suspecting that their reprieve might only be temporary, Benaud began by striking the ball boldly, aiming to save the follow-on – 95 runs away – while the conditions remained in favour of the batsmen. The strategy seemed to be working well as he and Miller put on 73 runs for the seventh wicket. Miller stretched well forward, sweeping emphatically and productively. Laker responded by bowling round the wicket looking for an lbw dismissal, should Miller fail to connect with his expansive swishes. Miller remained unconcerned, once picking up a ball from Laker off his legs and casually depositing it into the crowd.

With bright sun now beaming on the verdant Headingley outfield, May turned to Bailey, but there was nothing in this pudding-like surface for him to exploit. So May reverted to Laker, switching him to the Kirkstall Lane end, in the hope that the prevailing breeze would assist his off breaks to drift towards the waiting leg-trap. With the follow-on target narrowing, May despatched short leg Oakman to the midwicket boundary to protect England's dwindling assets. May was then mortified to drop Benaud's mistimed pull off Laker. The match was slipping from his grasp. Emboldened by the let-off, Benaud chanced his arm once too often, and Oakman gathered his slog-sweep on the square-leg boundary (142-7).

With Maddocks' arrival, May went back on to the attack with close catchers crowded around the bat. It was sheer kidology, but it was sufficient to fool the untutored wicketkeeper. Looking for gremlins that weren't there, Maddocks played an indeterminate shot to the first ball he received from Lock, and prodded a catch to Trueman in the gully (143-8).

Reading the runes with alarm, Miller tried to slog Australia to safety. His massive lofted drive failed to connect, though, whereas Laker's off break did, knocking back Miller's off stump (143-9). Johnson then followed Miller's lead, slamming a ball from Lock to Richardson at deep mid-off (143 all out), prompting an ecstatic war dance from the bowler. This had been suicidal batting. Australia had required only 33 more runs to save the follow-on, and probably the match, and yet four wickets had been frittered away for a single run.

Unhesitatingly, May asked Australia to bat again. Perhaps imprudently, Johnson ordered the heavy roller, risking that the excess moisture might be brought to the surface thereby assisting the English bowlers more. As if to confirm his error, Trueman quickly produced a full-pitched delivery that moved into McDonald and hit his middle stump (10-1). However, Harvey, playing attractively in partnership with the adhesive Burke, then mounted a promising recovery. This seemed to be prospering before Burke uncharacteristically over-reached himself, and was bowled, while skipping down the wicket to Laker (45-2). This left Harvey and Miller to take Australia to the close at 93-2 – still 89 runs in arrears.

Tuesday 17th July dawned dank and gloomy. Much to May's alarm there were reports of thunderstorms in the vicinity. It was a case of *Darkness at Noon* as the scoreboard lights shone with grotesque brilliance. In tune with the glowering atmosphere, the wicket had a mucky brown appearance. More importantly, its menace had returned. From the first overs of play, both Laker and Lock managed to extract vicious turn and lift. Only with immaculate skill did Harvey and Miller survive.

Those playing and those watching constantly switched their gaze from the compelling action to the darkening skies. Everyone knew that another downpour would probably obliterate England's chances. May needed quick wickets. He didn't get them, though, as Miller and Harvey blunted the turning ball for 50 minutes. Harvey took his score to 50. He had made much bigger scores, but probably hadn't played a better innings.

Then Laker struck. His off break turned and spat. Playing back, the ball glanced off Miller's bat, flicked his pad and was clutched gleefully by Trueman in the leg-trap (108-3). Burge also played back mistakenly to Laker except that his bat did not intrude, leaving him plumb lbw (120-4). Benaud did not remain long, either, before being bowled by another malevolent off break from Laker (128-5).

Johnson came, saw and complained, but after careful examination of the murky light the umpires rejected his appeal against the light. Laker punished the Aussie skipper's presumption, despatching him with a ball that clipped the bottom edge of his bat, deflected off his boot, and flew to Oakman at silly mid-on (136-6). Before lunch could be taken the game was almost over. Lock hurled himself forward to dismiss Harvey, caught and bowled (138-7), and Archer was expertly pouched in the covers by Washbrook (140-8).

Lunchtime was torture for May. The rumblings of an approaching thunderstorm were all too audible. So, it was with huge relief that Maddocks and Mackay were dismissed quickly by Lock and Laker at the resumption of play without any addition to the score. England had won by an innings and 42 runs. May was off the hook, and he duly expressed his gratitude to "Gubby" Allen for picking Cyril Washbrook.

While the English were celebrating, the Australian public were grumbling, believing that the Headingley pitch had been 'doctored' to play to Laker's and Lock's strengths. The Pakistani Test captain, Abdul Hafeez Kardar agreed, but Bradman did not object, and neither did Arthur Morris. In Morris's Test journal *Operation Ashes* he confined himself to the observation that the English pitches were "very different" from those played on in 1948 and 1953. He was correct. By the mid-1950s county strips tended to favour the spinner. Tyson, who wore himself out on Northampton's featherbed, said so in his autobiography *A Typhoon Called Tyson*. Even average county slow bowlers enjoyed rich pickings.

If the state of the Leeds wicket aroused the Australians' concerns, the Manchester surface caused outright anger. According to author Alan Hill, the Old Trafford groundsman, Bert Flack, had been asked to remove all the remaining grass from the Test pitch. Flack explained to Hill that Tommy Burrows, the Lancashire Grounds Committee chairman, had asked him to do this although Flack believed that it was at "Gubby" Allen's behest.

Although Flack told Burrows that the match might not last three days if the grass was removed he did as he was told, albeit with strong misgivings. However, in his journal *Operation Ashes* Arthur Morris said that Bert Flack gave him a different account. Of course, Flack might have been more guarded in speaking with the Australian Morris, particularly while the game was being played, lest he became implicated in a wicket doctoring scandal.

Morris recorded Bert Flack as telling him: "I have made a mistake. I attempted to make a fast wicket, but it has turned out to be easy paced. The suggestion that I made the pitch under instruction is nonsense; it has never been hosed and the only time it was rolled was when there was rain. It hasn't got any pace because the moisture is too near the surface. But everyone makes mistakes...I don't think it will break until Saturday."

Keith Miller's biographer, Mihir Bose, discussed the alleged incident with Allen over 20 years later. In line with Flack's earlier account to

Morris, Allen denied giving any wicket 'doctoring' instruction, stating: "The Manchester wicket was definitely not cooked. [Cyril Washbrook told us] that it was going to be the best batting wicket of the series...But when I saw the wicket, it looked funny...the top had gone...[Washbrook] was taken aback. [He remarked] 'This wicket has completely changed character.'

"The chairman of the Grounds Committee said: 'Do you want some more grass cut off?' I said, 'It wouldn't break my heart, but ask the groundsman, not me. See rule seven.' This part of the story got around and everybody, particularly the Australians, said Allen was behind it. Actually what happened was that the groundsman put the marl on top only ten days before the match – far too late. When he started to water it a member objected and the top layer was not properly bound."

Certainly Allen's comment "it wouldn't break my heart" seems open to misinterpretation although the truth seems as opaque as in the alleged Melbourne watering incident. But whereas the changed character of the MCG pitch did not disadvantage either side, the Manchester strip proved highly advantageous to England. It was not a level playing field.

Seven years later, Alan Davidson wrote in his autobiography *Fifteen Paces*: "Where [the Test pitches] three years earlier had played soundly and often with pace, in 1956 they were shaven, bare and dusty...The very first delivery that Lindwall sent down in the Manchester Test brought up a puff of dust, the ball bouncing twice to the wicketkeeper. The pitch was a dull red strip in a sea of emerald...There could be no doubt that these wickets were specially doctored to suit Laker and Lock."

As Mihir Bose recalled in his book *Keith Miller: A Cricketing Biography*: "[The Old Trafford wicket] was bare of grass and at tea on the first day when the wicket was swept a dust cloud erupted...Johnson tried to rally his men: we can fight back, we need guts, we can save this match. Miller detached himself from the race form he was studying and said: 'Bet you 6/4 we can't.'"

Although the Australian press had campaigned for Miller to replace Johnson as captain, Miller refused to lead a *coup d'etat*. However, his loyalty did not stretch to endorsing Johnson's naive optimism. Most of the Australian team seemed convinced of the inevitability of defeat even before a ball was bowled.

With the Australian pace attack neutralised by the sluggishness of the wicket, the England batsmen made hay, racking up 459 runs in only 491 minutes – an almost unseemly rate of progress for 1950s Test cricket. It was England's highest innings total in an Ashes contest since 1948.

Cowdrey (80) and Richardson (104) put on 174 runs for the first wicket in little over three hours.

Then, yet another selector hunch came off as David Sheppard, on a brief sabbatical from the Anglican Church, scored a fine century (113), having played only four preparatory innings for his county, Sussex. Because of the benign batting conditions, Sheppard was spared any discomfort against extreme pace, but this was still a remarkable performance from someone so short of match practice. MCC's members must have been hugging themselves at England's success, particularly with amateurs filling the first five batting slots, albeit all of them performed pitch-perfect impersonations of professionals.

Not even the inevitable intrusion of Manchester rain could save the Australians as they succumbed limply to Jim Laker's spin and the ravenous leg-trap. It is highly unlikely that Laker's record match haul of 19 wickets will ever be trumped in any form of first-class cricket, let alone a Test match. Alan Davidson wrote in his autobiography *Fifteen Paces*: "In the end we had been well and truly 'psyched'. Laker only had to take the ball, and casually step out his short run to send a shiver of apprehension through our ranks.

"His accuracy was uncanny, the ball landing with pinpoint precision on the spot, sometimes breaking sharply towards the cordon of leg-slip sharks and sometimes fizzing straight through with no spin at all...[He only bowled two bad balls] Both were full tosses. Miller was missed off the first, Harvey caught off the second!"

According to Tony Lock's biographer, Alan Hill: "Laker was convinced that the ball with which he dismissed Neil Harvey, in Australia's first innings, was the crucial breakthrough. It ensured that England would go on to retain the Ashes. [Laker said] 'Neil was the finest left-hander I ever bowled against and in our many challenging duels in the past honours had gone very much his way. But, as luck would have it this time, I managed to bowl him a beauty first ball. From around the wicket I held it back sufficiently for the ball to drift in and pitch around the leg and middle stumps. It turned just enough to clip his off stump.'"

Richie Benaud commented to Hill: "There is no doubt that Lock bowled magnificently from a technical point of view in Australia's second innings. We couldn't lay a bat on him because he was pitching outside the right-hander's leg stump and the ball occasionally spun straight to slip."

Thirty years later, in a BBC radio interview, Trevor Bailey added: "The most remarkable thing was not that Laker took 19 wickets, but that Lock only took one. And the reason, of course, was temperament. The more wickets Laker took, the more Lock tried and tried, and the faster and faster he bowled. Meanwhile, Jim just carried on putting the ball on the spot and letting the pitch do the work...If Johnny Wardle had been at the other end there is no way that Laker would have taken 19 wickets...But an English county side on that pitch would have played better than the Australians."

Laker seemed to be so nonchalant about his amazing feat. After he took his final wicket he swung around, grabbed his sweater from the umpire, and sauntered off the field as if he was completing a net session. In the dressing room he was content to sit quietly in his chosen corner, taking only a sip of champagne, before changing and driving home.

En route to London he stopped at a pub. A crowd had gathered around the television which was showing highlights of his immense achievement. He was the talk of the nation, but no one recognised him as he stood at the bar, meditatively drinking his beer. How different was the life of a 1950s sports star before the corrosive blight of 'the celebrity' took hold.

Colin McDonald, the only defiant Australian batsman at Old Trafford, was quick to express his displeasure with the pitch. "England cheated," he exclaimed, maintaining that the pitch had been prepared specifically to suit their purpose. The appropriately-named Flack quipped, "Thank God Nasser has taken over the Suez Canal otherwise I'd be plastered over every front page like Marilyn Monroe."

At a rain-ravaged Oval, there was just enough time for Denis Compton to give the English public a final glimpse of his brilliance, with a sparkling innings of 94 runs, and for Laker and Lock to humiliate the tourists, yet again, with their black arts. The 12 hours lost to rain, though, meant that Australia was able to escape with a draw, having been reduced to 27-5 in their second innings, chasing a victory target of 228 runs.

In *Operation Ashes* Arthur Morris concluded: "James Laker was to Australia what the sunken road was to Napoleon at Waterloo. The Australians had plotted and planned to counteract a fast attack envisaged by Tyson and Statham. Yet Tyson did not appear in any of the first four Tests, by which time the blueprint for success had been torn to shreds; Statham bowled at Lord's with little result while the Manchester wicket of such blood-raising controversy never lent itself to speed.

"In the West Indian tour of 1955, Ian Johnson had explained, to interested technicians in the art of batting, that Australian blades had never been held so straight, and that the cross bat, which caused such a profitable harvest to Tyson, was a dreadful stroke of the past. The whole pattern for regaining the Ashes was based on the ability to cope with

Tyson and Statham. The name Laker did not enter the operation."

The 1956 Ashes victory was also a triumph for the England selectors. Although maligned, in retrospect, for their myopic and nepotistic selections during these immediate post-war years, in that drab, dank summer of 1956 their perspicacity was irrefutable as each one of their gambles came off spectacularly. Washbrook, Sheppard and even Compton, who had his right kneecap removed, made cheering returns from the cold, helping ensure England's third consecutive Ashes victory.

However, the euphoric national mood, which the Ashes victory fed, was soon punctured by the humiliation of Suez. Britain's lofty position in the post-war world order had become diminished greatly. What happened subsequently, on the football fields of Sweden and the cricket pitches of Australia, gave symbolic emphasis to its decline. War had indeed withered this once great imperial power. Ironically, in October 1956, just as the Suez crisis was intensifying, the Queen was invited to attend a Royal Premiere screening of the film *The Battle of the River Plate* – yet another wartime tale of stoical British heroism in the face of unappealing odds.

The new Elizabethan age myth, which the film purported to champion, was about to be shattered. With the United States anxious about growing Soviet influence in Egypt, and the value of sterling plummeting, the Americans were able to call, or more pertinently, stop the shots.

Their support of Britain's bid for further International Monetary Fund assistance was made conditional upon its prior military withdrawal from Egypt. The campaign ended less like the snarl of the bulldog, and more like a yap of a poodle.

In sympathy with its diminished status, over the next eight years the once expansive British Empire was dismantled with almost indecent haste. *Look Back in Anger* playwright John Osborne referred to this political shrinkage in his subsequent play *The Entertainer*. The play charts the antics of a washed-up variety entertainer, Archie Rice, whose desperate theatrical routines and seedy philandering not only reflect the fading British music hall tradition, but also, by symbolic inference, the country's waning global status. Off-stage, Archie's son loses his life in a forlorn military action, brought about by Prime Minister Anthony Eden's reckless pursuit of lost national prestige.

There was nothing mythical about British wartime bravery, particularly when the UK found itself almost alone in defying Nazi aggression in 1940. However, the 'new Elizabethan' makeover, which presented the British as essentially glorious, and always honourable in combat, was exposed as a hollow sham by Anthony Eden's military intervention in Suez. In

Laurence Olivier's patriotic, D-Day-inspired rendition of Shakespeare's *Henry V,* the King's blood-curdling threat, to the besieged inhabitants of Harfleur, is largely edited out, as if to signify the earnestness of the British Army's noble intentions as an invading and occupying force in 1944.

However, there could be no air-brushing out of Eden's brutal foray into Egypt in 1956, despite the preposterous propaganda put out by Pathe News that this was a "peace-keeping" duty. Before Suez, it would have been unthinkable for the UK's cinematic industry to produce a film such as *Yesterday's Enemy*. In this controversial 1959 drama, a ruthless British Army platoon commander ordered two innocent Burmese villagers to be shot, in order to coerce a confession of vital military intelligence from a suspected Japanese collaborator in their midst.

And yet this situation was probably much closer to the harsh reality of war than what was depicted in so many self-reverential British war films of the 1950s. Although Viscount Montgomery of Alamein remained a sturdy advocate of, what he believed to be, Britain's estimable moral reputation, at Suez, Britain was shown to be a very small island, shorn of virtue. As a result of its reckless, abhorrent action, Britain not only bade farewell to its status as a global power, it shattered any pretension it once had of higher integrity. In short, Britain could no longer claim to be a credible arbiter of what was, and what was not, cricket.

'THE DAY THE MUSIC DIED':
1957 – 1959

"I'm the last of the straight-arm bowlers."
Ray Lindwall, 1958/59.

"It's like standing in the middle of a darts match."
Jim Laker, Australia, 1958/59.

'THE TRIBE THAT LOST ITS HEAD'

'Singing the Blues'

If most members of the 1948/49 MCC party were unaware of apartheid's impact, eight years later Peter May's players had no such protection. Jim Laker wrote in his book *Over To Me*: "Before we left England, we were given the usual preliminary briefing by the president of MCC [Lord Cobham]. He reminded us of South Africa's problems, and told us that colour, as a topic of conversation, was strictly out. It was something never to be mentioned. He suggested that the safest thing we could talk about was the [recent] British Lions rugby tour...which had been a fabulous success. Partly on account of this tour, crowds throughout South Africa had a high opinion of British sportsmanship. Let it stay high [we were told].

"The colour problems of South Africa, even if you don't talk about them are not things which you can overlook completely. In some ways the South Africans, condemned for their approach to the situation by most of the civilised world, have got a complex about it. The atmosphere, to anyone with the least sensitivity, can often be most uncomfortable."

Colin Cowdrey added in his autobiography *M.C.C.*: "I would have to admit to my shame, that the word 'apartheid' did not have a prominent place in my vocabulary before my one and only tour to South Africa in 1956...[While on the boat to South Africa] a mysterious parcel was delivered containing a number of books and a message asking our manager Freddie Brown to give each player a copy...A few days later, just as mysteriously, our manager [was told] that we would be in trouble at Cape Town if we tried to get the book through customs...It was Father Trevor Huddleston's *Naught for Your Comfort*."

In *Naught for Your Comfort,* Huddleston, a novice in an Anglican religious order, provided a graphic and damning indictment of apartheid's cruelties, having spent much time assisting its victims and advocating their rights to the white authorities. Among his recollections was the ruthless eviction of black families from Sophiatown, which took place just before the South African cricket tour of England in 1955.

Trevor Bailey recalled, in a 1980s BBC radio interview, that the touring party was given an "intelligent, carefully researched and reasoned account of apartheid" by Professor Tomlinson. Bailey claimed that this helped him to make better sense of the make-up of South African society, and how apartheid had emerged. However, as much as Bailey intended to be open-minded on the subject, enjoy the spectacular South African scenery, and his hosts' warm hospitality, his attitude became progressively soured by the appalling injustices he experienced.

In his autobiography *Wickets, Catches and the Odd Run* he recalled that he had his first brush with the South African regime after he was told that the novel he was reading would be confiscated if he tried to bring it into the country. It was Nicholas Montserrat's 1955 best-seller, *The Tribe That Lost Its Head.* The story describes an escalating power struggle between white colonialists and the black indigenous people on a fictitious African island. Bailey rightly considered the threat of confiscation to be intolerable. He was then exposed to the injustices perpetrated by South African treason trials which, in his view, "came close to black farce, but not for those concerned".

He was also confronted with the plight of a black home care assistant, caught up in a civil protest against an apparent white abuse of power. He wrote in his autobiography: "The black community decided to boycott the buses in protest [against rising fares]...When I saw [an elderly home help] arrive exhausted, I naively enquired why she had not taken the bus. [She replied] 'If I had come by bus, they would have burned down my home the first time, and if I had done it again, they would have killed me.'" Bailey was horrified by her desperate situation.

Jim Laker and Alan Oakman were equally appalled by the callous attitude of a white South African policeman, who had attended a traffic accident, in which a black man had been run over by a car that Oakman was driving. Although the victim had a broken leg, and was clearly in great pain, the policeman bullied the black bystanders into confirming the victim was a drunkard, and, therefore, at fault for the accident, before calling for an ambulance. Although blameless, Oakman visited the man in hospital, giving him some money to help his family through his recovery period.

If it now seems inconceivable why MCC should not have condemned apartheid sooner, there seemed to be personal issues muddying the waters. In his article on the D'Oliveira affair, sports writer Rob Steen explained that MCC's president, Lord Cobham, had a South African mother, and substantial business interests in the Union, as had "Gubby" Allen. As for Peter May, while he opposed apartheid, he remained loyal to his white South African friends whom he considered to serve non-whites better than their critics recognised.

So, when Rev David Sheppard declared, in 1970: "I'm ashamed I was so late in coming to a realisation of South African evil," he offended May, his long-term friend, greatly. Sheppard had a point, though. By the time he had made his 'belated' confession, International Olympic Committee and FIFA bans had been imposed on South Africa for six years. Not that this impeded MCC who proceeded to tour South Africa in 1964, the very year in which the Olympic expulsion took place. A reciprocal South African tour of England then ensued in 1965, while the Australian cricket team toured South Africa in 1966/67 and 1969/70, whereupon all Test matches ceased to be played with the Republic until the 1990s.

Certainly, when Sir Donald Bradman made his blunt denunciation of the South African regime, in 1971, it was not before time. South African Prime Minister Vorster had expected Bradman to allow the planned tour of Australia to go ahead. However, Bradman asked him why black sportsmen were not allowed to play cricket. Vorster replied that blacks were intellectually inferior and had no finesse for the game.

Appalled by Vorster's ignorant and repugnant reply, Bradman asked if Vorster had heard of a man named Garry Sobers. Upon returning to Australia, Bradman released a one sentence statement: "We will not play them until they choose a team on a non-racist basis." Although Australia's record on racial integration in sport had much room for improvement, as had Britain's at that time, Nelson Mandela rightly applauded "The Don".

There was little likelihood of any leading British political or sporting figure making a similar stand during the 1950s. This nation's record on race relations had hardly been exemplary, anyway. As a further illustration of this, just over a year after this troubled tour of South Africa, race riots broke out in the poorer areas of Notting Hill and Nottingham. Here, racial tensions had been exacerbated by acute competition for housing and jobs, and complicated by sexual jealousies.

Colin McInnes' 1959 novel, *Absolute Beginners,* set during the Notting Hill riots, contains the observation: "I don't understand my country any more...The English race has spread itself all over the damn world...no one invited us...yet when a few hundred thousand come and settle among our fifty millions we just can't take it."

Presciently, Laker commented in *Over to Me*: "Given some decent coaching, I am certain the coloured communities of South Africa could raise a side good enough to play an extremely worthwhile game against a touring side. I think most English cricketers would welcome this idea; it would provide variety and the chance to do something positive for the game. But I can't see it happening. The South African Government's views on so revolutionary an idea as a cricket match between blacks and whites can be guessed. MCC, for their part, would never suggest such a thing, even if the idea appealed to them."

Cowdrey expressed similar regrets in his autobiography *M.C.C.* he wrote: "With priests I visited coloured townships outside both Johannesburg and Kimberley...We ran into a group of young Africans playing cricket. I asked the priest I was with if I should join the game. He said: 'They'd love it – but I think you better not.'"

Laker continued in *Over to Me*: "Certainly, as far as cricket is concerned, I believe South African racial policies have worked to the disadvantage of all. The South Africans have never seen Weekes, Worrell and Walcott, for example. No coloured side can visit the Union; nor can a South African side visit a coloured country...It doesn't end there. For the next tour to South Africa, in 1964/65, the chances must be on Raman Subba Row being in the form which demands selection. And yet I can't imagine Raman – Cambridge Blue, county captain, Test batsman – being picked. He is of Indian extraction; after a quiet word with MCC I imagine he would tactfully find himself unable to go for 'business reasons'."

Like other white South African Test players, Roy McLean and John Waite seemed not to support racial segregation in sport. They wanted to join Jim Swanton's international team on its Caribbean tour. In his book *Beyond a Boundary*, CLR James applauded the idea, but the West Indian Board of Control vetoed their inclusion, fearing the hostility of home crowds and press. They also refused Frank Worrell's attempt to take a black West Indian team on a tour of South Africa.

James rightly castigated the West Indian Board for their short-sightedness. While the presence of Waite and McLean in the West Indies would have represented a powerful refutation of apartheid, Worrell's proposed tour simply could not lose whether the South African government permitted it or not. If permitted, the calibre of black South African cricketers might have been showcased, exposing the irrationality of their exclusion from the national side. If refused, South Africa risked further reputation damage, and potentially adverse economic repercussions, too.

As for the Test series between South Africa and England in 1956/57, despite the absorbing fluctuations in fortunes, too much of the cricket played was calamitously dull. The series was brought to an ironic conclusion when England became hoist by their own petard, as they lost the deciding final Test on a 'beach' of a wicket.

Neither side batted well. England won the first Test at Johannesburg after Peter Richardson (117) spent almost nine hours over his century, which was then a new world record for the slowest Test ton. However, had it not been for his monumental effort, and Cowdrey's half-century (59), England would have been in a mess. Together, they contributed two-thirds of England's first innings total of 268 runs, putting together a 121-run partnership for the fourth wicket after Heine, Adcock and Goddard had disposed of new opener Bailey, Compton and May with only 48 scored.

Richardson rode his luck, though, as a fired-up Neil Adcock beat him four times in the first hour, but he survived grimly, renouncing anything directed wide of his stumps. In six hours of play on the first day, he crawled to 69 not out with England managing only 157 runs. With Goddard's negative leg-theory contributing to the funereal scoring rate this was bleak entertainment for the 24,621 Johannesburg crowd. But because the locals were so starved of Test cricket, 35,258 rolled up for the second day's play on Boxing Day, which concluded with Goddard and Keith helping South Africa to a position of strength at 91-1.

With Tyson confined to bed with tonsillitis England was reliant upon a three-man attack, but Statham, Bailey and Wardle reduced South Africa quickly to 141-7 before Tayfield, Heine and Adcock swung heartily to lift the hosts' first innings total to 215 all out.

Not that the 53-run deficit appeared significant, as Heine and Adcock subjected England to a torrid barrage of malevolent, rising deliveries. Richardson, Bailey and night watchman Wardle were shot out for just 37 runs. On the fourth day, Tayfield soon dismissed Compton (32) with a stunning catch off his own bowling. Compton had not been sure of the legitimacy of the catch, but walked once Tayfield insisted that he had grasped the ball cleanly.

May was once again dismissed cheaply, by Heine this time, with Endean taking a stupendous catch (14). Insole (29) clung on for a while, despite being discomfited by Heine's high bounce, but Cowdrey did not stay long, edging Adcock to gully (6). Although Evans slashed joyfully,

England was rolled over for only 150 runs on an apparently blameless surface. Their characteristic frailty was rendered insignificant, though, as Bailey and Statham tore a massive hole in the South African batting order. By the close, the home side had subsided abjectly to 40-7. England duly won by 131 runs on the final day.

England won the second Test emphatically, too. Cowdrey's fine century (101), plus contributions from Compton (58) and Evans (62), placed England in the box seat at 369 all out. Wardle then exploited the South Africans' inexperience in dealing with back-of-the-hand spinners. His 'Chinamen' spat and turned prodigiously on the firm, dry Cape Town wicket. Wardle accounted for 12 South African wickets at a cost of 89 runs as England romped to victory by 312 runs. Once again, the South Africans could muster no more than 72 runs in their second innings.

However, the third Test at Durban was a much closer affair. May won the toss for the third time in succession, and chose to bat. At lunch on the first day, things were looking pretty with England coasting along on 103-0. However, their advantage was then squandered by over-cautious batting. Tayfield was allowed to bowl 14 consecutive maiden overs which set a new Test record. In the three hours of play possible after lunch, England accumulated only 81 runs, losing four wickets. Helped by the pitch 'sweating' overnight, the South African pace men then hustled out four English batsmen on the following morning and May's side could only make a very disappointing total of 218 runs.

Despite more of Wardle's trickery, McLean and Goddard batted splendidly to take South Africa to 140-3 at the end of the second day. McLean went on to score a century (100), as South Africa established a 65-run first innings lead. Thanks to a determined unbeaten maiden Test century by Insole (110 not out), England was able to set South Africa a victory target of 190 in just over four hours. But with May concerned with saving runs, and the South Africans cautious about Wardle, neither side chanced their arms. South Africa finished on 142-6.

The balance of power then shifted decisively on the first day of the fourth Test, played once again in Johannesburg. Having won the toss for the first time in the series, South African captain Clive Van Ryneveld decided to bat. Thanks to McLean's 93, and additional fifties from Goddard (67) and Waite (61), South Africa made 340 runs in their first innings, at a rate of over three per over – a mad dash by this series' sluggish standards.

This total was good enough for the South Africans to establish an 89-run lead as May (61), Insole (47) and Compton (42) were the only

English batsmen to pass 20 runs in yet another tentative display of batting. The deficit would have been worse had the England tail-enders not put together 75 runs for the final three wickets.

Then it became South Africa's turn to squander their advantage through over-caution. The Springboks' openers, Pithey and Goddard, batted with such hesitancy that too much pressure was placed on their other batsmen to obtain quick runs and ensure there was enough time to bowl out England for the second time. For their part, England slowed the game down to a glacial pace with Wardle taking as long to complete an over as any of the faster bowlers. After being comfortably in command at 91-1, South Africa lost their remaining wickets recklessly, while just 51 runs were added. England was left with a winning target of 232 runs.

May's side seemed on course for victory at 147-2, assisted by another gritty innings from Insole (68). However, despite a fine half-century from Cowdrey, England lost a tantalisingly close game by 17 runs. Tayfield was the South African hero, taking nine wickets for 113 runs.

The relaid wicket used at Port Elizabeth for the final and deciding Test was not nearly good enough. The result of the toss was all important. Sure enough, South Africa won both the toss and a low scoring game by 58 runs, thereby sharing the series. Although England was hampered by the loss of the injured Wardle, it was doubtful whether even he could have saved his side. For Peter May it had been a series to forget. Troubled by Heine's bounce and out-swing, and Tayfield's subtle loop and changes of pace, he averaged only 15 runs in the five Test matches.

South African Test player Roy McLean remarked in his account of the series, *Pitch and Toss*: "May seemed to have little confidence in himself as captain or in his bowlers...[He] preferred to play safe by preying on our patience and forcing us to get ourselves out when the spirit had flagged. He could have achieved more by using his bowling strength as an attacking weapon. At 60-4 in the final Test...Lock came on to bowl with a defensive umbrella field...[However, MCC players] produced ground fielding considerably in advance of what we expected.

"Their catching, especially Cowdrey, Insole and Wardle, close to the wicket, matched us [when] we had thought we had a distinct advantage. Lock, of course, was already acknowledged as one of the finest fielders in any position. This made it even more incomprehensible why May failed to attack us...Neither side ran singles well...Unless the top order batsmen can be taking their singles regularly when boundaries are not procurable so that the score moves along at a reasonable rate of 35 runs per hour, the burden thrown on the middle order batsmen too often is intolerable."

The average run rate for this Test series was 2.4 runs per over or 32 runs per hour.

McLean felt that the English habit of playing on uncovered wickets inhibited natural strokeplay. He commented: "England, now the only remaining country to play Test matches on uncovered wickets, should fall into line with the others, cover her wickets, and so make the toss less of a lottery. It would prove less of a handicap to players from abroad in a wet English summer – and damp summers seem to come around pretty frequently in England."

McLean also pointed out technical shortcomings shown by the South African batsmen, as a consequence of their repeated exposure to fast, short-pitched bowling. He commented: "Many of us got into the habit of pulling the front shoulder away to make for an open stance [with the shoulder facing midwicket rather than mid-on]...This way I found it so much easier to combat the bumper.

"We got a fair dose of them in Australia...This meant that the off-side attacking stroke by a right-hander off the front foot does not have the left shoulder over the ball. Similarly, the stroke off the back foot is controlled almost solely with the right hand. To the bowler who moves the ball away from the right-hander, the dangers are doubled. I thus halved my effectiveness and doubled the bowler's target."

McLean lamented, too, the decline in standards of sportsmanship in Test cricket. He remarked: "Bailey stood his ground until given out. May had not walked on the previous day, although he knew he was out, and got the benefit of the verdict. Both sides were becoming guilty of the same stratagem.

"At the start of the tour, May publicly stated that he felt a batsman would contribute to good sportsmanship if he left the crease, knowing he was out, without waiting for the umpire's verdict. [However,] a leading South African player was believed to have said [before the first Test] that in his opinion the umpires were appointed to adjudicate, and that if players took it into their hands to dismiss themselves, they were usurping the rights of umpires. Upon such utterances vast changes can sweep through a game."

Jackie McGlew, who missed all five Test matches because of a shoulder injury, was commonly thought to be this unnamed 'leading South African player'. McGlew had been incensed by Peter May's reprieve in the 1955 series decider at the Oval. As much as McGlew was criticised for taking this stand, it is one that is commonly practised today. Even in the late 1950s, such hard-nosed 'professionalism' was not new. Bradman played to such standards.

The turgid play witnessed in this series aroused concern at Lord's. MCC's president Lord Cobham warned that spectators would be driven from the game if the players did not endeavour to provide them with more attractive cricket. Coincidentally, on 25th February 1957 an MCC Special Committee had presented its recommendations for securing the future welfare of first-class cricket.

Among its proposals, which were subsequently accepted by the Advisory County Cricket Committee, a month later, was the limiting of on-side fielders to five, of which not more than two could field behind the popping crease at the time the ball was bowled. This measure was taken to eliminate the curse of negative 'leg-theory'. The boundaries were also to be reduced to a maximum of 75 yards; umpires were to be urged to issue official warnings to bowlers thought guilty of 'time-wasting', and bonus points were to be awarded to county sides scoring at a faster run rate in their first innings.

A proposal for introducing a limited overs competition was shelved, though, because it was said that the commercial implications required further examination. Consequently, the one measure which might have had a dramatic effect in raising the game's appeal was set aside. Certainly, as far as Test cricket was concerned, nothing much changed until Frank Worrell's brilliant West Indians cast a shaft of glittering Caribbean sunlight upon the grey game during the early 1960s.

'NEVER HAD IT SO GOOD'

'All Shook Up'

On 20th July 1957, Prime Minister Harold Macmillan announced: "Indeed let us be frank about it – most of our people have never had it so good." Increased production in British major industries had led to a rise in wages, export earnings and investment. He added: "Go around the country, go to the industrial towns, go to the farms and you will see a state of prosperity such as we have never had in my lifetime – nor indeed in the history of this country."

It was true that the economic upturn and consumer boom of the late 1950s had made enormous differences to the lives of ordinary Britons, helping release women from domestic drudgery, and extending the range of luxury items and home comforts available to working-class families. Despite the glossy images of 'Swinging England', by the mid 1960s the British economic boom was foundering. Devaluation lay just around the corner. Britain's traditional industries – shipbuilding, coal mining, and steel, car and textiles production – had lost ground in the face of stiffer competition from abroad.

Nations that had been bombed and shelled into submission, just over a decade before, recovered quickly. Their radical modernisation programmes enabled their industries to become more efficient and productive, while their road and rail improvements delivered slicker and quicker transportation. By the late 1950s, West Germany and Japan began to overtake Britain. So, while Britain was producing its last steam locomotive, *Evening Star*, in 1960, Japan was developing its futuristic 135mph electrically-powered *Bullet Train*.

Harold Macmillan, who had replaced his beleaguered predecessor, Anthony Eden, sensed the winds of change. After the Suez debacle, Macmillan was convinced that British interests were better served by de-colonisation than by repression. At the root of his conviction was a fear that unrest in the Congo or Kenya might set off a military escalation, as had happened in Serbia in 1914. Not that the British Empire had been maintained principally by force, at least not since the Victorian period.

Unlike the embattled French colonialists, who vainly tried to use military means to suppress angry nationalist factions in Algeria and Indo-China, the stability of the British Empire rested largely upon a series of fragile, improvised and flexible local agreements. However, the delicacy of these arrangements became upset first through global conflict, and then through ham-fisted commercial ventures, such as the Tanganyika groundnuts fiasco.

Where British rule did degenerate into clumsy and brutal suppression of local conflicts, as happened in Nyasaland, and also in Kenya, where 160,000 citizens were detained, and 90,000 allegedly executed, tortured or maimed, these actions exacerbated discord among the indigenous people. As a result, a more fertile ground was prepared for propagating nationalist ambitions.

By the early 1950s, the Empire's economic value to Britain was declining rapidly. The vast majority of the British electorate seemed unperturbed by its eventual loss; the re-tagging of Empire Day with Commonwealth Day in 1958 passed almost unnoticed. There was, after all, inevitability about the decolonisation process although its speed proved to be more shocking. By 1964, the size of the former British Empire had shrunk by 96% with much of that reduction taking place during Macmillan's last term in office. With the newly-independent African states created along the lines of their colonial boundaries, with little respect for historic tribal territories, the legacy of such haste was often years of internecine strife.

But while the decolonisation process was accepted by many British people, the Conservative right was indignant at the prospect. Viscount Montgomery of Alamein voiced their unease when he claimed: "There is only one race under Heaven which could stand between the Western world and utter destruction. That is the British race to which we belong." What was really feared here was a loss of British international power. Certainly, Macmillan and his Colonial Secretary, Iain MacLeod, found it easier to relinquish Britain's colonial assets than surrender the proud world status which its imperial role had once bestowed.

Between 1950 and 1970, Britain's share of world manufacturing exports fell from over a quarter to barely a tenth. Given Britain's relatively small population and limited natural resources, it became impossible to sustain its Victorian Age supremacy as better endowed nations came up to speed. Yet to this day Britain has clung to a world policing role disproportionate to its size, and economic and political status. And expectations of British sporting supremacy remain – notably at football and cricket – irrespective of the degree of difficulty now involved in maintaining such ambitions.

Until the mid 1960s, Test cricket was dominated by English and Australian sides almost to the exclusion of all other rivals. Despite suffering occasional defeats, the England cricket team was then expected to beat sides from the West Indies, India, Pakistan, New Zealand and South Africa. But just as foreign competitors challenged and ultimately overtook traditional British industries, Test-playing countries, other than Australia, began to beat England with greater regularity. However, the process of decline was accelerated because English cricket, like British industry, failed to modernise with sufficient speed or scope, and suffered the consequences.

In the two years that preceded the fateful Ashes tour of 1958/59, such a gloomy prospect would have seemed unthinkable. England's crushing home victories over the West Indies in 1957, and the New Zealanders a year later, gave a false impression of its continuing invincibility, perhaps feeding a fatal complacency that was brutally shattered Down Under in the winter of 1958/59.

The West Indian tour of 1957 was sorely disappointing to everyone who had rejoiced at the Windies' vibrant performance seven summers before. For a brief time, only, did Ramadhin re-assert his hold over the non-plussed English batsmen. In the opening Test at Edgbaston, Ramadhin took seven wickets for 49 runs as May's side was dismissed for a paltry 186 in their first innings.

West Indian batsmen Collie Smith (161), Walcott (90), Worrell (81) and Sobers (53) then collared Trueman, Statham, Laker and Lock with such ruthlessness that they established what seemed to be a match-winning 288-run lead. When England replied, Ramadhin despatched Richardson and Insole with only 65 runs on the board, but after Close departed with the score at 113, May (285 not out) and Cowdrey (154) put together a massive 411-run stand which smothered the mystery spinner's threat.

Smothered is probably an apt term as Cowdrey employed his pads as much as his bat in defying the Trinidadian's wiles. Ramadhin bowled an incredible 98 overs during England's second innings, but with no further reward after Insole's dismissal.

Peter May told his biographer, Alan Hill: "Colin and I agreed that we must keep going forward and that Ramadhin must be played as an off-spinner. If it was the leg break, we just had to hope that it would miss everything...Sometimes we would decide that the leg-break was the one which he bowled slightly slower or higher, or from slightly wider of the stumps. But we were never sure."

After May declared, with England's second innings total standing at 583-4, there was enough time to rattle the previously dominant West Indian batsmen. In the 60 overs remaining on the final day, the tourists were reduced to a calamitous score of 72-7 with Laker and Lock imposing the stranglehold that Ramadhin had previously exacted.

Thereafter, England seized total control of the series, winning three Tests by an innings, and having much the better of the other drawn game at Nottingham. After his winter traumas, it was a buffet summer for May who made a further century at Nottingham (104) plus a fifty at Leeds. Cowdrey also went on to make another big hundred at Lord's (152), adding fifties at Nottingham and Leeds.

Others joined the party, too. At last Tom Graveney set aside his serial underachievement, providing two emphatic demonstrations of his immense ability. At Nottingham he made a stupendous double century (258), following this up with another big hundred (164) at the Oval. Peter Richardson also helped himself to a brace of centuries. With May's pace men and spinners proceeding to rout the West Indian batsmen, notably at the Oval, England seemed on top of the world.

Once again the spectre of 'doctored' wickets was raised, this time by Clyde Walcott after Worrell's opening delivery at the Oval had raised "a puff of dust". In *Over to Me*, Laker refuted the charge, accusing the West Indians of giving up hope on the basis of a hasty judgement, and producing a "gutless" performance. Having lost their captain, John Goddard, at the end of the first day due to influenza, the West Indians were dismissed twice for scores under one hundred. Laker had match figures of five wickets for 77 runs in 40 overs while Tony Lock took 11 wickets for 48 runs in 37.4 overs. Whether 'doctored' or not, the wicket certainly favoured Laker and Lock – and not for the first time.

It had been a miserable summer for the "Three Ws". Although all three managed at least one innings of note, particularly Worrell with his immense knock of 191 not out at Nottingham, they failed to impose themselves upon the series as they had done in 1950. And once again there was the vexed issue of the West Indian captaincy.

West Indian independence was moving inexorably closer, but its cricket team had yet to appoint a regular black captain. In his book *Cricket from the Grandstand*, Keith Miller struggled to make sense of the apparent colour bar, pointing out that Worrell had made a fine job of skippering Commonwealth tours in India. There seemed no sense in excluding him from the West Indian captaincy. And yet the 38-year-old white veteran, John Goddard, was re-appointed as the West Indian leader for the 1957 tour.

Everton Weekes had excitedly acclaimed his side's victory in 1950 as the "end of empire". Seven years on, this judgement seemed premature. And yet this catastrophic tour did prompt the West Indian board to turn finally to Worrell. However, because of his university studies he was not yet able to accept the position. With perfect timing he accepted the role for the 1960/61 tour of Australia where he conducted himself admirably in a memorable, closely-fought series.

As preparation for the impending Ashes contest, a team from New Zealand was invited to contest five Test matches with England in the sodden summer of 1958. As if the huge imbalance in strength was not enough to cope with the poor New Zealanders had to contend with a succession of rain-affected wickets. Wally Hadlee's touring party of 1949 was strong enough to resist an under-strength England side on largely true, sun-baked surfaces.

In 1958, the Kiwis had neither the batting strength nor the experience of their predecessors, although their seam attack, notably the 6ft 5in Tony MacGibbon, posed problems for most of the English batsmen. England won the series easily. Had rain not wiped out two days of play at the Oval, then the series would have probably ended as a 5-0 whitewash.

Yet England had only batted with conviction in two of the five Tests. Since Cowdrey had ceased to be an opening partner for Richardson, seven batsmen had been auditioned for the role – Trevor Bailey, Brian Close, Don Smith of Sussex, David Sheppard, Mike Smith of Warwickshire, Arthur Milton of Gloucestershire, and Willie Watson. Milton scored an unbeaten century on debut, but his two Test innings against the Kiwis were insufficient to prove his worth.

It was an unsatisfactory warm-up series for the greater challenge ahead. Meanwhile, the Australians had emerged from their much more exacting South African tour with a 3-0 series victory. It was clear which side was the better prepared for the Ashes contest ahead.

By 1958, English first-class cricket was ailing badly. The Annual Report of the Warwickshire County Cricket Club summed up its malaise thus: "[This season] will go down to posterity as a depressing year in practically every way. The weather was almost continuously threatening and frequently wet and cold; the tempo of the game slowed to a degree where in the early stages of many games it was difficult to define actual movement; the Laws of the game were more than ever disregarded, and throwing and dragging by bowlers became all too commonplace (the younger generation were found to be needlessly employing them in junior games) and most depressing of all, no apparent action to rectify the position; as a culminating result there was a very great diminution of public interest, and County match aggregate gates fell from just over a million in the season before to practically half that figure.

"There can be little doubt left in the minds of those who administer the game...that the changes instituted twelve months ago almost entirely failed in their purpose, and that further legislative action must now be taken...to ensure that the Laws of the game are upheld, and if necessary an incentive given to ensure that the bat is applied to the ball with the basic idea of scoring runs... Unless this is remedied soon, most players will have lost the ability through lack of practice, to play strokes, and the game will face an age of strokeless batsmen opposed by throwers and draggers – a complete prostitution of the art of cricket."

Peter May concurred, reiterating Cyril Washbrook's proposal for playing zoned County Championship games at the weekend only. Almost heretically, May urged that the distinction between amateurs and professionals should be dropped, with everyone paid by the match, as was the case in Australia, with outside jobs being permissible for all players. With the 1960s about to blow in, it could be said or sung that 'The Times They Are a-Changin'.

'THROWN OUT'

'It's All In The Game'

Controversy mired the 1958/59 Ashes tour even before it began. May accused Laker of not trying to bowl out Kent in a county game at Blackheath. Laker was so incensed at the charge that he withdrew from the tour party. A tense mediation process followed, initiated by Denis Compton, and assisted by MCC officials Billy Griffith, "Gubby" Allen and Ronnie Aird. It was May who broke the deadlock, though, by offering Laker the olive branch.

Laker felt honour had been restored, and agreed to tour. However, the underlying tension resurfaced at the start of the voyage, when Laker announced his decision to retire at the end of the 1959 season on account of his arthritic right forefinger. The timing of his announcement was hardly propitious. It could not have failed to lift Australian spirits. The problem was compounded when Laker withdrew from the decisive Adelaide Test because of this troublesome finger, prompting an angry denunciation from MCC tour manager Freddie Brown.

There was also the tumult concerning Johnny Wardle's exclusion from that tour party after he had been reprimanded by Yorkshire for writing an ill-advised newspaper column, criticising his captain Ronnie Burnet and other team members. According to Laker, Brown caused friction, too, with his imperious edicts on how the players should dress and behave.

In his book *Fred Trueman: The Authorised Biography*, Chris Waters commented: "Trueman liked Brown as much as he liked 'Gubby' Allen, whom he loathed. He felt they epitomised the pompous nature of English cricket in the days of amateurs and professionals, gentlemen and players.

Trueman branded Brown 'a snob, bad-mannered, ignorant and a bigot'. He said that Brown was rude whenever he spoke to him and treated him with contempt." With May taking a back-seat role when off the pitch, the aggravation between his players and Brown was allowed to fester to the detriment of team morale.

Above all else, the MCC party was exposed to the dual spectre of Australian throwing and 'dragging'. According to Huw Turbervill, author of *The Toughest Tour: The Ashes Away Series Since The War*: "Three Australian fast bowlers – one a converted spinner – were either throwing the ball at the English batsmen at startling speed or dragging the toes of their back feet over the return crease so they could release the ball closer to the batsmen. Six-foot five-inch Gordon Rorke did both.

Tom Graveney recalled: "[Rorke] was huge, and he threw it at you. There were no crash helmets back then. All you had to do was stand there and fend it off... He had the longest drag you have ever seen. His front foot went six feet beyond the popping crease."

Trevor Bailey said of fellow offender Meckiff: "He managed to break the batting crease with his back foot which intimates that he got pretty close to you...Were the England team angry? Yes! [Meckiff] was the worst bowler ever to represent Australia." May added: "Englishmen who fell to Meckiff's speed and lift were hardly happy at being victims of deliveries that began with a bent arm and finished with a pronounced wrist-whip."

Peter May's biographer, Alan Hill, added: "Trevor Bailey had raised the issue [of Ian Meckiff's suspect action] at a team meeting. 'This man throws,' declared Bailey. 'I can assure you that if nothing is done, he will win at least one Test match for Australia. If we are going to complain, we must do it before he becomes lethal.' Richardson considers that Peter May must share some of the blame for not pursuing his players' fears."

Nevertheless, as Hill explained in his biography of Tony Lock: "The need for diplomacy was paramount on the 1958/59 tour. Throwing was a disfiguring feature in [almost] every state."

Speaking in a later ABC documentary on the series, Bailey reckoned that only Queensland was exempt from this charge. The South Australian team had two, apparently – Trethewey and Hitchcocks who were renamed by some members of the MCC party as 'Tre*threwey*' and '*Pitch*cocks'. Bailey recognised that English team were hardly well-placed to cast the first stone having Lock "throwing away" and Loader with a suspect faster and slower ball. With wonderful understatement, Peter May told his biographer Alan Hill, "Having a ball thrown at you from 18 yards blights the sunniest disposition."

Jim Laker recorded in his book *Over To Me*: "I vividly remember batting in the Brisbane Test with Meckiff on at one end and Burke at the other. 'It's like standing in the middle of a darts match,' I told Neil Harvey. Neil doubled up. It was about that time that Meckiff had one of his wild spells. Norman O'Neill, from the boundary, sent a fine throw right on top of the stumps. 'Put Norm on,' yelled a wag in the crowd, 'at least he can throw straight!'

"It's easy to see why the Australians are very wary of changing the law. They run the risk of cutting most of their main bowlers out of the game. I remember Ray Lindwall at Brisbane telling everyone 'I'm the last of the straight-arm bowlers [he was a renowned 'dragger' though]. That's why they are taking me on the tour of India – just so they have got someone to bowl if all the others are no-balled.'"

As for one of the so-called villains of the piece, Ian Meckiff wrote in his biography *Thrown Out*: "I have a permanently bent elbow...Like most fast bowlers I get most of my pace from my wrist action...Being slightly double jointed in the shoulders...this gives me added strength and bowling power. I have the support of the umpires in five countries...

"Benaud was furious when he heard about the attacks of the English writers...[*Sunday Pictorial* journalist] Alf Gover claimed I did not bowl a 'legal delivery' and added it was 'ridiculous that a player with this action should be the agent of England's destruction'...

"[During the second Test] With Bailey's dismissal, which was my third wicket at a cost of 11 runs, a new outcry went up against me. Now I was charged with bowling bodyline! According to the Melbourne morning papers, England's sensational collapse, and my bowling, had eclipsed even the Soviet moon rocket in two of London's three evening papers...

"Bailey took films that were shown to MCC...It has been proved on film that at times I did bowl with a bent arm, but it has also been proved on film that some of the most renowned straight-arm bowlers in modern cricket history also bowled with a bent arm at times...It's a pity [Bailey] didn't spend his time more profitably by working out a way to improve England's fight against Australia...I find it pretty hard to live up to this reputation as a monster because by nature I'm an easy going casual sort of person..."

Writing in the *Melbourne Herald*, former Aussie captain Ian Johnson joined the squabble. Not only did he indict Lock and Loader for throwing, he preposterously accused Statham and Trueman of producing 'jerky' deliveries, too, claiming that both employed a 'whip lash' wrist movement at the point of delivery. Of course, Johnson's action had been considered to be suspect also. On this glum tour the throwing uproar became more feverish by the day.

Meckiff recounted in his biography the pain he experienced in being caught up in this controversy. He wrote: "For a person who played cricket for the sheer love of the game, the violence of the throwing attacks levelled at me...came as a shock...My father and mother were pestered... my wife was continually upset...We even found that little kids named my young son Wayne 'Chucker'...One day I was giving some schoolboys a few hints... As I rolled my arm over a kid screamed out, 'no ball!'...The strain finally told on me and I had to seek medical advice."

There was no doubt that Meckiff suffered badly on account of his international success, and his eventual demise, in 1963, was unnecessarily cruel. Like the South African fast bowler, Geoff Griffin, he was 'called' for throwing while representing his country, leaving him with no option but to announce his immediate retirement from the game. The clean-up process, which followed this notorious Ashes Test series, was unforgivably harsh on both Meckiff and Griffin, whose exits could have surely been managed without either of them enduring a public execution.

Besides, England did not lose their world 'crown' in 1958/59 on account of foul play. As with England's humiliation in Dubai and Abu Dhabi 53 years later, the questionable action of an opposing bowler was no more than a sideshow. May's side did not lose 4-0 because of controversial umpiring decisions, either, although there did seem to be rather a lot of these; nor did they lose because of their appalling luck with injuries.

May's team lost the 1958/59 Ashes series – just as Andrew Strauss's side lost the 2012 series with Pakistan – because they did not play as well as their opponents. Only May and Cowdrey batted consistently well during the 1958/59 series, while Statham and Laker largely carried an underperforming bowling attack. Despite giving his all to the cause, Trueman was unlucky, but Tyson was simply a spent force. Tyson's three Test wickets cost a pricey 64 runs each. Bailey, with only four Test scalps, did not do any better while Lock's five victims cost a whopping 75 runs apiece.

Tony Lock's biographer Alan Hill wrote: "[Lock] found the concrete-like Australian wickets on the 1958/59 Ashes tour not at all to his liking. Ted Dexter remarked: 'The Australians treated him like a straight bowler and, with his angle of approach, would whip him through midwicket. Then he tried to pitch the ball a bit wider and was hit on both sides of the wicket.'"

The greatest indictment of England's performance lay in their woeful batting. Not once did they reach a score of 300. In fact, they only exceeded 250 runs on two occasions. Despite all the froth about 'throwing', almost 70 per cent of England's wickets fell to irreproachable straight-armed bowlers. The untarnished left-arm quick Alan Davidson and the blameless leg-spinner Richie Benaud shared 55 of the 97 English wickets taken in this series.

English journalist EM Wellings concluded: "[With regard to fielding, the Australians] were much faster on the ball, more sure of their handling, more adept at the half catch, and their brilliant throwing served to accentuate English weaknesses...Lock and Trueman were the only two whose consistent throwing accuracy compare...Another striking Australian advantage was that they took many singles that the English batsmen would have missed. Because they invariably ran the first quickly, they also had twos instead of ones and threes instead of twos.

"Richardson did not overcome his weakness outside the off stump [Clyde Walcott reckoned that Richardson always looked likely to be caught at gully before he had reached ten]. Watson was much too slow in his reactions to fast bowling. Subba Row, leaden footed, was bamboozled by googly bowlers. Milton, who began to make encouraging progress after a bad start, returned to his hesitant ways. Dexter...was clearly too immature for such cricket...England never bowled more than 67 overs in a five-hour day [equivalent to 89 six-ball overs, or 18 per hour] and dropped as low as 51...Australia could be as dilatory...This series was a time wasting crawl and had I been a free agent I would not have crossed the road to watch it, much as I love cricket."

Neville Cardus was equally lugubrious in his estimations. In an article entitled "Cricket, the Game" Cardus wrote: "Frankly, I am glad that England's long run of success has been rudely interrupted; another triumph would have concealed yet again certain deficiencies, some of them deplorable...Nobody complained against May's defensive methods so long as Tests were won at the expense of weakish opposition...[Despite the widely-expressed belief that this was the strongest England team for many years] the vulnerability of May's contingent stuck out miles – suspect batting against the new ball and hardly a technical batsman left after the fall of the fifth wicket. Injuries to Milton and Watson merely emphasised fundamental deficiencies...May is not accustomed to batting as a leader against heavy odds, not accustomed to handling men made to feel inferior.

"[In 1956] he was lucky with wickets patriotically prepared at the

Oval and Old Trafford...For years, English batting in county cricket has been sadly lacking in mobility of footwork and in mastery of attacking strokes. Boundaries were shortened to encourage a free swing of the bat – with the result that out-fielding amongst our players has lost power to throw, and lost the habit of pursuit...But the shorter boundary has not prompted average English batsmen to increase their capacity to drive in front of the wicket.

"In Australia, even Mackay, a spineless change bowler on a good wicket, was allowed to send down maiden after maiden...The main cause of poor strokeplay amongst English batsmen is the untrustworthy wickets in county cricket...it is no accident that England's two best batsmen developed their methods on the excellent turf of Charterhouse and Tonbridge.

"Because of poorly prepared pitches bowling in England is dependent upon the swinging propensities of the new ball...Only Jim Laker is a really class off-spinner and where is the slow left-hander clever enough to bear comparison with Lock...Neil Harvey told me in 1956 that he seldom received a ball not on his legs in a Test match. The modern idea apparently is that if a batsman shows form on a good wicket, bowlers should at once resort to negation, to an attack pitched beyond the range of his scoring strokes...Bowlers must be compelled every ball to try to get a wicket."

According to Freddie Trueman's biographer, Chris Waters, "May's report criticised several players. Raman Subba Row was 'a disappointment to me'; Ted Dexter made 'stupid mistakes in every department'; Jim Laker had a 'large chip on his shoulder' and was 'too self-centred'; Peter Loader was 'temperamental at times, which is rather tiresome' [whereas Trueman] was the greatest success of the tour. He was wonderfully loyal in every way... he was always in the game – batting extremely sensibly, catching well and bowling with every ounce of effort...I would recommend Trueman for an extra bonus.'" Battered by Benaud, bruised by the press, and afflicted by illness, an exhausted Peter May seemed to lose his appetite for the game. Sadly, 1962 would be his last full season of first-class cricket.

Trueman was back in the fold, though. Waters added: "In his post-tour report to MCC, Brown was subtly reproving of Trueman. 'The only player who needed any correction was Trueman but...he was always willing to listen and he took notice of things told to him and proved himself popular with the rest of the team.'"

While Ian Meckiff continued to plead his innocence, at least for a few more years, Tony Lock was led to repent several weeks after the Ashes were lost. While he was in New Zealand, on the second leg of this winter tour, he was shown a slow motion film of him bowling during the 1958 home Test series against the Kiwis.

His biographer Alan Hill stated: "It showed beyond doubt that he threw. Dexter recalled: 'There was much hilarity from the England players, but, when the lights went up, there was the absolutely ashen-faced Tony Lock. He was stunned and very quiet and was not prepared to speak to anybody.'"

Thereafter, Lock resolved to abandon the jerky style that had caused so much controversy. In its place, a smooth, legitimate action re-emerged that would eventually gain him rich rewards on the unforgiving Australian pitches during his later years with Western Australia.

As with any major national defeat, there was much wringing of hands. The *1959 Playfair Cricket Annual* editor Gordon Ross wrote: "Professional cricket today lives off the field; it derives great revenues from the televising of Test matches; many countries thrive on incomes from running sweepstakes, and top players make a good deal of money from lending names to articles and books and various forms of advertising media.

"Yet surely this structure is not a house built upon solid foundations; supposing that the BBC should decide that they are no longer interested in broadcasting or televising a certain series...It is up to the counties to make concerted efforts so that cricket can stand, if only a little uneasily, upon its own feet. To do so they must... 'Give the public what they want and not what one thinks they ought to have'!"

At least the throwing and dragging problems, which beset the 1958/59 Ashes series, prompted a review of the current regulations. By 1959, the throwing controversy was not confined to Australia. Ramadhin, yet to confess his 'sins', was still playing Test cricket for the West Indies. Geoff Griffin was about to make his Test debut for South Africa, despite being 'called' in the Currie Cup.

Neil Harvey alleged that the Indian off-spinner Jasu Patel was a blatant offender during the Australians' 1959/60 tour. England's Donald Carr alleged that he had seen several 'throwers' in Pakistan, too, during his Commonwealth team's visit in the mid 1950s. Several English county bowlers were cited as alleged culprits, apart from Lock and Loader. And as far as 'dragging' was concerned there were renowned offenders within the English county circuit. Because the game's administrators had been reluctant to grasp the nettle, the problems had proliferated. It was a sour end to England's reign as Test match kings.

A TROUBLED TEST TRIUMPH

etween 1953 and 1959 the England team was top of the world at Test cricket, and yet its triumph was sullied by throwing and 'dragging' controversies. Had a more decisive lead been taken by MCC, when these concerns were first identified, then the scandal, which engulfed the Ashes series Down Under in 1958/59, might have been averted. The state of English Test wickets also caused disquiet, not only because of the 'casino' effect brought about by the inclement British weather, but also because some wickets were thought to be 'doctored'.

It was not just the bowling or pitch preparation which were sometimes suspect, though. Even during England's period of supremacy, its batting was often unreliable, averaging only 267 runs per completed innings. Compare that figure with England's average score today which stands at around the 350 mark. Batting in the 1950s was frequently problematic, not helped by the poor state of the pitches. Because of this, the county game became defensively inclined, less attractive to watch, and less competitive as wickets were obtained so cheaply.

That said, the much-needed 'new professionalism', perfected at Test level by Len Hutton, but practised with equal diligence by top amateurs, such as Peter May, enabled England to regain a position of supremacy. However, an unwanted legacy of their grim competitiveness was a slide into over-cautious cricket, to the detriment of the game's entertainment value. As the South African Roy McLean and the Australian Neil Harvey demonstrated, if batsmen lost their appetite for, even, the quickly-taken single, then the game risked being reduced to unwatchable sterility.

Arguably, though, the greatest impediment to England's continuing success was the manner in which the game was run. It is hard to avoid the conclusion that England's triumphant interlude in the 1950s came about almost in spite of itself. Hampered by class snobbery, anachronistic fixations, an uncompetitive domestic game, unreliable playing surfaces and limited coaching opportunities for those from less privileged backgrounds, it was amazing that English cricket should have produced as many talented performers as it did. Nevertheless, with MCC clinging to its cherished past rather than investing in a testing future, it was almost inevitable that England's spell in the sun would be short-lived.

It has taken English Test cricketers over half a century to recover the world 'crown' that was lost at the Adelaide Oval in 1959. It was only after the appointment of Ray Illingworth, a curmudgeonly tough and tactical leader, in 1969, that the England Test team took back the Ashes in 1971. However, the world crown was not retrieved until after the Millennium, and not before English cricket was revolutionised, led by professionals as hard-nosed and determinedly focused as Len Hutton and Ray Illingworth.

Belatedly, English Test cricketers began to benefit from stricter disciplines and more fastidious preparations. These embrace: meticulous skills and fitness training, specialist batting, bowling and fielding coaching, forensic analyses of tactics and technique, detailed game planning based upon probing intelligence, comprehensive nutritional guidance, and careful and consistent selections, with a high premium placed upon robust mentality, inspired leadership and passionate teamwork. The modern player is expected to dedicate himself rigorously to the pursuit of individual and team excellence.

What a far cry this is from the recipe for success advanced by MCC in the immediate post-war years, which seemed to rest upon the notion of some swashbuckling 'gentleman'/'amateur' blazing away to glory with unfettered freedom. Even the most prominent amateurs of the time, such as May, Bailey and Cowdrey, took their cue from the ultra-professional Hutton, realising that success could only be obtained by disciplined, dedicated, shrewd and combative methods with the individual applying himself to a carefully-devised team plan.

And yet despite their heightened awareness, English cricket remained in the shadows for far too long, apparently ignorant of how it might restore its lost supremacy. It is not that it has lacked successful role models. The great West Indian and Australian sides made clear what needed to be done. It is only in recent times, though, that their messages have been fully grasped and acted upon successfully.

But there is nothing inherently conservative or reactionary about the game of cricket. By the 1950s, cricket in the Indian subcontinent had set aside its musty imperial connotations, having demonstrated how it might help fly the flags of freedom, democracy and equality, and heal the wounds of past segregation and conflict. In the West Indies, too, the post-war game helped propagate a less discriminative future. And yet in recovering Britain, MCC remained steadfastly reliant upon precedent as its guiding principle, wilfully ignoring the startling social and political changes impinging upon its domain.

Engulfed by blind complacency, MCC failed to address any of the major challenges presented to it during the 1950s which also included the throwing and 'dragging' controversies, declining public interest and the morality of playing cricket with a country wedded to apartheid. Instead, it insulated itself within an Edwardian cocoon oblivious to the massive changes taking place at home and abroad.

So, while England's supremacy was being over*thrown* in Australia, and the game deserted in droves by cricket-lovers bored with its dullness, MCC's tour manager Freddie Brown pontificated on dress code, correct terms of address and alcohol consumption. Surely, Nero has never fiddled with such gusto.

Deep within MCC's revered Victorian past, Benjamin Disraeli pronounced: "Change is inevitable in a progressive country. Change is constant." It was not a message that had much resonance at Lord's. However, why was it that MCC, of the 1940s and 1950s, failed to exercise better judgements? Its senior members and administrators were evidently intelligent men, some of whom had played the game at the highest level.

Of course, history is littered with examples of competent individuals, forsaking what their faculties are intimating, and choosing to see what they have presupposed to be true. During the Second World War, the radar operators at Pearl Harbor dismissed the rash of blips on their screen as sea birds because it seemed inconceivable to them that the USA should be attacked. Field Marshall Montgomery failed to grasp that Arnhem was a bridge too far, having presumed the German Army to be beaten despite overwhelming military intelligence to the contrary.

In Cleveland, during the late 1980s, an overzealous response to an alleged child sexual abuse scandal proliferated because professional discretion was lost in a febrile, Salem-like crusade. And, at Hillsborough in 1989, the police mistook crowd distress for mass disorder, not helped by the prevalent climate of fear and loathing on British terraces, or by their pre-match briefing which focused exclusively upon the officers' duty to combat any incidents of 'hooliganism'.

So, did MCC's members cling so limpet-like to a rose-tinted past, ignoring the mounting challenges of the present, simply because they felt so disconcerted or intimidated by the rapid changes taking place in British society? Joe Mercer's warning, issued in 1959, to his dynastic board of directors at Aston Villa FC, is perhaps pertinent here: "Tradition is a wonderful friend, but a dangerous enemy."

APPENDIX: ENGLAND TEST BATTING & BOWLING AVERAGES

June 1946-March 1959

Name	Runs	Batting avg	Wickets	Bowling avg
Hutton*	5,618	54.02		
Compton	5,373	48.85		
May* (A)	3,997	48.16		
Robertson	881	46.36		
Edrich (A) RFM	2,133	43.53	34	40.06
Washbrook	2,552	41.16		
Richardson (A)	1,623	40.58		
Watkins	810	40.50		
Cowdrey (A)	2,096	40.31		
Graveney	2,590	38.66		
Sheppard* (A)	608	38.00		
Simpson (A)	1,401	33.35		
Bailey (A) RFM	2,290	29.74	132	29.21
Yardley* (A)	805	27.76		
Watson	879	25.85		
Brown* (A) LBG	559	24.30	34	31.12
Ikin	606	20.89		
Evans+	2,439	20.49		

Appleyard OB			31	17.87
Tyson RF			76	18.56
Wardle SLA	653	19.78	102	20.39
Lock SLA			121	20.88
Laker OB	676	14.08	193	21.24
Trueman RF			103	21.90
Loader RF			39	22.51
Statham RF			140	24.83
Bedser RFM	714	12.75	236	24.89
Tattersall OB			58	26.08
Hollies LBG			44	30.27
Jenkins LBG			32	34.31
Wright LBG			108	39.11

Qualification: 500 runs or 20 wickets
England captain in period 1946-59 *, wicketkeeper +, amateur (A)
Bowling style: LBG leg break & googly, OB off break, RFM right arm fast medium, RF right arm fast, SLA slow left arm

REFERENCES

Absolute Beginners; Colin MacInnes; MacGibbon & Kee ©; 1959.

Anger and After: A Guide to New British Drama; John Russell Taylor; Methuen ©; 1962.

A Century of Great Cricket Quotes; David Hopps; Robson Books ©; 1998.

A Concise History of the Caribbean; BW Higman; Cambridge University Press ©; 2010.

A History of South Africa; Frank Welsh; Harper Collins ©; 2000.

Bomb Culture; Jeff Nuttall; MacGibbon & Kee ©; 1968.

Chronicle of the 20th Century; Derrik Mercer (Editor); Longman ©; 1988.

A Corner of a Foreign Field: The Indian History of a British Sport; Ramachandra Guha; Picador ©; 2002.

A Social History of English Cricket; Derek Birley; Aurum Press ©; 1999.

A Spell at the Top; Brian Statham; Souvenir Press Ltd ©; 1969.

A Typhoon Called Tyson; Frank Tyson; William Heinemann (reprinted by permission of Random House Group Ltd ©); 1962.

Anatomy of Britain; Anthony Sampson; Hodder and Stoughton ©; 1962.

As It Was; Fred Trueman; Pan Books (an imprint of Pan Macmillan, London ©); 2005.

Austerity Britain 1945-51; David Kynaston; Bloomsbury ©; 2007.

Australia 55; Alan Ross; Constable & Co Ltd ©; 1985.

Basingstoke Boy: The Autobiography; John Arlott; Fontana (reprinted by permission of HarperCollins Publishers Ltd ©); 1992.

Beyond a Boundary; CLR James; Yellow Jersey Press (reprinted by permission of Random House Group Ltd ©); 2005.

Bill Edrich: A Biography; Alan Hill; Andre Deutsch (reprinted by permission of Carlton Books ©); 1994.

Brown and Company: The Tour in Australia 1950-51; Jack Fingleton; Collins (an imprint of Harper Collins ©); 1951.

Cricket Campaigns; Norman Yardley; Stanley Paul & Co Ltd (reprinted by permission of Random House Group Ltd ©); 1950.

Cricket Cauldron: With Hutton in the Caribbean; Alex Bannister; Pavilion Books ©; 1990.

Cricket for South Africa; Jackie McGlew; Hodder and Stoughton ©; 1961.

Cricket from the Grandstand; Keith Miller; The Sportsmans Book Club ©; 1960.

Cricket Musketeer; Freddie Brown; Stanley Paul & Co Ltd ©; 1954.

Cricket My World; Walter Hammond; Stanley Paul & Co Ltd ©; 1958.

Denis Compton: The Untold Stories of the Greatest Sporting Hero of the Century; Norman Giller; Andre Deutsch (reprinted by permission of Carlton Books ©); 1997.

Diamonds, Gold, and War: The British, the Boers, and the Making of South Africa; Martin Meredith; Pocket Books ©; 2008.

End of an Innings; Denis Compton; Pavilion Books ©; 1958.

England Down Under: M.C.C. in Australia 1958-59; John Kay; Sporting Handbooks ©; 1959.

Everything Under the Sun; Jeff Stollmeyer; Hutchinson ©; 1983.

Family Britain 1951-57; David Kynaston; Bloomsbury ©; 2009.

Farewell to Cricket; Sir Donald Bradman; Hodder and Stoughton (reprinted by permission of Hodder Headline ©); 1950.

Fifteen Paces; Alan Davidson; Souvenir Press Ltd ©; 1965.

Fifty Years in Cricket; Sir Leonard Hutton; Stanley Paul & Co Ltd (reprinted by permission of Random House Group Ltd ©); 1984.

Flying Stumps; Ray Lindwall; Arrow Books (reprinted by permission of Random House Group Ltd ©); 1957.

Frank Worrell: A Biography; Ivo Tennant; Lutterworth Press; 1987.

Fred Trueman: The Authorised Biography; Chris Waters; Aurum Press Ltd ©; 2011.

Harold Larwood; Duncan Hamilton; Quercus ©; 2009.

Hurry on Down; John Wain; Secker & Warburg ©; 1955.

Hutton & Washbrook; AA Thomson; The Epworth Press ©; 1963.

Innings of a Lifetime; Ralph Barker; Collins ©; 1982.

Just My Story; Len Hutton; Hutchinson ©; 1956.

Keith Miller: A Cricketing Biography; Mihir Bose; George Allen &
  Unwin (an imprint of Harper Collins ©); 1980.
The Long, Slow Death of White Australia; Gwenda Tavan; Scribe
  Publications ©; 2005.
Look Back in Anger; John Osborne; Faber and Faber ©; 1978.
Lucky Jim; Kingsley Amis; Penguin Classics ©; 2000.
M.C.C.: The Autobiography of a Cricketer; Colin Cowdrey; Hodder
  and Stoughton (reproduced by permission of the publisher Hodder
  & Stoughton Ltd ©); 1976.
Mastering the Craft: Ten Years of Weekes 1948-1958; Sir Everton
  DeCourcey Weekes with Sir Hilary Beckles; Universities of the
  Caribbean Press Inc. (an imprint of Ian Randle Publishers ©); 2007.
Naught for Your Comfort; Trevor Huddleston; Collins ©; 1956.
Never Had It So Good: A History of Britain from Suez to the Beatles;
  Dominic Sandbrook; Little Brown ©; 2005.
Operation Ashes; Arthur Morris & Pat Landsberg; Robert Hale Ltd ©;
  1956.
Over to Me; Jim Laker; Frederick Muller Ltd (reprinted by permission of
  Random House Group Ltd ©); 1960.
Peter May: A Biography; Alan Hill; Andre Deutsch (reprinted by
  permission of CarltonBooks ©); 1996.
Peter May's Book of Cricket; Peter May; Cassell & Co ©; 1956.
Pitch and Toss; Roy McLean; Hodder & Stoughton ©; 1957.
Playfair Cricket Annual 1949; Peter West (Editor); Playfair Books Ltd
  ©; 1949.
Playfair Cricket Annual 1951; Peter West (Editor); Playfair Books Ltd
  ©; 1951.
Playfair Cricket Annual 1953; Peter West (Editor); Playfair Books Ltd
  ©; 1953.
Playfair Cricket Annual 1954; Gordon Ross (Editor); Playfair Books Ltd
  ©; 1954.
Playfair Cricket Annual 1956; Gordon Ross (Editor); Playfair Books Ltd
  ©; 1956.
Playfair Cricket Annual 1957; Gordon Ross (Editor); Playfair Books Ltd
  ©; 1956.
Playfair Cricket Annual 1959; Gordon Ross (Editor); Playfair Books Ltd
  ©; 1959.
Richie Benaud: Cricketer, Captain, Guru; Mark Browning; Kangaroo
  Press ©; 1996.
Room at the Top; John Braine; Arrow; 1989.

Rough Guide to Cult Fiction; Paul Simpson, Helen Rodiss, Michaela Bushell (Editors); Rough Guides ©; 2005.

Rough Guide to Cult Movies; Paul Simpson, Helen Rodiss, Michaela Bushell (Editors); Rough Guides ©; 2004.

Rough Guide to Cult Pop; Paul Simpson (Editor); Rough Guides ©; 2003.

Saturday Night and Sunday Morning; Alan Sillitoe; Harper Perennial ©; 2008.

Shadows Across the Playing Field: 60 Years of India-Pakistan Cricket; Shashi Tharoor, Shaharyar Khan; Roli Books ©; 2009.

Stiff Upper Lips and Baggy Green Caps: A Sledger's History of the Ashes; Simon Briggs; Quercus ©; 2006.

Sixty Years on the Back Foot; Sir Clyde Walcott; Orion Books; 2000.

Sweet Summers: The Classic Cricket Writing of JM Kilburn; Duncan Hamilton (Editor); Great Northern Books ©; 2008.

Ted Dexter Declares: An Autobiography; Ted Dexter; Stanley Paul ©; 1966.

Ten Great Innings; Ralph Barker; Chatto & Windus ©; 1965.

Test Match Diary 1953; John Arlott; James Barrie (an imprint of Random House Group Ltd ©); 1953.

The Ashes; Ray Illingworth & Kenneth Gregory; Collins ©; 1982.

The Ashes: Highlights Since 1948; Peter Baxter, Peter Hayter; BBC Books ©; 1989.

The Ashes Captains; Gerry Cotter; The Crowood Press ©; 1989.

The Bedsers: Twinning Triumphs; Alan Hill; Mainstream Sport ©; 2001.

The Complete Who's Who of Test Cricketers; Christopher Martin-Jenkins; Macdonald Queen Anne Press ©; 1987.

The D'Oliveira Affair: Forty Years On*; Rob Steen; Bodacious.com ©; 2008.

The Faber Book of Pop; Hanif Kureishi, Jon Savage (Editors); Faber ©; 1995.

The Fast Men; David Frith; Van Nostrand Reinhold ©; 1975.

The 50s; Peter Lewis; Cupid Press ©; 1978.

The Fight for the Ashes 1956; Peter West; George G Harrap ©; 1956.

The Great Captains; AA Thomson; The Sportsmans Book Club ©; 1967.

The Heart of Rock and Soul: The 1001 Greatest Hits Ever Made; Dave Marsh; Da Capo Press ©; 1999.

The Medium Is The Massage: An Inventory of Effects; Marshall McLuhan, Quentin Fiore; Penguin Modern Classic ©; 2008.

The Neophiliacs; Christopher Booker; Collins ©; 1969.

The Toughest Tour: The Ashes Away Series Since the War; Huw Turbervill; Aurum Press Ltd ©; 2010.

The Tribe That Lost Its Head; Nicholas Monsarrat; Cassell & Co ©; 1956.

The Ultimate Hit Singles Book; Dave McAleer (Editor); Carlton Books ©; 1988.

The Twentieth Century in Poetry; Michael Hulse, Simon Rae; Ebury Press ©; 2011.

The 1951-55 Conservative Government and the Racialisation of Black Immigration; Bob Carter, Clive Harris, Shirley Joshi; Policy Paper in Ethnic Relations Number 11, University of Warwick Centre of Research in Ethnic Relations ©; 1987.

Thrown Out; Ian Meckiff, Ian McDonald; Stanley Paul & Co Ltd (reprinted by permission of Random House Group Ltd ©); 1961.

Tony Lock: Aggressive Master of Spin; Alan Hill; The History Press Ltd ©; 2008.

Under My Skin: Volume One of My Autobiography; Doris Lessing; Flamingo ©; 1995.

Walking in the Shade: Volume Two of My Autobiography; Doris Lessing; Flamingo ©; 1998.

Why Are You So Fat? Cricket's Best Ever Sledges; Gershon Portnoi; Pocket Books, Simon & Schuster ©; 2010.

Wickets, Catches and the Odd Run; Trevor Bailey; Willow Books (reprinted by permission of Harper Collins Publishers Ltd ©); 1986.

The Wisden Book of Test Cricket 1876-77 to 1977-78; Bill Frindall; Macdonald & Jane's ©; 1979.

* Also presented as a sports and politics conference paper titled *M.C.C., English Complicity and The D'Oliveira Affair – The Elusiveness of Truth* which appeared, too, in The *Wisden Cricketer* magazine in 2008.